GUY GIBSON

AND HIS

DAMBUSTER CREW

1943, REALITY : Gibson (on steps) and his crew before the take-off

1954, RE-CREATION : Trevor-Roper (played by Brewster Mason), Pulford (Robert Shaw), Deering (Peter Assinder), Spafford (Nigel Stock), Hutchinson (Anthony Doonan), Gibson (Richard Todd), Taerum (Brian Nissen)

Actors playing Guy Gibson and his crew recreate the wartime Dams Raid photograph for the 1955 film, *The Dam Busters*. (*News Chronicle*, 31 May 1954)

GUY GIBSON

AND HIS

DAMBUSTER CREW

CHARLES FOSTER

While every effort has been made to trace the owners of copyright material reproduced herein, the publishers will be pleased to rectify any errors or omissions in any reprints or future editions.

First published 2023

The History Press
97 St George's Place, Cheltenham,
Gloucestershire, GL50 3QB
www.thehistorypress.co.uk

British Library Cataloguing in Publication Data.
A catalogue record for this book is available from the British Library.

ISBN 978 1 80399 213 6

Typesetting and origination by The History Press
Printed and bound in Great Britain by TJ Books Limited, Padstow, Cornwall.

Contents

List of Illustrations

1

Introduction

In Michael Anderson's 1955 film *The Dam Busters* (still regularly repeated on British television), there is nearly half an hour of running time before we first meet lead character Guy Gibson and his crew. It's mid-March 1943 and their Lancaster aircraft is seen landing in daylight after a night-time raid on Germany. The pilot Gibson, played by Richard Todd, and his flight engineer John Pulford (Robert Shaw) exchange a line of jargon: 'Rad shutters auto.' 'Rad shutters auto.'

The engines are switched off and Gibson then wipes his face with his silk scarf, shouting, 'Brakes off' through the cockpit window. Then we see seven young men clamber out, happy because they know that they have now finished their 'tour' of operations and can go on some much-anticipated leave. They board a small lorry which has bench seats, some puffing away at lit cigarettes, even though they are only a few feet from the fuel tanks and engines. An airman is holding the lead of Gibson's dog, who has been waiting by the stand. The dog is released, runs up to its master and has its stomach tickled. 'Good boy,' it's told, repeatedly. It's going on its holidays and can chase rabbits. They are interrupted by a bit of joshing from the crew. 'Come on, skipper, you'll miss the bus,' one shouts.

In the film, all seven men in this scene are given the real names of Gibson and the crew with whom he will fly later on the Dams Raid, and are played by actors who closely resembled them. However, this is where the film deviates from reality since, with one exception, the men who would fly on the Dams Raid on 16 May 1943 were not those who had been in his previous crew in 106 Squadron two months earlier. The only man who had flown with Gibson in 106 Squadron was his regular wireless operator, Robert Hutchison, but even he was not in the crew which bombed Stuttgart under Gibson's command on the night of 11 March. He had finished his 'tour' of thirty-three operations a fortnight before and was on leave.

The next scene in the film opens with the officers from Gibson's crew having a post-operation breakfast and engaged in a bit more repartee. They are making plans for a trip to London the next day, where they will take in a show before they disperse on leave. They will get a train after lunch. 'You can count me in,' says Gibson. But someone then comes up to Gibson with an order: he must report to Group HQ at 1100 the following day. He looks pensive. We cut to the next morning, and Gibson is driving up to Group HQ in his own car with his dog. He meets the Group Commanding Officer (CO) and is asked by him to undertake just 'one more trip' under conditions of great secrecy. Gibson will command the operation, in a new specially formed squadron, but it will mean putting off his leave. He can't be told the target yet but it will mean low flying, at night: 'You've got to be able to low fly at night until it's second nature.' He goes to another room with a different senior officer and starts the process of selecting who will join the new squadron and then discusses whether or not to bring his own crew with him. 'No,' he concludes, 'they've had a hard tour. Must be sick of the sight of me by now. I'll leave them alone.'

He drives back to the squadron's base, and bumps into his rear gunner Richard Trevor-Roper (Brewster Mason) outside the mess. 'Hurry up, skipper, you'll miss the train,' he says. Gibson replies that he won't be joining them in London, he's going to form a new squadron. 'Before your leave?' asks Trevor-Roper, incredulous.

'You tell the boys, will you, Trevor?' says Gibson and walks off.

He's then seen in his bedroom packing a bag, only to be interrupted by Trevor-Roper and another crewmate, Harlo Taerum (Brian Nissen, a British actor putting on a Canadian accent). 'This new squadron. Are you going to fly with it?' asks Trevor-Roper.

'Of course,' says Gibson. Taerum asks him if he isn't going to need a crew, to which he replies saying he will get one.

'Do you want to get rid of us?' he's asked.

'I didn't say that,' he says.

'Well, we've just held a committee meeting,' says Taerum, 'and it's the general opinion that it's not safe to let you fly about with a lot of new people who don't know how crazy you are. It's the general opinion that you will need us to look after you.'

'Well, if that's what you want to do, all right,' Gibson replies. 'But I think you are the crazy ones, the whole bunch of you.' The camera zooms in to show his face; he's obviously pleased with their loyalty. The whole scene is a typical passage of dialogue from the pen of scriptwriter R.C. Sherriff, disguising wartime emotional attachment with semi-humorous banter. And, of course, it's completely fictional.

Thus is the myth perpetuated that Gibson and his old crew moved from his previous posting, commanding 106 Squadron at RAF Syerston, to his new job, setting up what would soon be called 617 Squadron at RAF Scampton. This myth was created by just one line in Paul Brickhill's 1951 book *The Dam Busters* (the source for Sherriff's script), which simply says that Gibson had brought his own crew to Scampton.[1] This is a line that Brickhill obviously never checked. The first chapter of Gibson's own book, *Enemy Coast Ahead*, written in 1944 but not published until 1946, eighteen months after his death on operations, is slightly more nuanced on the subject.[2] In the course of its eight pages, readers are introduced to all six men in his crew as they fly towards the German dams on the night of 16 May

---

1   Paul Brickhill, *The Dam Busters* (Evans, 1951), p.51.
2   Guy Gibson, *Enemy Coast Ahead* (Michael Joseph, 1946), pp.19–21.

1943, but for how long Gibson had known them, with the exception of Hutchison, is not spelt out.

There has been some debate about whether Gibson wrote the text of *Enemy Coast Ahead* himself, or whether it was ghost-written by a professional writer. The majority of the manuscript probably came directly from him: he was given use of a recording machine and typing facilities while on a desk job in the Air Ministry in early 1944, and the breezy style sounds like the authentic voice of a 25-year-old bomber pilot with plenty to say. That said, small amounts of material from two separate 1943 articles published in an American magazine and the *Sunday Express*, and almost certainly ghost-written by professional writers, appear in the book almost word for word. We don't know now how much of this first chapter was written by Gibson, but it's obvious that the text never went through the hands of a sub-editor or fact-checker.

In the course of this opening chapter, Gibson says a few words about each of the men in his Dams Raid crew, mostly using nicknames. 'Spam', the bomb aimer Flg Off Fred Spafford, was a 'grand guy' from Melbourne, Australia, and 'many were the parties we had together; in his bombing he held the squadron record'. He had done about forty trips and 'used to fly with one of the crack pilots in 50 Squadron'. 'Terry', the navigator Flg Off Harlo Taerum, was a 'well-educated' Canadian from Calgary and probably the most efficient navigator in the squadron. He had flown on about thirty-five operations. 'Trev', Flt Lt Algernon Trevor-Roper, the rear gunner, came from 'a pretty good family and all that sort of thing', had been to Eton and Oxford and had done sixty-five trips. He was one of the real squadron characters who would go out with the boys and get completely plastered, but was always up on time in the morning. 'Hutch', the wireless operator Flt Lt Robert Hutchison, who 'had flown with me on about 40 raids and had never turned a hair' was one of those 'grand little Englishmen who have the guts of a horse'.

All these were officers, but the remaining two had been non-commissioned officers (NCOs) when they first joined up with

Gibson, which might explain why he seemed to know so little about them. 'In the front turret was Jim Deering of Toronto, Canada, and he was on his first bombing raid. He was pretty green, but one of our crack gunners had suddenly gone ill and there was nobody else for me to take.' George Deering's commission as a Pilot Officer had actually come through in mid-April, but the flight engineer, Sgt John Pulford, was an NCO. He is merely described by Gibson as a Londoner, and a 'sincere and plodding type'.

There are so many errors in this account of these six summaries that it's almost tedious to list them all. All the figures for numbers of previous operations are wrong. In real life, Spafford had thirty-two, Taerum thirty-two, Trevor-Roper fifty-one and Hutchison thirty-three (eighteen with Gibson). Contrary to Gibson's description, George (not Jim) Deering was not at all 'green': he had an impressive record of thirty-two operations in 103 Squadron before being sent on training duties, where he flew on two more. Also, it was not a last-minute decision to use him as the front gunner, replacing someone who had gone ill: Deering had first flown with Gibson on 4 April and had been on nearly all the crew's training flights, and nobody in the crew had fallen ill. Pulford's operational career isn't mentioned, but he had racked up thirteen operations in the three months' experience he had built up in 97 Squadron. When it comes to geography, Spafford was from Adelaide, rather than Melbourne, and Pulford from Hull, not London. There are further mistakes in the description of Trevor-Roper. His first names were Richard Dacre, not Algernon. This error has persisted since, to the annoyance of his family, and has been repeated in many books and on countless websites. Also, he was educated at Wellington and the Royal Military Academy in Woolwich, rather than Eton and Oxford.

So these were the seven men who flew in Lancaster AJ-G on the night of the Dams Raid. Five of them met Gibson for the first time in March or April 1943 and this was the first and last time that all seven would fly together on an operation. Sixteen months later, on 19 September 1944, Gibson and his navigator were both killed when the Mosquito aircraft they were in crashed in the Netherlands in still-uncertain circumstances while co-ordinating a raid. Gibson had left the completed manuscript of *Enemy Coast Ahead* behind in London, with five of the six names above listed in the book's appendix, the Roll of Honour. They appear on page 14 of the first edition in the following manner:

MY CREW
Missing, night September 15, 1943
F/O Spafford   'Spam'
F/O Taerum   'Terry'
F/Lt Hutchison   'Hutch'
P/O Deering   'Tony'
F/Lt Trevor-Roper   'Trev'

Even here there are more errors. It was the first four who died on 15 September 1943, killed flying on a bombing operation with Gibson's successor as Commanding Officer of 617 Squadron, Wg Cdr George Holden DFC. By this time, Trevor-Roper was no longer with the squadron, and was not killed in action until 31 March 1944. And to compound Gibson's lack of knowledge about Deering, he is given another nickname, 'Tony'.

John Pulford isn't even ascribed the dignity of being present on Gibson's list. In fact, he served in 617 Squadron the longest of them all, having joined Sqn Ldr Bill Suggitt's crew in the autumn of 1943. The whole Suggitt crew died on 13 February 1944 in a crash following an attack on the Anthéor Railway Viaduct.

In this first chapter, Gibson does give us a few snippets of the private lives of the crew, and to his credit these would seem to be pretty accurate. We are told that Trevor-Roper's wife was living in Skegness, and was about to 'produce a baby within the next few days'. (His son was indeed born in the seaside town on 15 June.) Two more had girlfriends: Hutchison's was a 'girl in Boston' (the Lincolnshire Boston, that is). Taerum was 'in love with a very nice girl, a member of the Women's Auxiliary Air Force (WAAF) from Ireland called Pat'. He doesn't, however, tell us any more about Pulford, Deering or Spafford, although at least one of these also had a fiancée.

These six men – all of whom were decorated for their work on the Dams Raid – therefore have this mythic status of being 'Guy Gibson's crew'. This book explores the connections between them and their pilot and tells their collective story for the first time. We will trace the individual histories of all seven from birthplaces in exotic locations ranging from Milo, Canada, and Simla, India, to the Isle of Wight and Hull, document how they joined the air forces of three different countries, and examine the six weeks in the spring of 1943 during which they flew on their one and only operation together. And we will see what they all did after their participation in the historic raid that brought them enduring fame in the few months they had left on earth.

How This Book is Structured

As mentioned previously, the seven men did not all meet together until April 1943. Therefore, in the next seven chapters each of their lives before that date is examined individually, and further chapters follow on their first meeting, the background and training for the Dams Raid, the raid itself and the public recognition of the part each played. Thereafter, their paths began to diverge and so their individual stories are traced once more. Finally, after their deaths, all of which fell in one twelve-month period, we see how their service was immortalised in print and on screen.

2

Guy Gibson

Pilot

Located in a row of houses on a cliff-top road in the small Cornish fishing village of Porthleven is a fine three-storey dwelling built in Victorian times. Soon after the turn of the twentieth century this became the home of an upwardly mobile master mariner and businessman by the name of Edward Strike, his wife Emily and their seven children. The family had moved there from a small cottage in the village, as their situation had improved. To demonstrate their enhanced position in society, Mrs Strike liked to make sure her daughters acted as young ladies. They were always impeccably dressed and were in trouble if they didn't wear white gloves when going down to the village. As if to emphasise the distance they had come from their more modest birthplace, the four youngest girls were sent to a Catholic convent in Belgium for part of their education, even though the family were Methodists.[3]

In the summer of 1913, when the Strikes' fourth child Leonora Mary (known as Nora) was 19, a handsome bachelor called

---

3   Susan Ottaway, *Dambuster: The Life of Guy Gibson VC* (Thistle Publishing, 2017). This book is the source for much further information in this chapter.

Family home of the Strike family, Porthleven, Cornwall. (Author photograph)

Alexander James Gibson (known throughout his life as A.J.) arrived in Porthleven on leave from his job in India. He had been born in 1876 to a Scottish father living in Russia with a local wife and was sent home to Edinburgh Academy for his schooling. He then prepared for entry to the Indian Forest Service (IFS), which had been set up in 1843 by an ancestor of the same name, studying at the Royal Indian Engineering College in Staines, Middlesex. He took up his first job in the Kangra division of the Punjab in 1898.[4]

Young men joining the IFS were expected to remain single but as they rose through the ranks they were allowed to contemplate marriage, and at this point in their lives many used the opportunity of being on home leave for several months to look for a bride. Gibson fitted the pattern, and when he attended a concert in the village one

---

4   Richard Morris, *Guy Gibson* (Penguin, 1995), p.4. This book is the source for much further information in this chapter.

evening, he was immediately struck by a singer in the choir. This good-looking girl was Nora, and she had a fine contralto voice. Later he would discover that she was also a talented artist, and he then decided that she would be a fine match.

He sought her out, and they soon began a very chaste relationship. At first, Mr and Mrs Strike were horrified that their teenage daughter was set on marrying a man so much older than herself. Although he seemed civil enough, there was an air of mystery about him. Nora, however, was determined and her parents relented, and on 2 December 1913 they put on an extravagant wedding for the couple in the village's Wesleyan Chapel.

A.J. and Nora set off for a honeymoon in Paris before sailing for India. It was in France that Nora discovered there was another side to her new husband. He insisted on taking her to a brothel where he used the services of a prostitute so that she could see what was expected of her in married life. This man-of-the-world attitude was an introduction to what was to follow in her new home, thousands of miles from Cornwall. When back in his own adopted country, A.J. would prove to behave somewhat differently than in England.

Their new base was the town of Simla, in the Himalayan foothills, the summer capital of the government. Nora enjoyed the retinue of servants which came along with A.J.'s social status: cooks, bearers, uniformed orderlies and an ayah for the children who followed in quick order. Alexander Edward Charles ('Alick') was born in June 1915, Joan Lemon in August 1916 and, two years later, Guy Penrose on 12 August 1918. Guy was the name of a family friend; Penrose was derived from the well-known manor house near Porthleven.

Although A.J. expected Nora to put up with his own extra-marital liaisons, he was not happy when she turned the tables. A series of handsome young officers began to pay attention to her and there was tension between the couple. This didn't impact on the children's behaviour, brought up as they were largely by the servants. For them it was a childhood full of happy times and exotic experiences.

The Gibson children first set foot in England in the summer of 1922, the year when Guy reached his fourth birthday. They were brought back to Cornwall on holiday by their mother and stayed in their grandparents' house in Porthleven, having many encounters with cousins and other relatives while exploring the delights of a traditional Cornish seaside holiday. Meanwhile, back in Simla, A.J. had been promoted to a more senior job shortly before his family took their holiday and was even more absent than before when they returned home in the autumn. Tension grew as the couple become more detached from each other, and as time went by it became obvious that the marriage would not last. Alick was now old enough (by the standards of the time) to be enrolled in a British boarding school so Nora decided that she would bring him to England, along with the other two children.

It was not a good trip back from Bombay. The weather was poor, and the three children squabbled. When they landed in England, Nora quickly found herself in difficult financial circumstances, since A.J. had not provided them with much in the way of support. Unwilling to call on her own family, Nora and the three children eventually moved into a suite at the Queen's Hotel in Penzance, and Nora sent Alick and Guy as day pupils to a local prep school, the West Cornwall College. She obviously discounted the need to get Joan educated, an attitude still all too common in the 1920s. There was more: she had got used to the heavy drinking culture while socialising in India, and she carried on the habit after having returned home. She also began an 'ill-concealed affair'.[5] Only just 30 herself, she was already exhibiting the behavioural tendencies which were to prove so problematic for the rest of her life.

Alick went to Earl's Avenue School (later renamed St George's School) in Folkestone as a boarder and in 1926 Guy joined him. During school holidays, the children lived a nomadic life, partly spent with their mother, partly with their grandparents and other

---

5   Morris, *Guy Gibson*, p.10.

relatives. Porthleven was an idyllic place for small children and it instilled in Guy a love for the seaside and small boats that lasted into adulthood. Sporadic episodes of bad and/or dangerous behaviour by their mother marred the school holidays. On one occasion, Nora decided to drive the boys back from Cornwall to school in Folkestone. By that time, she had moved to London so she also had Joan, who was living with her, in the car. Near Amesbury in Wiltshire, she was driving too fast, both her front tyres blew out and the car flew off the road and down an embankment. Nora suffered broken ribs, but the children were miraculously unhurt and had to continue their journey by train.

Meanwhile A.J. had returned to the UK, taking up a job with the Department for Scientific and Industrial Research in London, where he also rented a flat. He saw the children occasionally, but relations were inevitably strained. He did, however, pay the fees for Alick to move on to second-level education, so he was enrolled in St Edward's School in Oxford at the beginning of the Easter term in January 1930. Guy would follow him there, aged just 14, in September 1932.

The 1920s and 1930s were a buoyant period for public schools, growing both in the numbers of schools and the pupils who attended them, as an expanding middle class knew that the education they provided was 'the route to esteem and success'.[6] St Edward's School, founded in 1863, was typical of public schools of the era, with a headmaster (known as the Warden), who was both High Church Anglican and a prolific user of corporal punishment. This was Rev. Henry Kendall, still in the first decade of his leadership of the school but who would provide the inspiration and astute financial sense which played a crucial role in cementing its status and providing for its future in the years that followed.

Both boys were in Cowell's House under the house mastership of A.F. ('Freddie') Yorke, who taught science. Widely regarded as a

---

6   Malcolm Oxley, *A New History of St Edward's School* (Oxford, St Edward's School, 2015), p.254.

humane and thoughtful man (at least by the standards of the time) he came to occupy a quasi-paternal role in the life of the Gibson boys, shielding them from newspaper reports concerning their mother's escapades and helping with accommodation over the holidays. A.J. had now bought a house in Saundersfoot in Pembrokeshire, near that of a lady friend who had already borne him a child. His other children would occasionally stay there and, even though relations with his father were still difficult, Guy found the area so congenial that in the future he would spend many holidays there. Nora's sister Gwennie and her husband, also based in South Wales, helped out with accommodation and Guy developed a special bond with them.

Guy Gibson's time at St Edward's was not particularly distinguished, either academically or on the sports field. 'Corps' (army training) was compulsory one afternoon a week, as were games on the other days. He played rugby to a reasonable level, making the Second XV as scrum half, a decision-making position that perhaps predicted that he would reach a commanding role in a service career. But he was only a 'house' prefect, so his opportunities for leadership were limited.

However, it was at school that he first became interested in flying, one of many young men and women of the time who found it fascinating. This was the era of the Schneider Trophy and the Flying Flea, of Amy Johnson and Jim Mollison, whose exploits were well covered in the national press. A schoolmaster, Maitland Emmett, had a Bristol fighter aircraft which he had bought for £15 and kept in a field near the school, and this may have sparked his interest. Small wonder that an 18-year-old would want to explore how to take up flying as a career.

Gibson decided that he would like to be a test pilot and with this in mind wrote for advice to Captain Joseph 'Mutt' Summers, chief test pilot at Vickers-Armstrongs. About seven years later they would meet for the first time. Summers told him that the best way of getting trained would be to join the RAF. Gibson decided to do so, but his first application was refused – apparently, he was too short – so he tried again a few months later. This time he was accepted, so he must have grown a little in the intervening period. Not long after his eighteenth birthday, in November 1936, he was sent on the No. 6 Flying Training Course at Yatesbury in Wiltshire. This was a civilian course, involving both ground drills and flying and lasting just a few weeks, run under the RAF Expansion Scheme. Men who qualified were then recruited directly into the RAF and given a short service commission, so by 31 January 1937 Gibson was an acting Pilot Officer. After a week's leave, and this time in uniform, it was back to Wiltshire and No. 6 Flying Training School in Netheravon. On 24 May 1937, after more training in Hind and Audax biplanes, forty-two new pilots were awarded their wings. Their training finished on 31 August, but it had not been without hazard. Two trainee pilots were killed when their Audax crashed near Sutton Bridge on 4 August, a salutary warning of the perils of flying.

Gibson's first posting was to 83 (Bomber) Squadron at RAF Turnhouse in Scotland, in September 1937. He was assigned Plt Off Anthony ('Oscar') Bridgman as a mentor and was taken aloft by him shortly after arrival. They ended up flying low over the area, including a 'beat-up' pass near a sanatorium that had patients diving for cover. Gibson enjoyed the experience and delighted in retelling the experience many times over the ensuing months. The story, as they say, gained much in the telling.

Six months passed with not much happening except yet more training. Then, in March 1938, 83 Squadron was transferred a couple of hundred miles south, to the newly built RAF station at Scampton, Lincolnshire. The location was much more to Gibson's taste. He was much closer to his brother Alick's new house in Rugby and he would visit there often. Alick, who had an engineering job in the town, had started a relationship with a local young woman, Ruth Harris, and they became engaged in August that year. Guy meanwhile went out with several other women, but none for any significant length of time. With potential girlfriends as well as with others in his life, he was gaining a reputation for impetuosity and for wanting to be the centre of attention. As would be the pattern throughout his service career, this behaviour would be welcomed by some and shunned by others.

Gibson's time in 83 Squadron lasted three years, from September 1937 to September 1940, and Gibson devotes nearly half of the text of *Enemy Coast Ahead* to the third year, the first of the war. He began this twelve-month period as a 21-year-old Pilot Officer, estranged from both his parents with no steady girlfriend. He would end it as an experienced Flying Officer with a full tour of thirty-seven completed operations and engaged to be married.

In September 1939, the atmosphere among the young members of the Officers' Mess at Scampton was a 'settled and socially homogenous community'[7] – very similar to that of the middle ranks of a house at a public school: boys in their third and fourth years who are no longer 'fags' but don't have the responsibility of being prefects. Gibson writes about several of the characters: Oscar Bridgman, now his flight commander, a 'tremendous character' with a quick temper. Jack Kynoch, a tall, swimming champion, with not too much sense of humour. Mulligan and Ross, two Australian boys who did nearly everything together. Ian Haydon, married to a 'very pretty' girl called Dell, to whom he 'shot back' to Lincoln to be with her every night that he could manage. Someone called just 'Silvo' – 'What a chap!' And Pitcairn-Hill, a straight-faced and true Scot who had played rugger for the RAF. 'We were proud of ourselves we boys of A Flight, because we were always putting it across B both in flying and drunken parties.'[8]

Gibson doesn't, of course, write about how he fitted into this boisterous crowd. He was now more than two years into his RAF service, past the initial time allotted to his short service commission that had been renewed due to the widely expected outbreak of war. Seen as someone who liked to be the centre of attention,

7   Morris, *Guy Gibson*, pp.28–9.
8   Gibson, *Enemy Coast Ahead*, p.34.

challenging, sometimes thoughtless, he also had developed a tendency to criticise and call out ground crew, many of whom had come to dislike him vehemently.

By this time, the squadron was flying in Handley Page Hampdens, a twin-engined medium bomber. With enclosed cockpits and a four-man crew, they were among the most technologically advanced aircraft in the service. The crew consisted of a pilot, a navigator/observer, a wireless operator/mid-upper gunner and a rear gunner. It would be another three years before the four-engine heavy bombers would come into operation, although production on these had started in the period after the Munich crisis in 1938.

Gibson was on leave, sailing off the Pembrokeshire coast, when the Germans threatened to invade Poland and it became obvious that war would soon come. Finally, on 31 August, his leave was interrupted. The day's events form the second chapter of *Enemy Coast Ahead*: a telegram arrived, Gibson's leave was cancelled and he had to return to his unit immediately. His friend Freddie Bilbey offered him a lift in his Alvis, and the pair set off, fortified by beer and steak in Carmarthen, driving very fast and overtaking anything going too slowly. Freddie dropped Gibson off in Oxford, where they had more beer and a bottle of 'excellent 1938 Burgundy', and he completed the journey to Lincoln by train, arriving at Scampton at 4 a.m. There followed two days of intense activity, punctuated by the squadron gathering around the wireless to listen to the latest news. On Sunday, 3 September, Neville Chamberlain made his fateful broadcast to the nation. As his voice faded away, Sqn Ldr Leonard Snaith, the squadron's Commanding Officer (another man who had also played rugger for the RAF), broke the silence. 'Now's your chance to be a hero, Gibbo,' he said. So, a few hours later, Plt Off G.P. Gibson walked up to 83 Squadron's Hampden L4070, climbed in and went to war.

Snaith led a section of six Hampdens from 83 Squadron to attack German warships in the Schilling Roads and at Wilhelmshaven, on the North Sea coast. The weather was awful, and navigation proved very difficult. Eventually, the raid was abandoned and the aircraft returned to base, although landing at night – which Gibson had never done before – proved difficult. It might have been Gibson's first operation, but it would prove to be his last for four months, and this period would become known as the 'Phoney War'.

Gibson had been due to be the best man at his brother Alick's wedding to Ruth Harris two days after the war started. Originally scheduled for November, the date had been brought forward because of uncertainty as to when Alick's regiment would be posted, and the ceremony had been booked in Rugby register office. Gibson was resigned to missing the event, but on his way into the mess the morning after the unsuccessful raid, he bent down to pat the station commander's black Labrador. The dog bit him hard on the hand, and he needed five stitches. Given sick leave and with his arm in a sling, he set off for Rugby straight away, where he enjoyed a drunken ceremony in a hotel bar swollen by other revellers.

When he returned to Scampton, he found that preparations were being made for the squadron to move to Ringway in Manchester (now the city's commercial airport), in case the Germans started bombing well-known Bomber Command bases. The panic only lasted ten days, they returned to Scampton and he would stay there most of the next year until he completed his first tour of operations in September 1940.

Despite the outset of war, there was no action at first. But there was more intensive training, punctuated by the occasional leave, which he mainly spent with Alick and Ruth. One night in early December, he went with them to see a revue called 'Come Out to Play', starring Jessie Matthews, in the New Hippodrome theatre in Coventry. In the chorus was a 28-year-old dancer called Eve Moore, and Gibson was immediately smitten.

His behaviour thereafter was that of the traditional stage-door Johnny. He 'went round' after the show, sending a message up to her dressing room, then taking her for supper and plying her with drinks. He then insisted that they meet again for lunch the next day, and he went to the show once more that evening. Another supper followed: 'I think you are a humdinger, and I want to be with you as much as possible,' was his clincher of a chat-up line.[9]

Performances of her revue were suspended for Christmas, so Eve returned home to her family in Penarth, just outside Cardiff. Having wangled a flight to the nearby airfield of St Athan, ostensibly a ferry trip in a Hampden to have new equipment installed, Gibson turned up unannounced on her doorstep, very keen to pursue their relationship. A few days later, he was back in Penarth on the night when his mother, Nora Gibson, suffered a terrible accident after standing too close to an electric fire in her bedroom in London and her dress going up in flames. Taken to hospital, she died of burns and shock on Christmas Eve. It's not known when or how Gibson found out the news. He hadn't seen his mother since he'd left school, and he heard little from his father. None of the three Gibson children attended the funeral in Golders Green: Alick and Guy by choice, it seems, and Joan was given the wrong time by their father, A.J. However, the trust that had been settled on the children reverted to them and each received a sum of money. A.J. was quick to contact his son Guy, pleading poverty and asking for the money to be returned to him.[10]

Part of the squadron moved to RAF Lossiemouth in February 1940 to assist Coastal Command in 'sweeps' of the North Sea, searching for enemy submarines. Gibson flew on two of these, his first operational flying for five months. His section almost caused a major incident when it wrongly identified two Royal Navy submarines and tried to bomb them. Fortunately, the bombs missed and exploded harmlessly. On the journey north by train, Gibson had managed to see Eve in a new performance of 'Come Out to Play' in Glasgow.

It was not long after the return to Scampton that the Phoney War stopped. The Germans invaded Norway and Denmark on 9 April,

---

9   Jan van den Driesschen with Eve Gibson, *We Will Remember Them* (Erskine Press, 2004), p.15.
10 Morris, *Gibson*, pp.47–8; Ottaway, *Dambuster*, pp.49–51.

leading to attempts by the RAF to lay enormous minefields between Jutland and the Danish islands in order to disrupt the German navy. These 'gardening' operations were interspersed with 'ploughing' (actual bombing of targets in Germany), and Gibson flew on ten of these in April and May. The end of this period coincided with the invasions of Belgium, the Netherlands and France and then the replacement of Chamberlain and the Conservatives by Churchill and a coalition government: the 'Ten Days in May' seen as a major turning point in the war by historians ever since. 'The Finest Hour' was soon to follow the 'Gathering Storm', as the remnants of the British Expeditionary Force converged on the beaches of Dunkirk to await evacuation back to England.

Gibson survived a collision with a barrage balloon cable on a trip to bomb Hamburg on 17 May, and a fortnight or so later he was on a week's scheduled leave with Eve in Brighton as the Dunkirk rescue operations began. It emerged later that Alick and his Warwickshire Regiment were one of those units to make it safely home.

Returning to Scampton, he then embarked on what would be so far the most strenuous part of his war, with sixteen operations in the months of July, August and September. Many of the squadron members mentioned earlier had been killed by the time he went on his final trip in 83 Squadron, an attack on Berlin on 23 September. Those lost included Pitcairn-Hill, the Aussie pair of Ross and Mulligan, Haydon and 'Silvo', whose full name turned out to be Flg Off Kenneth Sylvester. To cap it all, his friend Oscar Bridgman failed to return from the Berlin operation, and this had a profound effect on Gibson, although it would later emerge that Bridgman was in fact a prisoner of war. Gibson had flown on thirty-seven operations, thirty-four in the previous five months.

The overall cost had been mighty. Fifty men had been lost from 83 Squadron, only twelve of whom were prisoners, but Gibson had been awarded the Distinguished Flying Cross (DFC) and, more importantly for his subsequent career, he had been noticed. Air Vice Marshal Arthur Harris, who will crop up later in this chapter, was the Air Officer Commanding (AOC) of 5 Group at this time. Gibson may only have been a relatively junior officer, but Harris wrote just eighteen months later that he was 'without question the most full-out fighting pilot in the whole of 5 Group when I had it'.[11]

Gibson was posted to RAF Cottesmore as an instructor in 14 Operational Training Unit, but he hardly had time to unpack his bags. He went down to Wales to see Eve and proposed to her under a tree while walking home on a wet night. The engagement was announced on 8 October.

On his return he found out he was on the move. There was a chronic shortage of experienced pilots for the RAF's night fighters, run by 12 Group, and its Commanding Officer, Air Vice Marshal Trafford Leigh-Mallory, had sent out a request for help. Harris explained his response in the same correspondence quoted above. He had chosen 'a hand-picked bunch of which Gibson is the best' and Gibson had agreed to give up his training period and take on something more interesting. Harris had struck a remarkable bargain: 'when [Gibson] had done his stuff on night-fighters' he would give him 'the best command within my power'.

This deal would take some sixteen months to play out. In the meantime, Gibson set off for RAF Digby to join 29 Squadron as a flight commander along with a promotion to Flight Lieutenant. He arrived there on 13 November to a somewhat hostile reception, as he was a bomber pilot promoted above a bunch of 'glamour boys' in a fighter squadron. The atmosphere thawed quite quickly, however, and eight days after his arrival he was allowed to fly a Blenheim to Cardiff in order to get married.

In wartime, the time between engagement and ceremony was often short, and the Gibson–Moore wedding was no exception. The Moore family liked to do things properly (after all, Eve was marrying

---

11 Letter, Harris to Air Vice Marshal J. Slessor, 22 March 1942, Harris Archive RAF Museum. Quoted in Morris, *Gibson*, p.72.

a public-school-educated officer). So they arranged a traditional church ceremony to take place on 23 November in All Saints Church in Penarth, with a reception afterwards in the Esplanade Hotel. Eve told her father on the way to the wedding that she thought Guy would be famous one day. His reply was that she shouldn't be too ambitious. The only Gibson relatives there were his Aunt Gwennie, her husband John and another cousin, Leonora. Alick and Ruth were stuck in Northern Ireland with Alick's regiment and a baby son. His sister Joan was also unable to attend. Whether A.J. was even invited is not clear. He had recently remarried, to a woman thirty years his junior.

The couple set off for a brief honeymoon in Chepstow. Their hotel overlooked the Severn Estuary and they could see flares in the distance in the direction of Bristol. There was obviously work to be done in Gibson's new job but this time there was no parting at the end of his leave. The new flight commander and his wife travelled onwards to his new station, the satellite airfield of Wellingore, 10 miles from Lincoln.

Things did not go well. Finding decent accommodation was nearly impossible, and Eve was left on her own for much of the time. While she sat in a grim isolated cottage Gibson was getting used to flying in a Beaufighter, which needed a two-man crew and a new approach to operational flying. The second crew member operated the Aircraft Interception (AI) radar set, a big technological advance at the time, which had been designed to track enemy aircraft in flight. The skilled AI operator could then direct the pilot to chase down and attack the enemy. With a maximum speed of 320mph, the Beaufighter was faster than most German bombers. However, flying it required a change of mindset for a pilot used to the structures in Bomber Command. Now he needed to take instructions from the AI operator, who was usually junior to him and often an NCO, rather than an officer.

It took a while for Gibson to adjust, and the cold and miserable winter weather didn't help. He and his operator saw some 'bandit' aircraft and chased a few of those. But they didn't get any hits until in February he finally teamed up with Sgt Richard James and the pair began to score some successes. In the squadron's Operations Record Book, flights were referred to as 'X-patrols' and over the next eleven months the pair notched up some seventy-eight of these (the official records disagree with Gibson's logbook over the exact number). James regarded Gibson very highly, and the reverse was also true. They even had the occasional drink together, and at one party in the Sergeants' Mess where the officers had been invited Gibson said to him: 'You know, James, you and I have reached the stage now that if anything comes over we are pretty certain to shoot it down.' He went on: 'One of these days your name and mine will be spread across the front page of the Daily Mirror.' James wasn't so sure, he didn't want to go on to Bomber Command with his skipper, even though he thought that Gibson had always been considerate to him, never bombastic or arrogant.[12]

During this period, 29 Squadron moved to West Malling in Kent, a place much more to Eve's taste. She had driven all the way from Lincolnshire in the couple's car – a fairly terrifying journey for an inexperienced driver – but they had found a comfortable cottage and now had a wide circle of friends and social activities. There were even revues and shows in which she could perform.

However, Gibson's tour on Beaufighters was about to come to an end. He had been promoted to Squadron Leader in June, and he wanted to get back to flying bombers. Although he had flown on a large number of patrols, he himself thought that he had only achieved an average rate of success, at least compared with some of his squadron colleagues. Unfortunately, Air Vice Marshal Harris had also moved to become Deputy Chief of the Air Staff so, for the moment, there was little that Gibson could do to call in Harris's side of their bargain. Gibson was therefore posted to RAF Cranfield in Bedfordshire, as Chief Flying Instructor in

---

12 Van den Driesschen, *We Will Remember Them*, p.155.

51 Operational Training Unit, and he took up his position there on 1 January 1942. They gave up the cottage in Kent and Eve went back to her parents' home.

Gibson spent two and a half months instructing at Cranfield, flying several different aircraft types but not many likely to see front-line service. His logbook entries manage to convey the boredom he seemed to be feeling, although on one day he borrowed a Lysander to fly to West Malling for a party, hosted by the legendary Gladstone ('Glad') Bingham. He owned a local paper business and had a reputation as a regular host for RAF personnel in the district. He was active in the Scouts, as Gibson had been in his youth, and he and his wife Gladys had also given Guy and Eve a young dog, a black Labrador, so they bonded over this.

Meanwhile, wheels were turning in the corridors of power in Whitehall. Air Marshal Sir Richard Peirse was effectively sacked as AOC Bomber Command, the last straw in a poor period in charge being a disastrous raid on Berlin in November 1941 which he refused to call off despite strong meteorological advice. He was replaced by Arthur Harris, who would remain in charge for the rest of the war. It had already been decided that 5 Group would be the first to be re-equipped with the four-engine Lancaster bomber, taking over from the twin-engine Manchester, made by the same manufacturer, Avro, and Harris wanted the squadrons which made up the group to have more dynamic leadership. Within a month of arriving at the Command's base at High Wycombe, he made good his promise to push Gibson forward for advancement. On 22 March he wrote to Air Vice Marshal Slessor, Commanding Officer of 5 Group:

I am sending you almost immediately S/Ldr Guy Gibson. I understand that Fothergill who commands one of your Lancaster squadrons, though a good organizer is not a fire eater, and I am sure you will agree that these fine squadrons ought as far as possible to have the absolute pick. Gibson has only been a S/Ldr for a year, but I desire to give him acting W/Cdr rank and command of a Lancaster squadron as soon as he can convert.[13]

Wg Cdr Charles Fothergill was the Commanding Officer of 207 Squadron, based at RAF Bottesford. Lancasters were being fed through to squadrons as soon as they came off the production lines. The first had been delivered to 44 and 97 Squadrons early in the New Year of 1942. No. 207 Squadron was next in line, scheduled to be followed by 61, 83 and 106 Squadrons. In the event, Slessor made his own decision, and sent Gibson to 106 Squadron, to replace Wg Cdr Bob Allen.

Harris's accession to the head of Bomber Command, which coincided with the arrival of the four-engine heavy bomber, can be seen as a turning point in the offensive war against Germany. He rapidly became adept at public relations, and over the rest of the war released a stream of statements which made him probably the best-known service commander in Britain. His famous 'reaping the whirlwind' comment was made in a speech filmed for newsreel in early June 1942. Apparently, he had first used the phrase in a remark to Air Chief Marshal Portal as they watched the London Blitz together:

> The Nazis entered this war under the rather childish delusion that they were going to bomb everyone else, and nobody was going to bomb them. At Rotterdam, London, Warsaw and half a hundred other places, they put their rather naive theory into operation. They sowed the wind, and now they are going to reap the whirlwind.[14]

Gibson's time at 106 Squadron, carefully co-ordinated by the RAF's sophisticated public relations operation, would become an important

---

13 Letter, Harris to Air Vice Marshal J. Slessor, 22 March 1942, Harris Archive RAF Museum. Quoted in Morris, *Guy Gibson*, p.99.
14 Newsreel shown in cinemas, June 1942.

part of the overall narrative created by Harris. He arrived at RAF Coningsby, the squadron's home, on 1 April 1942, and took a flight in a Manchester on the very first day. Although he seemed determined to ease himself into his new role as a squadron commander, he did make some initial mistakes which did not endear him to many of those under his command. Summoning all the non-commissioned aircrew to a meeting, he gave them all a rocket when they didn't stand up as he entered the room. This did not go down well, especially with those who were a good bit older than him and who had been putting themselves in the front line for many months. It wasn't long before he became known as the 'Boy Emperor'.

The squadron, however, had one of the best reputations in Bomber Command. Bob Allen had been its Commanding Officer for a year and was well regarded. Coningsby was also seen as a well-run station: 106 Squadron shared it with 97 Squadron, who already had the use of Lancasters, looked at enviously by the 106 Squadron members. It also had a new Commanding Officer, Wg Cdr Joe Collier.

In the meantime, the Manchester would have to do. Gibson took some time to familiarise himself with flying the bigger bomber and put himself on the operational list for the first time on 22 April, with a 'gardening' trip to the Radishes field. His first bombing flight was to Rostock three days later. April 1942 would prove to be an excellent month for the squadron, with eighteen nights of bombing and only two aircraft lost.

May brought about two more operations for Gibson in Manchesters, the first another 'gardening' trip and then an operation on 8 May to bomb the Heinkel works at Warnemünde, which met heavy resistance. This was the first time that Plt Off Bob Hutchison flew in Gibson's crew as its wireless operator, although it wouldn't be until July that he became part of his regular crew.

The month also saw the arrival of the first Lancasters. Gibson first flew in one, as second pilot with Sqn Ldr Charles Stenner when they took R5845 for a one-hour 'type experience trip' on 6 May, between the two Manchester operations. However, he then fell ill and was in Rauceby Hospital for two weeks. There he had a sinus operation designed to clear up his intermittent ear problems and was sent on a further two weeks' convalescence, which he spent with Eve, partly in Cardiff but also in Portmeirion in North Wales. He flew himself back from RAF Llanbedr on 30 June (which he recorded in his logbook as 31 June) in an Oxford which had been ferried down to the base by Sqn Ldr Francis ('Robbie') Robertson and Flt Lt Bill Whamond.

While Gibson was away, the squadron had participated in Harris's big innovation, the first Thousand Bomber Raid. Some sixteen of the total muster of 106 Squadron crews took part. Harris wanted to show the Chiefs of Staff and the politicians the power that had been built up in Bomber Command: a 'spectacular' that would 'impress his superiors, attract the admiration of the Americans and Russians who were now Britain's allies, bring cheer to British civilians and frighten Germany'. He reckoned that, with careful planning, he could get a thousand or more aircraft to drop their bombs on one target in ninety minutes and that would do the trick.[15] He only had around 500 front-line aircraft – the rest had to come from various training units. A huge effort was made to get enough crews and aircraft ready and the force was assembled by 26 May, ready to mount the attack on 30 May.

The particular innovation which made such a massive raid possible was the introduction of the 'bomber stream'. All aircraft would fly the same route out and back, at the same speed, with each one being allotted a height band and a time slot to avoid collisions. The force would then pass through the minimum number of German night fighter boxes. As each box controller could direct a maximum of just six interceptions per hour, the theory was that they would be overwhelmed by the sheer numbers.

The target was Cologne. The aiming point for the 153 aircraft from 5 Group was the square in front of Cologne Cathedral. Area

---

15 Patrick Bishop, *Bomber Boys* (Harper Press, 2007), p.97.

bombing – Harris's controversial technique which has been frequently criticised since – was to take place on a grand scale.

In bombing terms, the Thousand Bomber Raid was a great success. A total of 1,455 tons of bombs were dropped. More than 12,000 non-domestic buildings and nearly 40,000 dwelling units were destroyed or damaged. The human casualties hit a new record: almost 500 people were killed on the ground in Cologne, of whom only fifty-eight were from the military. Of the 1,047 aircraft eventually despatched, 41 were lost, an 'acceptable' 3.9 per cent of the attacking force.

Of the men who would eventually fly in Gibson's crew, just three took part in the first Thousand Bomber Raid. Bob Hutchison as wireless operator in 106 Squadron in Flg Off Worswick's crew, Harlo Taerum as navigator in 50 Squadron in Plt Off Roy Calvert's crew and George Deering as rear gunner in 22 Operational Training Unit in Plt Off Klassen's crew.

Other new personnel began to arrive on the squadron. One was the 20-year-old Flg Off John Hopgood, who had been posted to Coningsby at about the same time as his new Commanding Officer and, while Gibson was away, he had undertaken more training hours on the new Lancasters. For a few weeks he would become important in training many of the other pilots, including flying with Gibson on 4 July. Another was Sqn Ldr John Wooldridge, given command of one flight. An unusual character, with a flamboyant handlebar moustache, he was a talented composer who had studied under Sibelius. But he was also a determined and disciplined pilot, and was popular with members of his flight. One of those who joined his flight in Gibson's absence on sick leave was David Shannon. Only just turned 20, he had superb flying skills, and it wasn't long before he was flying in a Lancaster with Gibson as they both got used to the new aircraft. In July, the pair flew together on five operations attacking Wilhelmshaven, Danzig, Essen, Hamburg and Düsseldorf.

Another who joined the squadron at this time was Plt Off Richard ('Wimpy') Wellington, who came from an expatriate family living in Brazil. He would stay on the squadron until the end of January 1943, chalking up an astonishing thirty-five operations before transferring to Pathfinders and notching up twenty-five more. He never really got on with Gibson on a personal level, although he always 'had the highest admiration for him as a squadron commander'.[16]

Under Gibson's command, 106 Squadron became a regular VIP destination for senior politicians and journalists and it was on 25 July, a week after the Essen operation, that Gibson took the Air Minister, Sir Archibald Sinclair, and three senior officers aloft to 'see a crack station', as he put it in his logbook. The crew avoided an embarrassing moment when an unnamed new flight engineer feathered all four engines by mistake.

Bomber Command was also developing new techniques, and Gibson's outfit was often in the front line for these. One such was the use of a new Stabilised Automatic Bomb Sight (SABS), whose expert bomb-aiming instructor, Sqn Ldr D.S. Richardson, he took on an unsuccessful raid on the warships in the Baltic port of Gdynia.

Gibson, Hutchison and other aircrew in a group in 106 Squadron. (Hutchison family collection)

---

16   R.A. Wellington, *Pathfinder Pilot* (Pen and Sword, 2020), p.53.

Although the members of his crew changed regularly, it was about this time that Gibson built up a core team of four men, all of whom would eventually take part in at least half of his tour of operations. As we have seen, Plt Off Bob Hutchison, his wireless operator, first flew with him on 8 May. The others were Plt Off Frank Ruskell (navigator) with nineteen sorties, the first being on 8 July; Flt Lt Brian Oliver (mid-upper gunner) with fourteen, the first on 27 August; and Flg Off J.F. Wickins (rear gunner) with twenty-three, starting with Gibson's very first operation with the squadron, on 22 April 1942.

However, Gibson nearly always flew with a new man sitting beside him in the Lancaster's drop-down canvas seat. As will be discussed in the next chapter, the arrival of the heavy bombers had prompted a change in policy at the highest level, with the new trade of flight engineer taking on the workload previously entrusted to a second fully qualified pilot. Gibson got into the habit of taking a different man – a newly arrived pilot or flight engineer – to fill this role in his subsequent operations. He didn't always bother to record their names in his logbook, but they are listed in the squadron Operations Record Book. From this we can see that the first flight engineer to fly with him, on a 'gardening' trip to the Baltic on 8 August, was Sgt E. Russell.

The squadron moved to RAF Syerston in October 1942, in order to facilitate the installation of concrete runways at Coningsby. In overall charge of the Syerston station was Gp Capt Gus Walker, a very popular figure who had great leadership skills. Shortly after the move, Sqn Ldr John Searby joined 106 Squadron, scheduled to take over as B Flight Commander. On his arrival on the station, he had a brief conversation with his new counterpart on A Flight, Sqn Ldr Charles Hill, before Hill set off on an operation targeting Cologne. Hill and his crew were all killed that night, crashing at Menden. Gibson had also flown on this operation, so he and Searby had a rather terse conversation the following morning, as Searby recalled after the war:

He had been flying the previous night and was under some strain. He asked me what I had been doing before joining him – and heard me out with obvious distaste – impatient and barely polite. He was a small man – with a fresh complexion, and I thought, cocky as they come. I was brief but he cut in:

'You can forget all that – it means nothing. Anything you may have done before you came here is nothing. This is the real thing.' He got up from his desk and walked to the window, hands thrust deeply into the pockets of his uniform jacket. Then, 'Ops are what count here – and anyone who doesn't like it can get out.'

I began to dislike him, but sensed this was a bad moment.[17]

Two days later, on 17 October, the target was the Schneider Armaments Factory near Le Creusot in France. This had to be a daylight operation, the theory being that this would minimise civilian casualties in an occupied nation. Harris assigned the entire 5 Group, all nine squadrons, to attack the target with Wg Cdr Leonard Slee, Commanding Officer of 49 Squadron, in overall command. The squadrons all trained for the operation for several days previously flying in formation and at low level. The results, however, were mixed, with some of the bombing falling short, but only one aircraft was lost.

This raid was covered in the press, part of the Air Ministry's publicity strategy. Several photographs, taken by Plt Off Frank Ruskell, Gibson's navigator, were released to the press.[18] Another unofficial one was taken by Bob Hutchison, and is shown in Chapter 5.

More press publicity would follow a week later, with a photographer invited to cover the return of 106 Squadron back to Syerston after a long-distance raid on Genoa. Gibson took part in this raid but doesn't appear in the pictures. However, David Shannon and his navigator Flg Off Revie Walker, who would later take part in the Dams Raid, are prominent.

---

17 John Searby, *The Everlasting Arms* (William Kimber, 1988), p.26.
18 Clive Smith, *The Great Men of 106 Squadron* (Admiral Prune, 2022), p.80.

On 8 December Gibson was in the control tower overlooking Syerston's runway, accompanying the station commander Gp Capt Gus Walker (no relation to Revie Walker). Twenty-three aircraft from both 106 and 61 Squadrons were on the perimeter track getting ready to take off on a trip to Turin. Further away from the tower, Lancaster K, one of 61 Squadron's spares, was being prepared in case one of the designated aircraft developed a last-minute fault. Its bomb bays were still open, and a carrier packed full of ninety incendiary bombs suddenly dropped onto the hard-standing. Some of the bombs ignited.

Watching through binoculars, Walker and Gibson saw the flames. Worried that there was a 4,000lb 'cookie' on board which might explode, Walker rushed down to his car and set off to the seat of the fire. A station fire tender was also on its way. Through the binoculars, Gibson saw Walker gesticulating to the ground crew to get out of the danger zone and then grabbing one of the long-handled rakes for himself to try to remove the flaming incendiaries.

Then the cookie exploded, with such power that it was felt 20 miles away at the hospital at RAF Rauceby. 'We turned away, trying not to think of the horrible sight,' wrote Gibson. 'We thought that Gus had surely been blown sky high. But he was too tough for that. He had been bowled over backwards for about 200 yards; he had seen a great chunk of metal swipe off his right arm just below the elbow, but he had picked himself up and walked into the ambulance.' Gibson goes on to give us more details in his usual *Boy's Own Paper* style. According to him, before Walker left for the hospital, he asked Gibson to look for his severed arm because he was wearing brand new gloves. He also said he would be back in two months.[19]

Gibson doesn't tell us anything about the aftermath to this accident, but it was the cause of something which would have a profound effect on him. One of the two nurses in the mobile Burns and Crash unit despatched from Rauceby to deal with casualties was a

---

19 Gibson, *Enemy Coast Ahead*, pp.217–18.

WAAF with the rank of Corporal, Margaret North. Her account, as recounted to Richard Morris in the 1990s, makes it clear that Walker was much more seriously injured than Gibson implied, hardly in a state to walk into an ambulance. He was taken to Rauceby in the ambulance and a surgical amputation was carried out. Gibson was one of the worried spectators gathered around the scene.

The next day, Gibson went to visit Walker in the hospital, and came across North again, her uniform covered by a plain surgical gown. After some banter and a request for information about the work done in her unit, he asked her out for a drink. She hesitated, knowing that relationships between officers and other ranks was frowned upon. She explained, but all he replied was, 'Bugger that. We'll go anyway.' They talked for a long time, and it became a pattern for the next few weeks: they would meet for a drink and she listened to him as he got everything off his chest, including his relationship with Eve. He would also ask questions about her work and was fascinated to hear the details of how severely injured air crew were treated.

By this time, the autumn of 1942, Gibson's marriage to Eve may have been only two years old but it was foundering. She lived in a flat in St John's Wood in London, and he would occasionally spend some leave there, but they quarrelled often and were not faithful to each other. But the relationship with Margaret North, which developed over the next couple of months, was different. It remained platonic throughout, even though North plainly adored him. Gibson behaved, as Richard Morris says, with 'uncharacteristic circumspection', making no advances. It was Morris who first interviewed her in the 1990s and published an account of their time together in his biography of Gibson. His telling of the story, with its references to fantasies of honeysuckle cottages and seaside visits, makes heart-breaking reading. What could she do? Maintain an intermittent relationship with an attached man, or acquiesce to the attentions of suitors who had the advantage of not being married?

Things eventually came to a head. She began seeing another man, a Sgt Figgins, and he wanted to marry her. Gibson tried to persuade her not to go through with it, but in the end she did and the wedding went ahead on 20 February 1943, in Quarrington parish church.[20]

Four days after Walker's accident and the first meeting between Gibson and North, the 12 December 1942 edition of *Illustrated*, a magazine published by Odhams Press, arrived on the nation's news-stands. On the cover was a full-page colour photograph of Plt Off James 'Jimmy' Cooper of 106 Squadron at the controls of Lancaster W4118, which featured nose art of a cartoon mouse bearing the name 'Admiral Prune'.

The article tells the story of a mining operation on 16 November 1942. Under the headline 'Mines were laid in enemy waters', the writer, Carl Ollson, conveys the background in matter-of-fact prose. Photographer Jack Esten's pictures show the pre-raid activity: the mines being fused, checked and winched up into the bomb bay, and the pilot and navigator getting prepared.

The article doesn't mention Gibson in the text, but he is shown in a photograph on page 5 of the magazine, alongside Gus Walker. This is actually a cropped version of another photograph released by the Air Ministry at about the same time so it may not have been taken on the day. In the full-size version, Walker is flanked by his two squadron commanders, Gibson on the left and Wg Cdr Richard Coad, Commanding Officer of 61 Squadron, appears on the right.

The magazine also notes that the squadron used several jokey 'Admiral' names and corresponding nose art on its aircraft. This prac-tice had started in 1940, while Gibson was at 83 Squadron, and had been invented by a member of this squadron's ground crew, Douglas Garton. The first one named in 83 Squadron was Admiral Ben Foo, and many other Admiral names then joined the fleet.[21] Gibson brought the nicknames onto the Beaufighters of 29 Squadron and thence to 106 Squadron's Lancasters. Admiral Prune (W4118) was

---

20 Morris, *Guy Gibson*, pp.126–34.
21 Morris, *Guy Gibson*, p.61.

The multi-page feature on 106 Squadron in the 12 December 1942 issue of *Illustrated* magazine. (*Illustrated* magazine, 12 December 1942, Clive Smith collection)

not, as some people have claimed, Gibson's personal Lancaster. Although he liked flying it, there are several examples of operations where it was flown by other pilots while he flew a different Lancaster. Altogether, Gibson only flew W4118 on six operations – a similar number of times to the occasions when it was captained by John Wooldridge and John Searby (six and seven respectively).[22]

The publication of the four 'Admiral' nose art pictures in *Illustrated* magazine nearly caused an international incident, as Richard Wellington explained in his recently published memoirs. His wireless operator, Sgt George ('Titch') Webster, had painted an artistic Walt Disney-style Dumbo on the side of one of their regular Lancasters, and it needed a name. After a lot of indecision, it was suggested that Wellington choose 'something rude in Portuguese' to reflect his Brazilian upbringing. He gave it the title 'Admiral Filha da Puta', adapting a common insult. Sometime after publication the magazine was shown to Brazilian President Getulio Vargas by someone who hoped he would be outraged. He took the opposite view, however, finding it amusing and requesting more copies be sent to him.[23]

The New Year of 1943 heralded a change in the national mood. The second decisive battle of El Alamein, ending in November 1942, had been the first major victory by the Allied armies and its propaganda value was immense. At Bomber Command headquarters Arthur Harris and his staff decided that it was time to start a new campaign against the German capital. Buoyed up with new technical inventions and the fact that they could now send hundreds of four-engine bombers with much greater loads out on one single day, two operations were mounted on Berlin on both 16 and 17 January, the first attacks there for fourteen months. Gibson flew on the first of these, leading the 106 Squadron detachment in an overall force of 205 aircraft, 190 of which were Lancasters. In Gibson's aircraft was BBC correspondent Richard Dimbleby, flying on the first of the twenty operations he would undertake by the end of the war. His recording apparatus had been installed in the aircraft's body. Although his report wasn't broadcast until the following Monday, 25 January, the

22   Smith, *Great Men of 106 Squadron*, p.35.
23   Wellington, *Pathfinder Pilot*, pp.67–8.

next day's *Daily Express* carried a piece about the Berlin raid, written by one of the other journalists who had been invited to Syerston for the occasion. A photograph of Gibson smoking a pipe was included, but the emphasis was on two of the squadron's other crews, those skippered by Plt Off David Shannon and Flt Sgt Lewis Burpee. It may be a coincidence that these two pilots were later brought to 617 Squadron to take part in the Dams Raid.

Gibson's next operation was not until 14 February – an attack on Milan – and there would be only three more in 106 Squadron after this. On 25 February, his crew went to Nuremberg, the last trip in 106 Squadron for wireless operator Bob Hutchison, who finished his tour that day with thirty-three completed operations. They went to Cologne on 26 February and finally to Stuttgart on 12 March. This day saw the first operation for a nervous young Canadian pilot, scheduled to fill the second pilot seat along his squadron commander. He met Gibson in the bar of the Officers' Mess that afternoon:

'You must be Thompson,' he said, walking across the room and extending a strong hand. Before I could acknowledge he said, 'My name is Gibson, will you have a drink?' 'Thank you sir, a half of bitter would be fine.' The barman drew a glass as Gibson turned to the adjutant and I heard him say, 'Maybe he'll be another Joe McCarthy.'

I had met McCarthy during my incarceration at Grantham, where he had landed one day. He was from New York. I forgave Gibson for blurring the distinction between Canadians and Americans. He said, 'You're just in time, you'll be flying tonight.' I hoped he hadn't seen me gulp as I asked, 'With my own crew, sir?'

'No, you'll be coming with me, so get yourself settled in and I'll see you at briefing.' I had only a sip of the beer.[24]

---

24 Walter Thompson, *Lancaster to Berlin* (Goodall, 1985), pp.53–4.

There are discrepancies in the records as to who made up the rest of Gibson's crew that night. As well as Thompson, Gibson's logbook records Sub Lt Gerard Muttrie RN as bomb aimer, Flt Lt Norman Scrivener, the squadron's Navigation Leader, as his navigator and Flt Lt Brian Oliver as the rear gunner. The Operations Record Book agrees on these four. Gibson lists Sgt L.J. Hayhurst as the wireless operator and Sgt James Hargreaves as mid-upper gunner, but the Operations Record Book says that Flt Sgt D.H. Marshall was the wireless operator and Sgt J.R. Stone the rear gunner. Whoever filled all six seats, none of them would end up at Scampton as a member of Gibson's crew. As it happened, the flight was fairly uneventful, except that they lost power in one engine and flew most of the trip at only 4,000ft. They landed back at Syerston at 0240, and Gibson thought that his tour was over. He celebrated this event by spending quite some time compiling a summary table of his operational flying across a double-page spread in his logbook. He totted up all the hours he had flown in the various capacities, both day and night flying in both single and multi-engined aircraft. He then summarised his three tours:

1st Tour	Hampdens	242.20 hours	42 sorties (4 day)
2nd Tour	Beaufighters	199.10 hours	99 sorties (19 day)
3rd Tour	Mancs/Lancasters	201.00 hours	29 sorties (4 day)
Totals		642.30 hours	170 sorties

This was signed off by Gp Capt I. Bussell, the AOC of RAF Syerston, and dated 14 March 1943, a date which suggests that Gibson did have a little time to spare in his schedule on Saturday, 13 March, and compiled the table then.

The following day, Sunday, 14 March, he got in his car and drove to Grantham to meet Air Vice Marshal Ralph Cochrane, who made him an offer he didn't – or couldn't – refuse.

3

John Pulford

Flight Engineer

John Pulford was born on 24 December 1919 in Lorne Street in the Sculcoates area of Hull, the second child of George and Ada Pulford. He had an older brother, George, born in 1915 and three younger siblings: Thomas (b. 1922), Ivy (b. 1926) and Stanley (b. 1933). His father was a dockworker. The young John went to St Paul's School, a local elementary school, and left at the age of 14. He went to work for a large local business, the Paragon Motor Company, who had two premises in Hull and several more over the rest of the north of England. He started work as a lift attendant but the management recognised his potential and began training him as a motor mechanic.

In the months before the war broke out, the RAF stepped up its active recruitment of young men with mechanical experience. Many of those who would later take part in the Dams Raid in 1943 as flight engineers joined the service at this time, including two who relocated from Canada for this very reason. Pulford was another of those who answered the call. He signed up at the RAF recruitment centre at Padgate in Cheshire on 9 August 1939 as an 'Aircrafthand Fitter Mechanic and Fitter Radio'. After initial training he went into the

John Pulford photographed for 617 Squadron records. (Humphries family collection)

fitter mechanic stream in November. He qualified as a Fitter Mechanic in early 1940 and was then deployed to his first active role as ground crew with 10 Squadron at RAF Dishforth in Yorkshire in April 1940. Some five months later, he was sent first to RAF Shoreham and then RAF Kenley, a fighter station just south of London, and home to two squadrons of Hurricanes. This had been heavily bombed during the Battle of Britain, so his posting there was likely to be related to this emergency. In January 1942 he was posted to No. 1 School of Technical Training at RAF Halton, presumably for further training, and it must have been while at this famous establishment that he heard of the important decision taken by the Air Ministry.

The announcement was of a change of policy which led to ground crew fitter mechanics being trained to fly. Pulford's decision to apply led to him participating in the Dams Raid within nine months. The new heavy bombers – the Short Stirling, Handley Page Halifax and Avro Lancaster – were coming into service and each needed a crew of seven. Six of the positions were taken up by men with established skills: pilot, navigator, wireless operator, bomb aimer, mid-upper gunner and rear gunner. It was recognised that with four engines a second man was needed in the cockpit to monitor their performance. Initially this position was occupied by a fully qualified second pilot. However, getting to this level of skill took the best part of a year and the attrition rate among bomber crews meant that a lot of invested time and money was lost if a crew with two pilots was shot down or crashed. And, in reality, the role of a second pilot was often superfluous, with him rarely gaining any actual flying experience. Moreover, both the Avro Lancaster and the Handley Page Halifax had only one set of controls, the Short Stirling being the only heavy bomber with two sets. So in early 1942, it was decided that the second pilot should be replaced by a flight engineer. This new trade had been in existence in some squadrons since late 1940, with training being done at squadron level, but it became formalised in May 1942.

A new training establishment – No. 4 School of Technical Training – was set up at RAF St Athan in Glamorgan and courses were devised to take place there. Initially entrants to this course were recruited from ground crew who had qualified as either fitters or mechanics, although later in 1942 new recruits were accepted directly into the course. The training was type specific, as the skills needed to manage the engine performance of a Lancaster, Halifax or Stirling differed considerably. Flight engineers were also given some rudimentary training in flying skills, so that they could take the controls if their pilot was incapacitated. As with the other flying trades, each new flight engineer received an automatic promotion to the rank of Sergeant along with his 'E' flying badge when he qualified.

Pulford applied to become a flight engineer, as did his younger brother Thomas, and he arrived at St Athan on 9 September 1942. He finished the course in October and then had a brief stint on the books of 207 Squadron. He then joined 97 Squadron, based at Coningsby, early in December 1942. Sqn Ldr Eric Nind had also recently joined the squadron and took command of one of its flights. Born in 1911, he had been in the RAF since before the war and had been serving in 57 Squadron at its outbreak, taking part in the battle of France. He completed this tour and then went on instructional duties. Affectionately known by his colleagues as 'Windy Nindy', he set up a crew of mostly new men, which included Pulford as his flight engineer. The navigator was a 20-year-old Scot, Sgt William Wishart, who was embarking on an operational career that would see him rise to the rank of Squadron Leader and win the DSO, DFC and Bar before being killed on an operation in 83 Squadron in February 1945. (Wishart's pilot that day was Gp Capt Anthony Evans-Evans DFC, the station commander at RAF Coningsby.)[25]

Nind and Pulford's first operation together was a bombing trip to Duisburg on 20 December 1942, a relatively standard operation taking just over four hours. Over the following three months they went on a further twelve, including trips to Berlin on 16 January (the same operation in which Richard Dimbleby had flown with Gibson in 106 Squadron) and Milan on 14 February. There were a few changes in the personnel during that time, as well as the occasional substitution. In one, on two operations on 5 and 8 March Flg Off Grant ('Jock') Rumbles, normally in Les Munro's crew, flew as the navigator. Rumbles transferred to Scampton to join 617 Squadron on 25 March, along with the rest of the Munro crew. Their flight engineer, Frank Appleby, and Bill Radcliffe, who occupied the same position in Joe McCarthy's crew, would also have been known to Pulford.

Pulford's last trip in 97 Squadron was on 11 March, an operation targeted at Stuttgart, which was abandoned due to the failure of the aircraft's wireless system. Two weeks later, twenty-one men from the squadron were posted to the new 617 Squadron being formed at RAF Scampton, an event which must surely have caused comment among those left behind at Coningsby. The men transferred were three pilots, Flt Lt David Maltby, Flt Lt Joe McCarthy and Flt Lt Les Munro, each with a complete crew. As 97 Squadron had shown such compliance with the previous request it is perhaps no surprise that a few days later someone asked it to supply an experienced flight engineer for the new CO's crew. Whether Pulford volunteered or was merely told he was being transferred is not known but on 4 April, the 97 Squadron Operations Record Book shows him being posted to 617 Squadron. When he arrived at Scampton he must have immediately been taken to meet the rest of Gibson's crew, since it was the afternoon of that day when the entire seven-man crew flew together for the first time.

---

25 Kevin Bending, *Achieve Your Aim* (Woodfield, 2006), p.41.

4

Harlo Taerum

Navigator

Torger Harlo Taerum was born on a farm near the small town of
Milo in southern Alberta, Canada, on 22 May 1920, the eldest son of
the four children of Guttorm and Hilda Taerum. Guttorm Taerum
was Norwegian, and had immigrated to Canada as a young man,
where he had met Hilda Olson, also from a Norwegian family. They
had a farm near Milo, and their four children were all born there.
After Harlo came their daughter Eleanor, born in 1922, and sons
Lorne (b. 1924) and Verne (b. 1926).

Harlo had only just turned 11 when tragedy struck the family. His
father had gone fishing in the local lake on a Sunday afternoon. He
and some others were on the water's edge but saw a man and a boy
out in a raft capsize when the wind suddenly increased.

Guttorm Taerum swam out to provide assistance but disappeared
under the waves. Panicking, one of Hilda's brothers, Henry Olson,
jumped in to try to save him. But Henry couldn't swim, so they
both drowned. In one moment, Hilda lost both her husband and her
brother. Hilda was widowed with four young children to care for at
the start of a decade-long depression. Harlo was one of those children who had the emotional intelligence and wherewithal to assume

adulthood at the age of 11. He did most of the farm chores, worked part time at the hardware store and general store in Milo to support the family, and helped raise his three younger siblings.

Despite having to deal with this tragedy, Harlo was a brilliant student at the local Lake McGregor Elementary School and went on to keep up his academic standing with excellent results at Milo High School, as well as being a 'track, baseball and rugby football star'. When he left school, the family moved to Calgary and Harlo got work as a labourer. He also took correspondence courses while he contemplated joining the air force.[26]

By this time, the war had started and the Canadian news was full of what had happened in Europe when Taerum's parents' old country was invaded by the Germans. His response was to enlist in the Royal Canadian Air Force (RCAF), which he did on 19 July 1940 at the Calgary recruitment centre. Thereafter, his training wound its way through its various components, at each stage of which he achieved very good or excellent results. He got his navigator's badge and wing on 7 June 1941, when the awards were presented by the legendary Great War flying ace Air Marshal Bill Bishop, VC.

Final training followed and then, without being allowed to go home on a few days' embarkation leave, Taerum was told that he must report immediately to St Hubert airfield in Québec. He sent a telegram to his mother: 'LEAVING MONDAY NO ADDRESS NOT PHONING LETTER FOLLOWING LOVE HARLO.' The navigation skills he had developed in the classroom and on training flights were to be put to the test immediately, on a direct flight across the Atlantic. He was tasked with crewing for Captain H.C. Moody as they delivered a Lockheed Hudson coastal reconnaissance bomber to the UK. Taerum undertook a four-hour test flight in a Hudson on 25 July, and then on 30 July they picked up the aircraft they were due to deliver from St Hubert and flew with it to Gander,

---

26 Ted Barris, *Dam Busters* (Patrick Crean/HarperCollins, 2018), p.109. This book is the source for much further information in this chapter.

Telegram from Taerum to his family, announcing his sudden departure for the UK. (Bomber Command Museum of Canada)

Newfoundland. They set off from Gander at 1830 on 1 August, landing at Prestwick in Scotland the next day, having completed the trip in a record ten hours and forty-four minutes.

Having arrived in Britain in this slightly unorthodox manner, Taerum returned to the normal final stages of getting ready for operational flying. He was posted to 16 Operational Training Unit at RAF Upper Heyford on 23 August for training on Hampdens. Finally, two days after Christmas and now combat ready, he was sent to 50 Squadron at RAF Skellingthorpe, the only transferee from 16 Operational Training Unit to 50 Squadron recorded that month.

Just over a week later, he was on the front line. Allocated to the crew of the experienced Rhodesian pilot Norman Goldsmith, he took off on his first operation at 0320 on 7 January 1942 as observer in a crew which also included Sgt Robertson and Sgt Waldie. The target was Cologne, which they reached and bombed from 10,000ft. Another Hampden had left the ground just four minutes earlier, piloted by Sqn Ldr Lloyd and carrying Sgt Richard Trevor-Roper as wireless operator/air gunner. This was probably the first time that a pair of men who would eventually make up the Gibson crew on the Dams Raid had met, at least in the crowded environs of a briefing room. This was actually Trevor-Roper's twenty-third operation in 50 Squadron, and the last one he would fly for a few months.

A busy period followed, with Taerum clocking up eighteen operations in just over two months, all except one with Goldsmith. They were paired together on 12 February, detailed to attack the German battleships *Scharnhorst* and *Gneisenau*, which were trying to escape from Brest harbour, when their Hampden was hit by flak and suffered severe damage. The lead from the aircraft's Aldis lamp had to be called into emergency use to lash the pilot's handgrip to his control column, and they finally landed at RAF Horsham St Faith in Norfolk.

A month later, on 13 March 1942, Taerum undertook his last operation in a Hampden with Goldsmith. They attacked Cologne in what was described as a 'good trip'. Taerum flew on one final Hampden operation, navigating for Sqn Ldr Jeffs on a 'gardening' trip to Lorient on 24 March.

The squadron then began to receive its first heavy bombers, several of the not-very-reliable Avro Manchesters touching down at RAF Skillingthorpe. Taerum's logbook records a number of training flights in this period, mainly with Goldsmith, before they set off on their first operation. The first was a trip in Manchester R5778, a 'nickelling' (leaflet-dropping) operation over the Paris suburbs on 12 April 1942. The Operations Record Book lists Taerum's first operation in a seven-man crew, which comprised Flg Off Goldsmith, Sgt Wiseman, Flt Sgt Taerum, Sgt Waldie, Sgt Vernall, Sgt Johnson and Sgt Mogg.

Three days later, a slightly different crew flew with Goldsmith and Taerum on their second heavy bomber operation, a 'gardening' trip to St-Nazaire. It included a young mid-upper gunner on his first operation, Sgt Gordon Cruickshank.

He wrote up an account of this experience some time after the war, recalling that the crew included navigator 'Terry Tuirum [*sic*]

Taerum and another airman in 50 Squadron. (Bomber Command Museum of Canada)

a Canadian from Calgary'.[27] Understandably, Cruickshank recalled that he was very excited and that the operation had been a success, with four 'veg' laid from a height of just 800ft. At some point in the next few months, he shared a room with Taerum.

---

27 Gordon Cruickshank, 'Memoir Flight Lieutenant Gordon Cruickshank D.F.M. RAFRO', *IBCC Digital Archive* [accessed 9 September 2022] ibccdigitalarchive.lincoln.ac.uk/omeka/collections/document/17702.

Altogether, Goldsmith, Taerum and Cruickshank flew three trips together. The last of these was on 24 April when the target was Rostock. The second pilot on this occasion was Plt Off Leslie Manser, who would lose his life a few weeks later on the first Thousand Bomber Raid, targeted at Cologne, when he refused to abandon his aircraft after it was hit by flak. He controlled the aircraft for long enough for his crew to escape and then remained at the controls as it crashed. In October 1942, he was posthumously awarded the Victoria Cross for his bravery. Taerum may therefore be the only Second World War airman to have flown with two winners of the Victoria Cross.

Taerum and his colleagues had a fairly routine trip to Rostock, finishing for the moment his partnership with Goldsmith. Both men were coming to the end of their tours of operations, although there was a series of 'maximum effort' days in the pipeline requiring their attendance. On 31 May the first Thousand Bomber Raid was undertaken on Cologne and Taerum would fly with Plt Off Roy Calvert in Manchester L7525, while Goldsmith was second pilot in one of the first Lancasters to arrive at 50 Squadron, skippered by Flt Lt Wilkins. Taerum recorded in his logbook that their aircraft had been hit by flak and they returned on one engine.

On 30 June, Taerum was posted to 50 Squadron's Conversion Flight, as was Goldsmith, but the pair were reunited on two more operations. A force of 630 aircraft set off on 31 July to attack Düsseldorf, the first occasion when more than 100 Lancasters took part (113 in all). Flg Off 'Johnnie' Tytherleigh, who would fly on the Dams Raid in the Maudslay crew, was their mid-upper gunner. On 13 September, 446 aircraft attacked Bremen, with Goldsmith and Taerum among their number.

Taerum's time in the conversion flight seems to have been largely ground based from the time of this operation through to the New Year. His logbook records just one ferry trip from Scampton, on 25 September, with Mick Martin as the pilot. On 11 October he was posted to 1654 Conversion Unit (CU) at RAF Wigsley, carrying on instructional work. It seems that one of the classes with which he was involved was teaching students how to use the GEE navigational aid, since this was remembered years later by trainee Flt Sgt Ken Brown, who was later to fly on the Dams Raid as pilot of AJ-F.[28] It was while Taerum was still serving at Wigsley that he undertook two operations to Berlin, flying in a Lancaster with Martin, whose scratch crew also included Wg Cdr Irwin McGhie as his second pilot. The first trip, on 16 January 1943, resulted in a 'Boomerang' (an early return) when the crew turned round before reaching the enemy coast with a faulty intercom. The second, the following day, was more successful, although the aircraft was 'continually fired at by flak' and sustained some damage. They landed at RAF Docking in Norfolk.

Having been recommended for a commission by a number of different superiors in his initial training, it's perhaps a surprise that this wasn't sanctioned earlier than the beginning of 1943. However, the commission was then backdated to 2 October 1942, and Taerum was thus automatically promoted to Flying Officer six months later, on 2 March 1943. His record shows that he was actually on leave between 22 and 28 March, so it's not clear exactly where he was (although it is likely to have been London) when Gibson called Martin to invite him to the new project. It is likely that Martin was the man who suggested Taerum be recruited for the new squadron. The official record shows him being transferred on 28 March 1943, but his own personnel record shows that the posting occurred six days later, on 3 April.

---

28 www.bombercommandmuseum.ca/chronicles/ken-brown-cgm-dambuster/ [accessed 3 October 2022].

5

Robert Hutchison

Wireless Operator

Robert Edward George Hutchison was born in Liverpool on 26 April 1918, the oldest of the four children of Robert and Ada Hutchison. Their other children were Leonard (b. 1921), Colin (b. 1927) and Jean (b. 1929). Leonard died of cancer as a teenager. The family lived in the Liverpool suburb of Allerton.

Robert Hutchison Sr worked for the Hall Line, a freight shipping line, as its senior travelling freight representative. He was also active in the local Masonic lodge, the source of much of the business he brought to his company.

Hutchison won a scholarship to the famous Liverpool Institute, whose later old boys would include both Paul McCartney and George Harrison. After leaving school he worked in the principal accountant's department of the Mersey Docks and Harbour Board and he was also active in local dramatics and concert parties in the Allerton area. He applied to join the RAF shortly after the war began, and signed up at the recruitment centre at RAF Padgate in January 1940.

After initial training, he was sent for training as a wireless operator/air gunner at the Electrical and Wireless school at RAF Yatesbury in

Wiltshire, and then on to RAF Invergordon in the north of Scotland. This station was in close proximity to various naval and army establishments, and Hutchison spent much of his free time organising concert parties and other entertainments. The programme for one of these – 'NAAFFOLLIES' – is in the family archive, and it certainly seems as though he was one of the evening's star turns, appearing not only as the compere but also acting in sketches, such as 'What A Mess', and singing various songs, including 'The Only One Who's Difficult Is You', along with Miss Chamberlain of the Wrens.

Hutchison then moved on to specialist signals training back at Yatesbury before a trip to the Isle of Man for gunnery training at RAF Jurby. The final stage of training was on 7 September 1941 at 25 Operational Training Unit at RAF Finningley in Yorkshire, where he crewed up with Plt Off Horner, flying Hampdens. They flew together for the first time on 21 October 1941. It is likely that the rest of the four-man crew were Sgt Stanley Hewitt and Sgt Revie Walker, and that all four were posted together to 106 Squadron at RAF Coningsby on 6 December 1941. This cannot be verified, but the four men are the crew listed in the 106 Squadron Operations Record Book as flying together on their first operation on 15 December, just nine days after their arrival, in what was described as an operation for freshman crews. They flew in Hampden HT121 and dropped bombs on shipping in the harbour at Ostend. Whichever place they first met, there is no doubt that Revie Walker and Bob Hutchison became firm friends. Daniel Revie Walker (known to his family as Revie, but often called Danny in his RAF days) was a Canadian, from Blairmore in Alberta, and didn't have any close family living in the UK. Hutchison would invite him to accompany him back to his own home in Liverpool when on leave. Walker went on to join David Shannon's crew and completed a full tour in November 1942. He was working in a training role when Shannon got in touch and brought him back on operations in 617 Squadron. He and Hutchison must have been delighted to find themselves serving together once more.

Horner, Hutchison and Walker flew on four more operations together in January and early February but then Horner vanishes from the records. Walker and Hewitt are listed as flying in other crews on several occasions, but February marked the end of Hutchison's career in the four-man Hampden. The Avro Manchester was now coming into service in 106 Squadron, and Hutchison flew on his first operation in one on 24 March, one of a seven-man crew piloted by Plt Off John Worswick. He flew on five more Manchester operations with Worswick in March and April.

On 1 April, while Hutchison was getting acquainted with his new skipper and crewmates, the new squadron Commanding Officer arrived. Guy Gibson already had something of a reputation and, as we have seen in Chapter 2, he did not get off to the best of starts. He took a while to build a core of men willing to fly in his crew, but on his fourth trip, an operation to Warnemünde in a Manchester on 8 May, Hutchison flew with him for the first time. Gibson noted in his logbook that this was a 'hot trip', and the Operations Record Book agrees, recording that there was fierce opposition. However, they bombed successfully and landed back at Coningsby safely. Hutchison had been commissioned on 20 April, shortly after Gibson's arrival, which might also have brought him to the new CO's attention.

Gibson then went on sick leave followed by a period of convalescence, so Hutchison went back on Worswick's crew for the first Thousand Bomber Raid on 30 May. This was a one-off reunion, which was a good thing from Hutchison's point of view, as Worswick and all his crew were lost on their very next operation, bombing Essen on 2 June. Hutchison meanwhile filled in with Sgt Jones for two trips and Plt Off Ronnie Churcher for one.

Hutchison rejoined the Gibson crew on 18 July and thereafter was an almost constant presence in the wireless operator's station in his aircraft. Operations on important targets all over Germany followed as 106 Squadron became one of the most high-profile units in Harris's Bomber Command.

Hutchison and his fiancée, 'Twink' Brudenell. (Hutchison family collection)

The nearest town to Coningsby was the market town of Boston, a thirty-minute bus journey from the RAF station. Although he didn't drink, Hutchison had a girlfriend there named Beryl Brudenell, whose parents owned the White Horse Hotel. She was known to her family and friends by the nickname 'Twink'. Their relationship continued, even after the squadron moved to Syerston on 1 October which lies a good distance further away, between Newark and Nottingham. They would become formally engaged in June 1943, after the Dams Raid.

Back on the base, Hutchison and Walker's friendship grew. There are many pictures in the Hutchison photograph album from this time, and it's remarkable how frequently Walker features, along with his skipper David Shannon and indeed Gibson himself. Gibson is sometimes criticised for his abrupt manner, but he had a group of brother officers he was close to, and Hutchison definitely fell into this category.

For Hutchison and Gibson, the first operation from their new base was on 17 October. Gibson led the 106 Squadron detachment which was part of the daylight force which attacked the Schneider Armaments Factory at Le Creusot in France. Hutchison took his own camera to record the event. After having the print developed, he asked all his crewmates to sign the back in order to put a unique souvenir in his photograph album.

The week after this raid on French soil, they began a sequence of five trips to Italian targets, backing up the Allied campaign on the ground in North Africa, with operations travelling across the Alps to Genoa, Milan and Turin. These were Hutchison's last operations in 1942.

Back to work in the New Year, 106 Squadron was again sent to Germany. They flew on a trip to Essen on 11 January, and to Berlin five days later. This was the raid on which BBC correspondent Richard Dimbleby was a passenger, along with a load of recording equipment, which proved a bit of an obstacle for the crew crowded into their Lancaster's fuselage. His broadcast, several days later, was very well received, and Hutchison's family, listening at home in Liverpool, surely picked up the mention of 'Hutch, the radio operator' as he namechecked the men on board.

Hutchison was then recommended for the DFC, where the citation noted the 'numerous operational sorties' he had undertaken.

The daylight raid on Le Creusot, photographed by Hutchison. (Hutchison family collection)

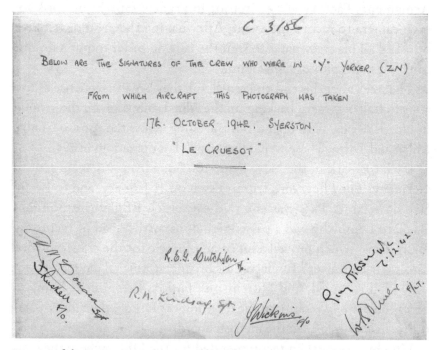

Reverse of the Le Creusot print, signed by Gibson, Hutchison and their crewmates. (Hutchison family collection)

It also specified an attack on Berlin in which he repaired defective electrical circuits in the mid-upper turret, despite the intense cold which almost rendered him unconscious during the work. As the Dimbleby trip was Hutchison's only ever operation to Berlin, this event must have occurred then. Presumably it didn't come to the broadcaster's attention.

The proud Hutchison family all made the trip to London for their son's award, and a large group gathered outside Buckingham Palace for the ceremony, including his parents, brother and sister and soon-to-be fiancée. Also present was Flg Off Revie Walker, who had already finished his tour in 106 Squadron, and was instructing would-be navigators in 22 Operational Training Unit.

Hutchison flew on three operations in February, trips to Milan, Nuremberg and Cologne. After the last of these, on 26 February, Gibson touched down on the Syerston runway one minute before midnight, and pronounced in his logbook that it had been a wizard prang and his 169th war flight. For Hutchison, it was a little fewer, but he had completed thirty-three operations in about fourteen months, including eighteen with Gibson. He had come to the end of his tour and would now be posted to a training unit.

Hutchison's posting came through in due course, but he was probably granted some leave first. His new job was at 1654 Conversion Unit at RAF Wigsley, where the instructors already present included Mick Martin and Harlo Taerum. The chummy Hutchison is likely to have made acquaintance with one or other of them in the few days he was there. So even if Gibson had lost track of where 'Hutch' had gone, when he rang Martin at Wigsley he was probably reminded.

The final entry on the page in Hutchison's logbook where he recorded his postings shows that he left 1654 Conversion Unit on 24 March 1943 and went to 617 Squadron the day after.

6

Frederick Spafford

Bomb Aimer

Frederick Michael Burke (later Spafford) was born on 16 June 1918 in North Adelaide, Australia, the only child of James Michael Burke, a tannery foreman, and his wife Vida Muriel, née Spafford. His parents both died when he was young. His father was just 41 when he died of a heart condition in 1923. His mother was described as having pulmonary tuberculosis for four years when she died in 1926 at the age of 36. Frederick, now 8, went to live with his maternal grandparents and on 19 September 1929 he was adopted by his maternal grandfather Frederick Blaker Spafford, a 70-year-old ironworker, and given his surname.

Little more is known about Fred's childhood. He went to Thebarton Boys Technical High School and when he left school he worked as a fitter at Austral Sheet Metal Company. His grandfather died on 25 March 1940, and so when he joined the Royal Australian Air Force (RAAF) later that year, he named his uncle Walter James Spafford as his next of kin. Walter was one of Vida's older brothers, born in 1884, and had a high-ranking career in public service. By 1940 he was South Australia's Director of Agriculture.

On 14 September 1940 Spafford enlisted in the Royal Australian Air Force on 14 September 1940 and went for training in wireless

Fred Spafford. (Helen Lakley)

at Ballarat, Victoria, and in air gunnery at Evans Head, New South Wales.[29] His record then shows that he embarked on a troopship to England on 25 May 1941 and was then registered at No. 3 Personnel Reception Centre in Bournemouth on 30 August. The ship must have gone round the globe by the longest route. Throughout his air force career Spafford was always known by the nickname 'Spam', reflecting the wartime ubiquity of the well-known luncheon meat. Whether he acquired the name in Australia, on the troopship or in Britain isn't known.

Things moved a little quicker then, since on 8 September he was posted to 25 Operational Training Unit at RAF Finningley. Here he would have picked up the skills necessary to fly in Hampdens when he went to war. And it wasn't too long before he did so, because he was posted to 83 Squadron on 13 January 1942, along with a number of other graduates from 25 Operational Training Unit. This was, of course, the squadron in which Guy Gibson had been serving at the start of the war, twenty-six months previously, and it was still located at RAF Scampton, as it had been in Gibson's time. The squadron had recently been equipped with Avro Manchesters, which necessitated moving from four- to seven-man crews, and this obviously presented extra opportunities for aircrew to fly.

---

29 Eric Fry, 'Spafford, Frederick Michael (1918–1943)', *Australian Dictionary of Biography*, National Centre of Biography, Australian National University, adb.anu.edu.au/biography/spafford-frederick-michael-11737/text20985 [accessed 4 July 2022].

One of these was Fred Spafford: he was only at 83 Squadron for about five weeks, but he went on four operations in that time, all in Manchesters piloted by Flt Lt David McClure. The first of these was on 31 January 1942, a trip to bomb the docks at St-Nazaire in Manchester L7423. The crew was Flt Lt McClure, Sgt Rayment, Sgt Ogilvie, Flt Sgt Taylor, Sgt Stead, Sgt Duffield and in the rear gunner's position, Sgt Spafford. This was the first operational trip in a heavy bomber by any of the seven men who flew in Gibson's Dams Raid crew. Three more trips would follow, the last 'gardening' trip to the Frisians on 16 February.

Five days later, five Australian air gunners and an Australian wireless operator were posted from 83 Squadron to 455 Squadron (RAAF), one being Spafford. Their new squadron had an unusual history. It had been formed on 23 May 1941 in New South Wales, Australia, as an RAAF squadron designated to take part in the European theatre of war. The main body of officers and airmen were then shipped to the UK, but before their arrival other personnel formed the squadron again on 6 June at RAF Swinderby in Lincolnshire. These were mainly drawn from the RAF, but RAAF men already in England were posted to it, as well as subjects of other Commonwealth countries. Those shipped from Australia arrived on 1 September. There were also a number of Australians who had come to Britain around the time of the start of the war to join the RAF, among whom was the young Plt Off Harold Martin, known to all by his nickname of Mick.

He might have only been a young Pilot Officer but Mick Martin was imbued with the buccaneering spirit and high standards which would set the style for this new squadron. The son of a doctor, he had come over to the UK in the year before the war to take up a place at medical school in Edinburgh. However, the war intervened, and he joined the RAF instead, where he rapidly became known as a superb pilot. A natural leader with a gregarious manner, he then built up a tribe who followed him devotedly into devil-may-care scrapes on the ground and exploits in the air. He was also someone who planned meticulously before every operation, polishing the Perspex on his canopy himself, as a smear could conceal an oncoming enemy fighter, and demanding the same high standards from those who flew with him. While Max Hastings wrote about him approvingly that he and his crew 'achieved an almost telepathic mutual understanding and instinct for danger',[30] some on the ground couldn't understand him at all, describing him as 'mad as a grasshopper'.[31]

Martin was very proud of the fact that on 18 February he and his crew – Plt Off Jack Leggo (observer) and Sgt Toby Foxlee and Sgt Tom Simpson (gunners) – made up the first all-Australian outfit to fly an operation over Germany. These four would fly together as the crew of AJ-P on the Dams Raid fifteen months later. Another key Australian officer at the time in 455 Squadron was Plt Off Bob Hay, another social animal who would turn out to be one of the best-known bomb aimers in the service.

Spafford and his colleagues arrived at the expatriate squadron on 18 February, the same day that the Martin crew caused head-lines down under when they attacked Cologne. Manchester aircraft were yet to arrive at Swinderby, so it was back to Hampdens for them. Spafford was placed into the crew of the veteran pilot Sqn Ldr Richard Banker DSO, DFC, who had joined the RAF in 1935. Spafford flew two operations with him, an attack on Kiel on 27 February and on the Renault factory in Paris on 3 March. He was then transferred to the crew of Flt Lt Roy, with whom he undertook three more operations.

However, things were about to change for 455 Squadron. Soon after the disruption of a move to RAF Wigsley, an even more extensive plan was revealed. On 17 April, instructions were received from 5 Group that the squadron was to 'cease to operate as a Bomber Squadron. Twenty crews were to proceed to Leuchars with appropriate establishment for a two flight Hampden Squadron

---

30   Max Hastings, *Bomber Command* (Pan, 1999), p.165.
31   Tom Simpson, *Lower than Low* (Libra Books, 1995), p.40.

for torpedo-bombing duties as a Unit of Coastal Command.'[32] This obviously did not go down well with many of the crews on the station: the next day it was announced that the transfer was to be delayed for a week, and the day after that, that the transfer was to be scaled back. The saga went on for several more days. On 20 April, the weary writer of the Operations Record Book recorded that the 'whole scheme was in the melting pot' and more lists were prepared. Finally, on 24 April, it was decided that a large number of aircrew who must have requested they stay on active bombing duties would be transferred in order that they could do so. Some went to 44 and 406 Squadrons but the biggest section of ten pilots and thirty-nine aircrew were sent to 50 Squadron. Among these were many Australians, including Martin, Leggo, Hay, Foxlee, Simpson and Spafford. There were parties in both the Officers' Mess and Sergeants' Mess to say 'Farewell to Wigsley'.

The arrival of this group at 50 Squadron's base at Skellingthorpe must have taken a while to assimilate, coming as it did at much the same time as the arrival first of Manchesters followed by the much-anticipated Lancasters. Training for a large number of crews to fly these, plus a move from Skellingthorpe to Swinderby, filled several weeks of the next few months. The switch to heavy bombers with a seven-man crew also provided more opportunities for ambitious young men like Fred Spafford, who put in for training in order to be remustered in the new trade of 'air bomber', the official name for what was usually called 'bomb aimer'. According to his personnel record, he achieved this status on 24 July 1942, but this was actually the day after he had flown with his new pilot and crew on what would be his tenth operation.

Spafford had been teamed up with Sqn Ldr Hugh Everitt, an experienced pilot who was the flight commander of the squadron's B Flight. The crew was made up of Sgt James Wolton (flight engineer, this being one of the first occasions that someone had filled

---

32   The National Archives (TNA), AIR 27/1897, April 1942.

this new role on an operational flight), Plt Off Bob Hay (navigator), Flt Sgt Donald MacDonald (wireless operator), Sgt Fred Spafford (bomb aimer), Sgt Joel Bogard (mid-upper gunner) and Plt Off Harold Gilleland (rear gunner).

Over the next three-and-a-half months Everitt took off on twenty-three operations, and Spafford and wireless operator Donald MacDonald were in his crew on all of them. James Wolton and Harold Gilleland only missed one trip each. Bob Hay was the navigator on the first seventeen. Together, they became something of a highly decorated star turn. Everitt himself would pick up a Bar to his DFC and the DSO for this sequence of flights, while Hay received the DFC, MacDonald a Bar to the DFM he had won in a previous tour, and Spafford and Wolton the DFM. Six medals for one crew in under four months may well be a record.

October was a particularly busy month with seven operations, the second of which was an attack on Aachen on 5 October. While over the target, the aircraft was hit by flak, causing petrol to leak from a fuel tank. Spafford was still able to drop his bombs successfully, whereupon they turned immediately for home. They made it as far as West Malling airfield, where they crash-landed without any injury to the crew. Three were decorated for this incident: Hugh Everitt with the DSO, wireless operator Donald MacDonald with a Bar to the DFM and flight engineer James Wolton with the DFM.

Twelve days later came the daylight raid on the Schneider Armaments Factory at Le Creusot in occupied France. Twelve 50 Squadron crews helped make up the ninety-four Lancasters which attacked the factory. Results were, however, mixed. Shortly after this, Everitt and his crew made two eight-hour trips to Italy in three days, the first to Genoa and the second in daylight to Milan.

Spafford's DFM came through in late October without any specific event being mentioned. The citation stated that this was being awarded because he was 'an air bomber of high merit. He has taken part in many sorties and, by his skill, has played a great part in the successes obtained. He has set a praiseworthy example.'

Without being named, on 28 August the crew had also taken part in an Avro Lancaster photo call, with exclusive access being given to a photographer for *The Aeroplane* magazine. Everitt was the pilot and other members of the crew can be seen in the close-up photographs.

Spafford became known as one of the squadron's most skilled bomb aimers. This was picked up by the assiduous RAAF press office in London, who were able to place a story in Spafford's hometown newspaper, the *Adelaide Mail*, on 31 October 1942, showing how the squadron had destroyed the rail station in Milan, with a bomb dropped by 'Sergeant-Pilot [*sic*] F.M. Spafford, of Wayville, who is a nephew of the Director of Agriculture Mr W.J. Spafford'.

The flyers may have worked hard, but there were occasional times they could unwind, and 50 Squadron's sizeable Australian contingent led the way in socialising, which mainly involved card schools and drinking. In his book *Lower than Low*, Mick Martin's gunner Tom Simpson records these activities in some detail, and names the main ring leaders as Toby Foxlee and Bob Hay. Spafford was close to both men, and it is hardly a surprise that he would be earmarked as a suitable bomb aimer when it came to putting together the Gibson crew a few months later.

All that was to follow, however. Spafford's November trip to Hamburg on 9 November was his thirty-second, and therefore the end of his tour. So, on 17 January 1943 he was posted to a training role at 1660 Conversion Unit, based at RAF Swinderby, and full of ex-50 Squadron colleagues. He was also recommended for a commission, which came through on 22 March. Spafford would serve in the conversion unit for little more than two months. He was on 'commissioning leave' in London at the end of March and bumped into Tom Simpson. Simpson had already been told by Mick Martin that a new squadron was being formed, and that Martin wanted Simpson to be part of his crew. Simpson probably told Martin about Spafford's availability, and he was then allocated to the Gibson crew.

Simpson and Spafford stayed with a Mr and Mrs Marvel in Bromley for two days and played golf.[33] Spafford also attended an event in early April at the Boomerang Club, a venue set up in Australia House in London's Strand for Australian service personnel, at which the guest of honour was the Duchess of Kent. (Her husband, the Duke of Kent, King George VI's younger brother, had lost his life in August of the previous year in somewhat mysterious circumstances on an RAF flight to Iceland.) According to the *Sydney Daily Telegraph*'s rather breathless correspondent, Elaine Berkeley, this was the climax of:

[T]he gayest day in the life of this popular club for Australian service men and women in London. The sad, sweet Duchess, accompanied by Lady Herbert, both wearing black fur topcoats, was received by Mr. and Mrs. Stanley Bruce and Sir Claude James, the club's president.' ...

Flight-Sergeant Freddie Spafford D.F.M., of Wayville, S.A., who talked for a long time to the Duchess, said 'She is so natural that I was completely at ease, though I wondered whatever I would say to her when I was told I was to be presented.'

Freddie told the Duchess that he would rather be home. 'It's too cold over here, Your Royal Highness,' I heard him say.[34]

If these dates are correct, then Spafford's arrival date at Scampton may have been incorrectly recorded.

33 Simpson, *Lower than Low*, p.78.
34 *Sydney Daily Telegraph*, 5 April 1943.

7

George Deering

Front Gunner

The Deerings are a family of Irish descent, from a Church of Ireland background living in the homeland of Roosky, near Monaghan town. Samuel Deering was born there in 1879, as was his wife-to-be, Martha Ballagh, a Presbyterian. By the turn of the century, both were working in the grim Cavan and Monaghan Lunatic Asylum, on the outskirts of Monaghan town. Samuel worked as an attendant, Martha as a maid. The institutions in which mentally ill people lived at this time were very poor and unenlightened by modern standards, and this facility was no exception. At the time of its construction in 1867 it was the largest asylum in Ireland.

Sometime in the early part of the twentieth century Martha Ballagh moved to Wallington in Surrey and Samuel Deering took up a new job in Woodilee Asylum in Lenzie, near Kirkintilloch in Scotland. The pair were married in Christ Church Presbyterian in Wallington in August 1905. The married couple then moved to Kirkintilloch, and Martha got a job nearby at a private asylum at Westermains. This was owned by Mr James Lawrie and was advertised as being 'A private institution for the Care and Treatment of a limited number of Ladies (exclusively) suffering under the milder forms of Mental Ailment'. She appears to have also secured accommodation in the premises. By the time of the 1921 Census, Westermains was recorded as being an annexe of Woodilee Asylum, Samuel as an attendant and Martha as a cook. George's birth certificate shows Westermains House as his place of birth and the whole Deering family were photographed on the steps outside the house when he was a small boy, with everyone dressed in their Sunday finery. The four Deering children were all born in Kirkintilloch: three girls, Sarah (b. 1906), Charlotte (b. 1908) and Margaret (b. 1917), followed by their only son, George Andrew, born on 23 July 1919.

In October 1925, the family left Scotland. Both Samuel and Martha had been born in Ireland, which was partitioned in 1922 into two separate entities: Northern Ireland, with six counties and still part of the UK, and the remaining twenty-six counties which formed the Irish Free State, a dominion under its own government. Although they were both natives of Co. Monaghan, a county in the Free State, they decided to move to Northern Ireland and they bought a fruit farm in Co. Armagh. The authorities at Woodilee were apparently very sorry to see the couple leave. Samuel was now in charge of the asylum's branch at Westermains, and he was presented with a gift and the hopes that both he and his wife 'would experience an almost complete recovery to health'.[35]

Whether the fruit farm business worked or not is not known, but in 1927 they moved again. The family decided to take advantage of the various schemes offering British citizens the chance of relocation to Canada and left via Belfast on the SS *Montnairn*, which docked in Saint John, New Brunswick, on 10 April 1927. They then moved to the city of Toronto, despite the fact that the schemes were largely aimed at providing workers for the agricultural provinces further west. Samuel found it difficult to get employment but the two older

---

35 *Kirkintilloch Herald*, 14 October 1925.

girls worked and brought in an income for the family. Margaret and George went to local schools.[36]

To add to their difficulties, in August 1930 Martha Ballagh died and Charlotte became the family's housekeeper. Samuel had a job as a watchman but had lost his savings in an unwise investment in the 1929 crash. The two younger children were still at school, with George finishing his education at Essex Street school, Toronto, in 1935, at the age of 16. He took a job at a shoe manufacturing company and stayed there until the war came. However, he also studied part time, first at business college learning shorthand and typing, and then at the Canadian branch of the Technological Institute of Great Britain, studying aircraft design, mathematics and applied mechanics. Another tragedy struck in 1939 when Sarah (known as Sadie), who was working as a stenographer, died suddenly of a heart attack aged just 33.

George Deering was a bright young man, doing well in his studies, and involved in a range of sports and other activities. He was active in a youth group based in an Anglican church and liked music of different types, even owning a guitar. He also had an interest in flying. He joined the Air League of the British Empire (which still exists as the Air League charity) and took flying lessons at the Toronto Flying Club, gaining his pilot's wings. So it was probably inevitable that when war came he would try to join the RCAF, and after applying in March 1940, he was signed up at Toronto Recruiting Centre on 1 July. Assessment of which stream he would join followed and, although he wanted to be a pilot, he was eventually sent to be trained to be a wireless operator/air gunner. He was posted for wireless training to Calgary, Alberta, and then to the Bombing and Gunnery School at Jarvis, Ontario. He was promoted to Sergeant in February 1941.

---

36 Chris Ward and Clare Bennett, *Dambuster Deering* (Bomber Command Books, 2020). This book is the source for further information in this chapter.

Deering after qualifying as a
wireless operator/air gunner.
(Deering family collection)

In April 1941, after a final course at RCAF Debert in Nova Scotia, the last staging post on the route to the port of Halifax, Deering embarked on a troopship to England, arriving on 19 April. After processing at the reception centre in Bournemouth, his next stop was more training at No. 2 Radio School, Yatesbury. A few weeks later, on 31 May, he took another step towards flying when he was posted to 21 Operational Training Unit at RAF Moreton-in-Marsh. Here the trainees learnt the intricacies of flying in a Wellington bomber, and the different skills required.

At the Operational Training Unit, Deering crewed up as an air gunner with three other trainees, Flt Sgt George Fitz-Gibbon (wireless operator), Sgt J.G. Smith (observer) and Sgt Loder (gunner) and waited to be posted to a squadron, where they would be given a pilot (or, more likely, where a pilot would select them as a suitable crew). Fitz-Gibbon was a fellow Canadian, from Fort Erie, Ontario.

The four transferred together on 16 August 1941 to 103 Squadron at RAF Elsham Wolds in North Lincolnshire. There they were assigned to be the crew of Flg Off Douglas Peck, who had been with the squadron since 16 June, flying as second pilot on three occasions. The Wellingtons of 103 Squadron had a crew of six: pilot, second pilot, observer, wireless operator and two air gunners. It was the normal practice for five of the crew to stay together from one operation to another, while new pilots just arrived on the squadron flew with them as the second pilot to gain experience. So it was on 11 September that Peck, with three operations, and his new crew who had none, were allocated another new pilot, Sgt S.S. Martin, for their first trip together. A total of four new crews, constituted in this way, were sent to attack Le Havre. In the event, it was a disappointing operation: due to low cloud only two aircraft were able to locate the target, and Peck's crew brought their bombs back to base.

The Peck crew would go on to fly on twenty-three more trips over the next six months, with Deering and Fitz-Gibbon flying on all of them and Smith on most. Loder left the crew and was replaced by Sgt F.T. Hooper about halfway through. Deering paid visits to all of Bomber Command's major targets over this period, ranging from Hamburg on the north coast of Germany to an attack on the Renault factory at Billancourt, near Paris in the south. He also notched up another operation, flying to Wilhelmshaven in Plt Off Wallis's crew on 16 December 1941, replacing one of his regular gunners.

Because he had undertaken three 'second dickey' trips at the beginning of his operational career, Douglas Peck finished his tour

Deering and crew in 103 Squadron. (Deering family collection)

with a trip to Cologne on 13 March. However, most of those who were flying in his crew at that point were still short of the target of thirty, including Deering, who now had a total of twenty-five. He, Fitz-Gibbon and Smith, who had now been together for six months, remained in the active crew taken over by pilot Flt Lt Clive Saxelby, who had returned to 103 Squadron for a second tour. He had been recommended for a DFC after his first, although it wouldn't be gazetted until May 1942.

Saxelby was a New Zealander but he had been commissioned into the RAF at the start of the war. He would have an eventful second tour, shot down on a raid in September 1942. He bailed out and became a prisoner of war. Imprisoned in Stalag Luft III, he was involved in the Great Escape but was still in the tunnel when the Germans discovered the dig. After the war, he stayed on in the RAF and was Commanding Officer of 617 Squadron from 1946 to 1947.

Deering, Fitz-Gibbon and Smith flew on six operations with Saxelby in a very busy twelve days. The first was a trip to Poissy, a suburb of Paris, on 2 April 1942. Raids on Cologne, Hamburg and two on Essen followed before this spell was completed on 14 April with an attack on Dortmund. Deering then fitted in another operation with Plt Off Ken Wallis, a trip on 18 April when the target was Hamburg. Unable to turn on the nacelle fuel tanks, the pilot abandoned the primary target and instead bombed the port of Cuxhaven. The front turret also developed a problem but fortunately the aircraft made it back to base safely.

This meant that Deering had done a total of thirty-two operations, twenty-four with Peck, two with Wallis and six with Saxelby, and his tour was over. Thereupon, Deering and Fitz-Gibbon were posted together to 22 Operational Training Unit at RAF Wellesbourne Mountford to take up training roles. Deering was given five days, leave before leaving 103 Squadron and ten days leave before starting at 22 Operational Training Unit. So he reported for duty at his new posting on 23 May 1942, ready to start instructing. However, the powers that be had other ideas and it would not be long before he was back in action.

Arthur Harris's first Thousand Bomber operation was scheduled for 30 May, with the target being Cologne. In order to get this many aircraft into the sky he needed to call on experienced crews from the training units and their sometimes rather old machines. No fewer than thirty-five Wellingtons would come from Deering's new location, twenty-five of these taking off from Wellesbourne Mountford with the other ten moved over to Elsham Wolds. Deering flew as rear gunner in a crew skippered by Plt Off W.C. Klassen, with Flt Sgt R.E. Walker, Plt Off G.R. Harsh and Flt Sgt G.H. Moon also on board. They took off on time, reached the target and bombed successfully from 15,000ft.

Senior officers were pleased with the results, so while all the aircraft and crews were all gathered in the right places a second massive operation was mounted on Essen two days later, on 1 June. This time, only 954 aircraft took off, but Klassen, Deering and the rest of their comrades were among them. However, their wireless equipment failed so they had to abandon the mission.

Having started his period away from the front line by taking part in two more operations, the rest of Deering's time at 22 Operational Training Unit seems to have passed relatively quietly. There was a constant throughput of young aircrew, many Canadian, to be trained so this might have added some interest. In early February he had been recommended for a commission and this was approved, so perhaps this added to his sense of urgency. Like many men who had survived one tour, he must have wanted to get back on operations. Heavy bombers were now streaming off the production lines and Bomber Command now had a much more powerful weapon which it could unleash on German targets. For a young man who wanted to carry on the fight, being confined to a backwater doing training on elderly Wellingtons must have caused him to glance enviously over the fence at the outside world.

At some point in mid-March 1943 – but we don't know how – George Deering found out that a new squadron was being formed in a different Bomber Command group at an airfield more than 100 miles from where he was currently situated. He appears to have been on leave between 19 and 25 March, so perhaps he met someone somewhere who had heard some gossip. It's also possible that he heard from fellow instructor Flg Off Revie Walker, one of the many other Canadians in the unit, that a new squadron was being formed, since it seems that Walker was contacted by David Shannon with the offer of a place as his navigator. Walker was also good friends with Gibson's wireless operator, Bob Hutchison. By whatever means he found out, we do know that Deering arrived at Scampton on or about 29 March and within six days he was climbing into an Avro Lancaster – possibly for the first time in his life – and setting off on a training flight which would mark his place in history.

8

Richard Trevor-Roper

Rear Gunner

Richard Dacre Trevor-Roper was born in Shanklin on the Isle of Wight on 19 May 1915, the son of Charles and Gertrude Trevor-Roper. He was the middle child of the family: one sister, Elizabeth, was born in 1914; the other, Anne, in 1916.

The Trevor-Roper family came from North Wales and had owned a large seventeenth-century house, Plâs Teg, and its surrounding estate for a considerable time. When Charles Cadwaladr Trevor-Roper – Richard's father – was born, in 1884, it was in the hands of his uncle, Charles James Trevor-Roper. Charles's parents George and Harriette moved to Bedford when Charles and his brother were still children. When Charles was 17, his uncle died and he inherited Plâs Teg.

Charles served in the Royal Welsh Fusiliers, a territorial regiment, between 1906 and 1910. He then embarked on an acting career, including touring with Harry (son of Henry) Irving and performing at the Savoy Theatre in the West End. By the time the war came he had married Gertrude Clabby and the couple had a baby girl, Elizabeth. They were living in London and Newbury, but he rejoined the army, taking up a commission in a battalion of the Hampshire Regiment. This was then a territorial battalion, serving on the home front in the Isle of Wight, which is why their second child, Richard, was born there in 1915.

In 1916, everything changed with the passing of the Military Service Act. Conscription was introduced and territorial battalions were sent over the Channel to the Western Front. Charles joined the 14th Battalion of the Hampshires in September as a Captain, and they were posted to Flanders. In mid-1917, his battalion formed part of the 116th Brigade ready to launch an offensive to capture a ridge near Ypres. The ensuing conflict, which became known as the Battle of Passchendaele and would drag on until November, started in July and Charles died on 3 August, from wounds probably received the previous day.

Gertrude Trevor-Roper therefore became a war widow with three small children. Worse, Charles had died intestate so the death duties for Plâs Teg were punitive. However, Richard was sent to Oriel House prep school in Flintshire and then to Wellington College, where there were many other boys whose fathers had died in the Great War.

Wellington College was originally founded to provide an almost free education to the sons of army officers who had died in service, and throughout its history has provided up to eighty places at a time for such students, known as Foundationers. Richard took up one of these places when he went to the college in September 1928. He was placed in Blücher Dormitory (House). While at college he played in the dormitory's rugby team, and became a dormitory prefect and Sergeant in the Corps. In his penultimate year he studied in what was known as the 'Army Lower Sixth', the stream designed for those boys who were destined for the service. He rose to the sixth form for his final year in order to take the exams to enter the Royal Military Academy in Woolwich, the usual pathway for young men wanting to be commissioned in the Royal Artillery, the Royal Engineers or the Royal Corps of Signals. Contrary to some of the material which has been circulated since this time about his school life, there is nothing in the Wellington College archives to indicate that he either left the school early or was disciplined before leaving.[37]

Richard left Wellington in December 1933 and then in February 1934 entered the Royal Military Academy (RMA) at Woolwich, with his age being very precisely recorded on the day of his arrival as being '18 years, 8 months and 14 days'.[38] He was in a class of sixty-two cadets, nearly all from public schools and many whose fathers who had been army officers. This was the last decade of the academy's two-century existence: it would close in 1939 at the outset of war and then be amalgamated with its equivalent at RMA Sandhurst when this reopened in 1947. The academy had many formal traditions including dining-in nights where the cadets wore formal dress. The military artist Amies Milner must have been invited to one of these and drew a cartoon-style portrait of Richard in his formal outfit.

The young Second Lieutenant Trevor-Roper was commissioned into the Royal Artillery on 29 August 1935. By 1937, he was serving in the regiment's 2nd Medium Brigade at Longmoor camp in Hampshire. However, he then resigned his commission with effect from 1 August 1937, and left the army.[39] The circumstances remain unexplained. He then ended up in casual employment, working as a scaffolder on building sites. Family folklore says that at some point he was involved in painting Blackpool Tower.

Two years later, with war about to arrive, he decided to apply to join the RAF. In a letter to his sister Elizabeth, sent on 29 August 1939, he told her what he had been doing over the previous months. He had managed to join up and was now stationed at RAF Cardington in Bedfordshire. Styled as 'AC2 Roper 652959', he wrote:

---

37 Wellington College Archives.
38 RMA Register of Cadets, RMA Sandhurst collection.
39 Army List, January 1937. *London Gazette*, 3 August 1937, p.4935.

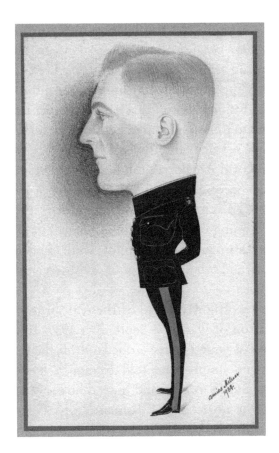

Trevor-Roper in mess dress at the Royal Military Academy, Woolwich. (Trevor-Roper family collection)

I have been to almost every RAF station in the south during the last fortnight. Their Lordships of the Air Ministry have decided that they don't really require me as a pilot and so four of us have decided to enlist and try our luck that way.

I am therefore here to be trained as a wireless operator. Its an absolutely wizard life of course, everything is in a hopeless muddle at the moment. Reservists are coming in every day at the rate of about 100 an hour and nobody has the vaguest idea of where to put them or what to do with them.[40]

---

40 Richard Trevor-Roper, letter to Elizabeth Hyde Parker, approx. 30 August 1939. Spelling and punctuation as in original. (Trevor-Roper family collection)

What Trevor-Roper is referring to was the decision to cease direct training for pilots in July 1939 because all the vacancies were filled, with 'about 180 undergoing training'.[41] The similar scheme for observers/air gunners didn't appear to have any limit on the numbers recruited and so it was by this mechanism that Trevor-Roper must have been recruited. Soon after he signed up, on 24 August 1939, all recruitment into the regular service officially ceased and every man after this date joined the Royal Air Force Volunteer Reserve with the rank of an Aircraftman Second Class (AC2), regardless of their schooling or perceived social status. Selection for pilot training and other aircrew was still going on through this scheme, but after recruitment as general aircraftmen would-be pilots were identified and moved into one channel and others into training as observers and wireless operator/air gunners.

In fact, Trevor-Roper was slightly ahead of the real surge that would follow the declaration of war on 3 September 1939. In the weeks following, thousands of young men swarmed outside the RAF recruitment offices, with many simply being told to come back later.

So at least he had managed to join up and indeed he moved on from Cardington (where he noticed that dismantled parts from Barnes Wallis's R101 airship were still on the site) within a few weeks. In a second letter to Elizabeth, an undated 'War Bulletin No. 2' written while he was at No. 2 Electrical and Wireless School at RAF Yatesbury, he wrote:

> Now let me tell you something of the life of an airman in war time England.
>
> I am here to learn Morse and wireless sets the sets are easy but morse is hell. I can take about 8–10 words per minute now, but we

---

41   RAF Air Historical Branch, Manning Plans and Policy, app. 1948, available at www.raf.mod.uk/our-organisation/units/air-historical-branch/second-world-war-thematic-studies/manning-plans-and-policy [accessed 1 November 2022].

have to pass out at 18–20 words per minute and I can assure you that's no mean task in the time they give us. Normally this is an 18-month course, we've got 17 weeks more, that's 21 weeks altogether!

I shall be in England all winter which is one good thing.[42]

He seemed to have settled in, he told his sister, partly because he had met up with six 'co-spirits', young men who obviously came from a similar background. 'We are known as the Mayfair gang and are thoroughly disliked by everyone else, mainly because we are better scroungers than them and never do a stroke of work. I spend most of my time when I am not struggling with morse, running a rugger team and an Amateur Dramatic Society.'

By the New Year the reality of what they had all signed up for had dawned on Richard and the many others in his intake. In another letter, he wrote about what he had done at Christmas where he had spent 'odd days' with a local family – the Carringtons – with whom he had become friendly, through their daughter Mavis, who worked as a Voluntary Aid Detachment (VAD) nurse and, usefully, had a car. The father of the house, retired Brigadier Robert Carrington, had also served in the Royal Artillery, so they had plenty to talk about: 'religion, love and war which seem to be the only things that matter these days'. From the letters, it's obvious that Richard and Mavis were toying with each other's affections, but Richard was determined to keep things cool.

He went on:

The Mayfair gang now only consists of three of us, two have got theirs. They went out to France just before Christmas and were both killed last week. Although the general public don't seem to realize it, the RAF are losing about 70 men per week. All of them of course air crew, that is pilots, observers, wireless operators and air gunners. As

---

42 Richard Trevor-Roper, letter to Elizabeth Hyde Parker, ND [? October 1939]. Spelling and punctuation as in original. (Trevor-Roper family collection)

I hope to be a wireless op. and an air gunman in six weeks the prospect of surviving a long war doesn't look too hopeful ...

There's been a sort of panic here. These unfortunate kids are just beginning to realise that they are here and what they are here for. They joined up in a blaze of patriotic glory and a bath of darling Mummies tears and they are just beginning to realize that they have taken on the most dangerous job in the world and that in a few weeks' time, so far as this world is concerned, a large percentage of them are going to be nothing but a name in a casualty list ...

Those few of us who have seen, at any rate, a little of the world beyond our family circle and who have learnt to take what's coming without cracking up completely, can do nothing for them, we are living on our nerves ourselves and all we can do is stand by and watch normal boys of 17, 18 and 19 turned into neurotic wrecks.

About one man in twenty failed to come back from Christmas leave. I suppose they are hiding somewhere. Poor devils it will be all the worse for them when they are found. It's got to the stage now where the authorities cut out all the casualty lists from the flying papers before they come into camp.

For God's sake don't repeat any of this drivel. We've got the finest Air Force in the world and when it comes to the point these chaps will live or die the [way the] proverbial Briton has always lived or died. But the waiting, the intensive, rather over intensive training and the general atmosphere of Yatesbury is too much for some of them.[43]

Trevor-Roper moved through various other training courses with the last being a posting to 16 Operational Training Unit at RAF Upper Heyford in August 1940, flying on Hampdens. In early October he moved from there to one of Bomber Command's most prestigious units, No. 50 Squadron at RAF Lindholme, to begin

---

43 Richard Trevor-Roper, letter to Elizabeth Hyde Parker, 7 January 1940.
    (Trevor-Roper family collection)

operations. 50 Squadron had re-formed in April 1937 under the RAF Expansion Scheme. On the day the war started, it reported that it had '23 officers, 20 airmen pilots, 42 aircrew and 184 non-flying staff'.[44]

By October 1940 the squadron had been in front-line combat for more than nine months and was under the command of Wg Cdr G.W. Golledge. Trevor-Roper's first operation was on 6 November 1940 as one of the eight aircraft detailed to attack various railway marshalling yards. He was the rear gunner in Hampden X3004, piloted by Flt Lt Donald Johnston, with the other members of the crew being Sgt Carthew and Sgt Howell. They left Lindholme at 0215 as one of the two attacking Hamm in Germany: the only one to reach the target, the other turning back early because of instrument problems. At Hamm they dropped their four 500lb bombs successfully from 11,000ft. Severe static and icing conditions were experienced on the return flight and the carburettors iced up. Nevertheless, the aircraft landed safely at 0920.

Trevor-Roper flew on one further operation with Flt Lt Johnston but in November, Sqn Ldr Gus Walker arrived on the squadron, and Trevor-Roper was allocated to him as wireless operator/gunner. Walker had been Commanding Officer of 16 Operational Training Unit while Trevor-Roper was in training there, so they may have come across each other earlier. Their first sortie was to Hamburg on 14 November 1940, with Plt Off Rendall and Flg Off Davies making up the rest of the crew. Flt Lt Johnston and his crew also took part in this attack. Walker reported that the attack had been successful.

This was the first of some nineteen operations undertaken by Trevor-Roper in Walker's crew. Wg Cdr Golledge left and Walker was promoted to Wing Commander and took over command of the squadron. Trevor-Roper's time in Walker's crew resulted in him being awarded the DFM, the citation picking out several

---

44 'No. 50 Squadron Royal Air Force In World War Two', downloaded from www.no-50-and-no-61-squadrons-association.co.uk/history-of-no-50-squadron/ [accessed 22 August 2022].

particular incidents, particularly a return from an attack on Bremen on 11 February 1941 when first the Marconi and then the TR9 transmitter failed. It goes on:

> After working at the TR9 set for an hour Sergeant Trevor-Roper made it operate successfully by tapping 2 volts off the main 12 volt circuit. Eventually the aircraft landed safely at OAKINGTON guided to the aerodrome in conditions of extremely poor visibility, with cloud height 200 feet, entirely by strength of the TR9 transmissions. Sergeant Trevor-Roper's skill undoubtedly ensured the safe landing of this aircraft.

It went on to say that in addition to being an outstandingly able wireless operator he had excellent gunnery skills, having on two occasions doused searchlights which had held the aircraft in their beams. He was an 'outstanding inspiration' to his own and other crew, it concluded. The DFM was gazetted on 23 December 1941.[45]

One of the last operations undertaken by Walker in 50 Squadron was on 12 October 1941, on the plastics factory at Hüls. The 50 Squadron Operations Record Book shows Sgt Trevor-Roper among the three-man crew, along with the recently arrived new pilot Plt Off John Hopgood and Flt Lt Undery. Hopgood's logbook, however, doesn't list Trevor-Roper in the crew on this day, recording the crew as himself as second pilot, Undery and Flt Sgt Hobson.

Walker left soon after to take up roles as station commander, first at RAF North Luffenham and then in April 1942 at RAF Syerston, along with a promotion to Group Captain. He arrived at Syerston in the same month as Guy Gibson, who had just assumed command of 106 Squadron, as we have seen earlier.

Five days after the Hüls operation, Trevor-Roper was commissioned for the second time in his life, and from then on is listed as Plt Off Trevor-Roper in the Operations Record Book's pages. With

---

45 *London Gazette*, 23 December 1941, p.7238.

Walker gone, he flew mainly with Sqn Ldr Lloyd but also with the new squadron CO, Wg Cdr Russell Oxley. Harlo Taerum had also joined the squadron and flew his first operations in January 1942. He and Trevor-Roper flew on the same operation on a couple of occasions, the first being a series of 'Scuttle Raids' on 7 January, where individual aircraft bombed built-up areas through gaps in the clouds, having been given a GEE positional fix. Trevor-Roper flew with Sqn Ldr Lloyd and Taerum with Plt Off Norman Goldsmith.

According to Gordon Cruickshank, another 50 Squadron air gunner, Trevor-Roper was now the squadron Gunnery Leader, although this isn't recorded in the Operations Record Book. This would explain why he was sent on a temporary posting to the Parnalls factory in Gloucestershire for two weeks in February on a 'Gun Turret Course'. Parnalls were the manufacturer of the Frazer-Nash gun turret, used in various wartime aircraft.

On 14 May, Trevor-Roper was posted to 50 Squadron's Conversion Flight, which was founded at about this time, although the exact date is obscure. The first Thousand Bomber Raid on Cologne took place on 30 May, and Trevor-Roper doesn't appear to have taken part in this but, on 25 June, by which time 50 Squadron had moved from Skellingthorpe to the new concrete runways at Swinderby, he took part in the third Thousand Bomber Raid from the new station. This was an attack on the Focke-Wulf factory at Bremen, and he flew as part of a scratch crew piloted by Flg Off Norman Goldsmith, Harlo Taerum's ex-pilot. Taerum was also on this raid, in a crew skippered by Plt Off Roy Calvert.

It was while Richard Trevor-Roper was in this part of his career that his second cousin Hugh Trevor-Roper chose to write about him in his diary.[46] The diaries were not transcribed and published until

---

46 Elizabeth, Richard and Anne Trevor-Roper were second cousins of the historian Hugh Trevor-Roper (1914–2003, later Lord Dacre), Patrick Trevor-Roper (1916–2004), the ophthalmologist and gay rights activist, and Sheila Trevor-Roper (1912–92). They were all great-grandchildren of Charles Blayney Trevor-Roper (1799–1871).

many years later, after his death in 2003, and bear all the hallmarks of the finicky, gossip-loving intellectual he undoubtedly was. At this stage in his life, he may have only been a junior officer in the Secret Intelligence Service, with a single publication to his name as a young history don at Oxford, but he had developed the acerbic style which he would later put to good use in his public lectures and books. So, in between entries about subjects as diverse as his friend Frank Pakenham (later Lord Longford) being 'shot in the bottom' by a fellow Home Guard and that he realised that he was 'repelled' by women when travelling on a bus in the Haymarket, he recorded some gossip about his kinsman:

> June 1942
>
> I've never met my cousin Dick Trevor-Roper of Plâs Teg, but whenever his name drifts into my ken it is attached to some exploit showing a proper spirit of enterprise and adventure – either controlling an extensive underground betting organisation as a schoolboy at Wellington, or speedtrack-racing, or climbing the outside of skyscrapers (if this story isn't apocryphal) or disgracing the name of Trevor-Roper by being cashiered from the Regular Army, or rehabilitating it by brilliant exploits in the RAF. I expect he's an awful bounder really, but among my drab and dreary relatives, who emerge occasionally from sordid suburbs or faded spas, he beacons from afar, and helps me to bear the burden of my name. So I look with relief from them to him, as one lonely mountain might eye another across a flat and featureless waste.[47]

It is interesting to speculate what might have caused Hugh Trevor-Roper to write this entry. It may have followed public notice of the award of Richard's DFM. His remarks, coming as they do from the pen of such a distinguished historian, have however caused

---

47 Hugh Trevor-Roper, *The Wartime Journals*, edited by Richard Davenport-Hines (Tauris, 2012), p.88.

the accounts of his cousin's life to be badly tarnished, and must be treated as repetition of gossip without any evidence from the primary sources. As we have seen, there is no record of Richard being expelled from Wellington for gambling activities. He left aged 18 and went straight to the Royal Military Academy at Woolwich as an Officer Cadet. Similarly, he was not 'cashiered from the Regular Army', although he did resign his commission. Unfortunately, in these times when fake news can travel around the internet while the truth is putting its boots on (to adapt a famous phrase), many people have since copied and pasted the Regius Professor of History's wartime gossip without checking the original records.

As his cousin Hugh's diary entry was then still secret, these remarks would not have concerned Richard. He was about to add some stability to his hectic social life by getting married to Patricia Edwards. The wedding took place on 5 September 1942 in St Andrew's church in Nottingham. Patricia was the daughter of Richard Edwards and his ex-wife Hilda Menzies.

Trevor-Roper stayed on instruction duties until the autumn of 1942, and then returned to 50 Squadron on 14 November, posted in from 1660 Conversion Unit, along with pilot Sqn Ldr Peter Birch DFC and rear gunner Sgt John Hartman. Trevor-Roper was in Birch's crew for a trip to Turin on 20 November, which was unsuccessful due to engine trouble, but flew to Stuttgart two days later. Like Trevor-Roper, Birch was on his second tour. His first had been in 207 Squadron, where he had won the DFC. On being posted to 50 Squadron for a second tour he had become the flight commander of B Flight.

Trevor-Roper's arrival at Skellingthorpe brought one of the squadron's widely acknowledged party animals back to operational service. Even though he was now married, with Patricia now pregnant and living not too far away in Skegness, he was obviously still dedicated to having some off-duty fun. At some point about this time (the record shows that he was a Flight Lieutenant, to which rank he was promoted in October 1943) his messmates invested him with the award of the 'Grog Gong', stating that he had 'always

Richard and Patricia Trevor-Roper on their wedding day. (Trevor-Roper family collection)

shown a sincere devotion to the bottle, and even though surrounded by Air Commodores, Group Captains etc can still drink himself into a perfect state of coma … From all his operations at the bar he has returned unscathed, and many times has removed the pants of more sober persons.'[48]

This letting off steam happened at the same time as the war progressed into a new phase, shared by all the men who later made up the Gibson crew. Birch's second pilot on an operation to Duisburg on 8 January was Flt Lt Henry Maudslay DFC, getting back in the saddle as he returned to operations at the start of his second tour. The first had also been undertaken in 50 Squadron. It was a relatively routine operation, although the aircraft had to take evasive action when attacked by a fighter. On returning to England, the weather had closed in over Lincolnshire, which necessitated the crew landing at RAF Tangmere, Sussex.

Birch and Trevor-Roper flew on the second of the pair of Berlin operations in January 1943 which received such press attention. Theirs was on 17 January, when they led a detachment of eight 50 Squadron crews, including that of Les Knight. Birch reported that they were attacked by fighters on two occasions. The first was an Me 109, fired on by rear gunner John Hartman, with the pilot taking subsequent evasive action. Fifty minutes later, three Ju 88s attacked simultaneously. One came in from the starboard bow direction, the two others from 500ft above, one on the port side, one on the starboard. Trevor-Roper engaged the starboard side attacker while Birch dived the aircraft from 17,000ft down to 2,000ft. This was enough to throw off the attackers, but necessitated the jettisoning of the bomb load, so the target was not reached.[49] Their return flight missed the advised track by a distance of 30 miles at ground level, but this did not matter as they didn't encounter any further opposition, landing safely after a trip of almost seven hours.

---

48   Trevor-Roper family archive.
49   TNA, Combat report, AIR 50/188/417.

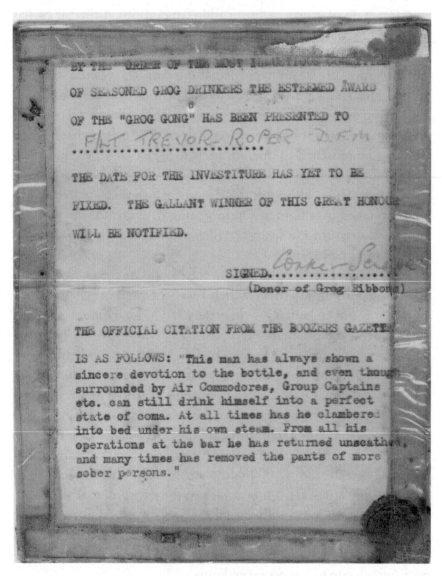

Trevor-Roper awarded the 'Grog Gong'. (Trevor-Roper family collection)

Trevor-Roper in the crew of Sqn Ldr Peter Birch in 50 Squadron. (Trevor-Roper family collection)

Altogether, Trevor-Roper would go on to fly on eleven operations over the four months he was in the Birch crew. His last was a trip to St-Nazaire on 22 March, a 'completely successful' operation according to the Operations Record Book. Their aircraft – decorated with Peter Birch's favourite 'Donkey' nose art – was forced to land at Woodhall Spa shortly before midnight due to misty conditions at Skellingthorpe. Also on this operation were the pilots Henry Maudslay and Les Knight and their crews, who would also join 617 Squadron and fly on the Dams Raid.

According to the 50 Squadron Operations Record Book, Maudslay, Knight and their crews were all transferred from Skellingthorpe to Scampton on 25 March but Trevor-Roper's posting is not listed on this day, or indeed on any other. Maudslay, incidentally, was surprised to be told the day before that he would be transferred, and even more surprised to find out that he would be a flight commander in the new squadron. He had time to write to his mother to tell her the news.[50]

Trevor-Roper is recorded as arriving at Scampton on 25 March, so perhaps he was on the Skellingthorpe bus. Whatever method of transport he used, his arrival at Scampton would mean that he was both the oldest and most experienced member of Gibson's crew. He had been on almost continuous active service since November 1940, and only his new skipper had more operations than him. He had certainly come a long way since he had taken the king's shilling as an Aircraftman Second Class in July 1939.

50 Robert Owen, *Henry Maudslay: Dam Buster* (Fighting High, 2014), p.248.

9

The Crew Comes Together

Guy Gibson stepped down as Commanding Officer of 106 Squadron shortly after finishing his second tour of operations as a bomber pilot at 0240 on Friday, 12 March 1943. He was having a lie-in the next morning when he was woken by Flt Lt Charles Martin, the squadron's adjutant, with a message that his next posting was to be to 5 Group headquarters in Grantham. There was no indication as to what job he would be required to do when he got there.

Gibson travelled the 17 miles from 106 Squadron's base at Syerston to Grantham the next day, Sunday, 14 March, returning in the evening for a farewell party. It appears that Cochrane told him on this visit that he would be setting up a new squadron, since he relayed this information to Charles Martin, who recorded it in the 106 Squadron diary, dating it that day.

The impression is sometimes given that Cochrane and Gibson had not met before this encounter, as Cochrane had only taken over command of 5 Group on 27 February. However, earlier in the war Cochrane had been Director of Flying Training while Gibson had served as an instructor, and he had been at Syerston on 11 March, the day on which Gibson flew on his last operation in 106 Squadron.[51]

---

51 Richard Mead, *Dambuster-in-Chief* (Pen and Sword, 2020), pp. 132–3.

If Gibson was told about his new role, then the information must have been given informally since it wasn't until Monday, 15 March 1943 that Air Chief Marshal Sir Arthur Harris officially chose 5 Group to undertake preparatory work on the Dams Raid. He sent a memo to the group's Air Officer Commanding, Air Vice Marshal the Hon Ralph Cochrane, telling him that he would need to set up a new squadron to undertake the operation, but emphasising that he should not reduce the efforts of his main force.

This was followed by two further memos written on Wednesday, 17 March sent by Harris's Senior Air Staff Officer, Air Vice Marshal Robert Oxland. The first was to the Director of Bomber Operations, Air Cdre Sydney Bufton, stating that Harris had decided 'this afternoon' that a new squadron should be formed.

The second memo was sent to Cochrane. It described the new Upkeep weapon: it was, Oxland said, a spherical bomb that if spun and dropped from a height of 100ft at about 200mph would travel 1,200 yards:

> It is proposed to use this weapon in the first instance against a large dam in Germany, which, if breached, will have serious consequences in the neighbouring industrial area … The operation against this dam will not, it is thought, prove particularly dangerous [*sic*], but it will undoubtedly require skilled crews. Volunteer crews will, therefore, have to be carefully selected from the squadrons in your Group.[52]

It is worth noting that Oxland called the weapon a spherical bomb, but it was soon changed to a large cylinder, much the shape and size of a cricket pitch heavy grass roller. At first, the cylinder was enclosed in a wooden sphere, but this proved impractical so was not used.

---

52 TNA, AIR 14/840.

This second memo led to a circular being sent by 5 Group to all its squadrons, asking them to provide a pilot and crew for a new squadron, for a special one-off operation. No copies of the circular survive, but it would seem to have specified that the crew should be experienced, even perhaps have completed a full tour. Individual squadron commanders interpreted this circular in different ways, as has been documented in the relevant sections of my earlier book, *The Complete Dambusters*.[53]

Gibson seems to have been at 5 Group HQ while all the paperwork was going on, and on Thursday, 18 March he was summoned again to Cochrane's office. This time, Gp Capt 'Charles' Whitworth, the Commanding Officer of RAF Scampton, was also present. There was space available at Scampton at the time, since there was only one unit based there, 57 Squadron. Despite the 106 Squadron adjutant's note from four days before, it was at that meeting that Gibson was formally asked to do 'one more operation' and told that he would be commanding a new squadron.

Gibson probably arrived at Scampton three days later, on Sunday, 21 March, before any pilots or other aircrew had been posted to the station. But the news had travelled fast, since some of the administrative staff may have been ready to start including Flt Lt Charles Pain, who had been posted by 5 Group to be the new squadron's adjutant. Gibson fell out with him almost immediately – the exact cause isn't known – and arranged for him to be removed. He asked for him to be replaced by Flg Off Harry Humphries, whom he knew from Syerston and whom he reckoned was ready for a promotion. Humphries had been Syerston's Committee of Adjustment Officer, the man who dealt with the admin duties when an airman had gone missing and was either dead or a prisoner of war ('posted to No. 1 Depot RAF Uxbridge, Non Effective, Missing' as would be noted in the official records). Humphries duly turned up on 1 April, with a promotion to Flight Lieutenant.

---

53   Charles Foster, *The Complete Dambusters* (The History Press, 2018), pp.43–71.

It is likely that it was around this time that Gibson telephoned a few people he knew personally. Two were pilots from 106 Squadron, John Hopgood and David Shannon. He had flown with both of these, and liked and trusted both. Another was Joe McCarthy, whom Gibson had heard about because he was a close friend of another of his 106 Squadron pilots, Don Curtin. Curtin and McCarthy were both American citizens, friends from New York City, who had joined the RCAF together in 1941. They went through training together but had been separated when going on active service: Curtin to 106 Squadron, McCarthy to 97 Squadron. Curtin had flown on more than twenty operations before being shot down and killed in February 1943.

Another of Gibson's phone calls was to Harold ('Mick') Martin, who was just coming to the end of a spell as an instructor at 1654 Conversion Unit at RAF Wigsley. Several months previously Gibson had met him at an investiture and they had discussed low-flying methods, so he was an almost automatic choice for the project. There is evidence that Martin immediately began to pull together much of his old crew from his time in 50 Squadron. They had all dispersed to instructional jobs, but were happy to go back to flying with their charismatic skipper. His navigator, Jack Leggo, had completed a full tour and had a DFC, collecting it at Buckingham Palace on the same day as Martin himself. Both his gunners, Toby Foxlee and Tom Simpson, had also completed tours with Martin in the cockpit. Leggo, Foxlee and Simpson were all Australians but Ivan Whittaker, his most recent flight engineer, came from Newcastle upon Tyne and had flown with him for several months. Add in another Aussie from 50 Squadron, Bob Hay, widely recognised as an excellent bomb aimer, and New Zealander Len Chambers as wireless operator, who had thirty-seven operations in 75 Squadron, and you had one of the 'experienced crews' that the 5 Group memo had asked squadron commanders to provide. Leggo and Hay, both extrovert personalities and each with DFCs and a formidable number of operations, were quickly appointed as the new squadron's Navigation and Bombing

Leaders respectively. Gibson had met Hay in December 1942 when, as Group Bombing Leader, he came to speak to 106 Squadron about the new bomb sight which was going into action.

Having sorted out their own crew, Martin and Hay would seem to have been involved in head-hunting a crew for Gibson himself, bringing in three men who had served with them on 50 Squadron. For a period in the summer of 1942, in a rest from his bomb-aiming duties, Hay had flown as the navigator in Hugh Everitt's 50 Squadron crew with another Australian, Fred Spafford, as the bomb aimer. Spafford turned out, unsurprisingly, to be another extrovert and would fit in with Gibson's crew. Spafford, in his turn, had been at 50 Squadron since April 1942, and overlapped with Canadian naviga-tor Harlo Taerum for several months. Taerum was also well known to Martin, having been at the same 1654 Conversion Unit at RAF Wigsley since October 1942, and had been part of the crew he took on two operations to Berlin on 16 and 17 January 1943. As well as all this, Taerum had overlapped with Richard Trevor-Roper for the first six months of 1942. They may not have flown together, but they had certainly known each other. Trevor-Roper had actually joined 50 Squadron as far back as October 1940 and most of his first tour was undertaken in the crew skippered by squadron CO, Wg Cdr Gus Walker, so he, too, would undoubtedly have been well known on the station. Trevor-Roper had been on instructional work for several months but had rejoined 50 Squadron in November 1942, and was back on operations, flying in Sqn Ldr Peter Birch's Lancaster crew. Trevor-Roper's upper-class manner and reputation as a hellraiser might also have endeared him to Gibson, as would be the fact that he was well known to Gus Walker, whose accident as witnessed by Gibson we have already discussed.

Meanwhile, at 1654 Conversion Unit at RAF Wigsley, where Martin was notionally still an instructor, an experienced wireless operator had just turned up expecting to undertake instructional duties. This was Robert Hutchison, recently in Gibson's crew at 106 Squadron. A meticulous noter of dates in his own logbook,

Hutchison recorded his arrival at Wigsley on 19 March 1943, and his departure for Scampton six days later, on 25 March. He may well have received a phone call at Wigsley from Gibson, or perhaps the astute Martin spotted the connection and put the two back in touch. Also, as he had been the Signals Leader at 106 Squadron, he could fill this role in his new unit.

So that was four of the skipper's crew sorted, although they would take several days to organise themselves and travel to their new station. Gibson needed this help from Martin, Hay and probably others because he was busy with his own schedule. On Wednesday, 24 March, he found out a little bit more about the task he was being asked to undertake. Satterley called him over to Grantham again and told him that a driver would take him to 'an old country railway station' near London from where he should get a train to Weybridge in Surrey, where he would be met. In *Enemy Coast Ahead* he describes this as happening after most of the aircrews had arrived at Scampton, but in reality it was before.

From the anonymous station near London, Gibson caught his train to Weybridge, and there to pick him up was Mutt Summers, Vickers-Armstrongs' chief test pilot, to whom Gibson had written for advice as a schoolboy when deciding on a career. They had never met in person. Summers drove him to Burhill Golf Club, which had been requisitioned by the government to give Vickers a drawing office away from the main factory, and he was introduced to its assistant chief designer, Barnes Wallis. Everything at the golf club was cloaked in secrecy, with special passes being demanded at every checkpoint.

Wallis and Gibson hit it off quite well, but it was awkward for Wallis since Gibson was not on the list of people to whom he was allowed to divulge the target. However, he was able to tell him something about the requirements – the weapon would have to be dropped at night from low height into water at a speed of 240mph. Then he showed him some of the films he had been hawking round Whitehall just a month or so earlier.

When Gibson wrote *Enemy Coast Ahead* in 1944 everything about the Dams Raid was, of course, still a closely guarded secret. So this description of what he saw for the first time that afternoon is very imprecise:

> When [the aeroplane] got to about two hundred feet it levelled out and a huge cylindrical object fell from it rather slowly towards the water. I was amazed; I expected to see the aircraft blown sky high. But when it hit the water, there was a great splash and then – it worked. That's all I can say to describe it – just that it worked, while the aeroplane flew over serenely on its way.[54]

One can only speculate what Gibson said to himself about the way in which the 'bouncing bomb' worked. He describes himself as going back to Scampton deep in thought, as well he might.

In the meantime, Martin arrived at Scampton and seemed to carry on his unofficial role as a personnel officer. He sorted out several unattached aircrew who heard the gossip about a new squadron being formed and wangled themselves a transfer to Scampton, looking for work.[55]

One of these unattached men would seem to have been George Deering, an experienced air gunner. On 29 March, five days after Gibson's trip to Burhill, Deering turned up. He had been undertaking training duties in 22 Operational Training Unit at RAF Wellesbourne Mountford, and he was allocated to Gibson's crew. This was completed on 4 April by flight engineer John Pulford, who was thirteen operations into his first tour with 97 Squadron when he was posted to Scampton.

---

54 Gibson, *Enemy Coast Ahead*, p.251.
55 These included George Chalmers, who became the wireless operator in Bill Townsend's crew. Source: Max Arthur, *Dambusters: A Landmark Oral History* (Virgin, 2008), pp.15–16. Martin may also have paid a part in the recruitment of Ken Brown and his crew from 44 Squadron, who had passed through his hands at 1654 Conversion Unit.

Gibson's logbook states that he took his full crew out for the first time on 1 April, on a local training flight lasting one hour. He records the crew as:

P/O Tearom [*sic*]
P/O Stafford
F/Lt Trevor-Roper
F/Lt Hutchison
P/O Deering
Sgt Pulford

However, the date of 1 April is almost certainly an error. Both Hutchison and Taerum are notably meticulous logbook keepers, and neither recorded a flight on 1 April. Indeed, they both independently record their first trip with Gibson in their new squadron as taking place on 4 April. Hutchison notes this as a 'low-level X country' lasting one hour twenty-five minutes and Taerum as 'Local-Base-Sheffield Area' for one hour twenty minutes. Gibson records the flight as a 'Lake near Sheffield' lasting one hour twenty minutes. Because he seems to think this is his second flight with his new crew, he just writes the single word 'Crew' in the relevant column, a description he repeats for the next six weeks.

Add to the logbook entries the evidence that Spafford was on leave in London at the beginning of April, playing golf with Tom Simpson, and that Pulford's transfer isn't recorded until 4 April, it is most likely that 4 April was the first time all six of his crew flew with their new skipper. However, the fact that he lists them all in his logbook on the earlier date, even if it's wrong, would suggest that he regarded them as the crew he had settled on for the upcoming operation.

It's interesting to speculate what they all made of each other as they clambered into a 'borrowed' Lancaster, No. W4940, on this April afternoon. Even those who hadn't flown with Gibson before had probably all heard of him, since squadron COs tended to have reputations which spread beyond their individual commands. Hutchison, of course, knew Gibson well, but doesn't seem to have come across any of the others. Taerum and Trevor-Roper had met, and Taerum had also met Spafford, so the three of them had 50 Squadron banter to rely on. Deering and Pulford would have been the odd ones out, but Deering was Canadian so had something in common with Taerum even though one was from a big city and the other from the prairies. Pulford was the least experienced; as a Sergeant in a crew with six officers and also a working-class Yorkshireman who had left school at 14, he probably felt somewhat excluded. His new skipper's occasional irritability would not have helped.

If they ever got round to sharing lists of operations then they would have discovered some common experiences. The first Thousand Bomber Raid – now nearly a year ago – was probably a formative event for those who had taken part, and Taerum, Deering and Hutchison had all flown on this. Gibson, Hutchison and Spafford had all flown on the Le Creusot trip in October 1942. And Gibson, Hutchison, Taerum, Trevor-Roper and Pulford had all been to Berlin in January 1943, although only the first two had had their participation recorded for posterity by the BBC. Even without their pilot, the six men had clocked up 193 operations between them.

They might also have discussed what two of their number would be doing as the new squadron's trade 'leaders'. Hutchison would be responsible for the wireless operators as the squadron Signals Leader and Trevor-Roper for the gunners as the Gunnery Leader. The other two leaders, the Australians Bob Hay for Bombing and Jack Leggo for Navigation, would come from Mick Martin's crew. The presence of all four leaders in these two crews would cement their positions in the squadron's pecking order.

10

The Plan to Attack
the German Dams

In the course of his meetings with Barnes Wallis, Gibson was let into the secret which had been a long time in the planning. This chapter will examine how the plan was developed. Two dams, the Möhne and the Sorpe, controlled the water flow in the heavily industrialised Ruhr valley, and had been identified well before the war started. Air Ministry planners argued that if both were destroyed the valley's power stations could be neutralised. However, the Ministry also recognised that in order for a successful attack to be mounted three separate developments needed to occur. There needed to be an explosive device of sufficient size, an aircraft big enough to carry it and aircrew who could be trained in any special delivery method.

Committees were set up and papers were written and circulated, but no conclusions were reached. However, an attack on the dams remained on the agenda. Significantly, in July 1940 Air Marshal Sir Charles Portal, at that stage the Air Officer Commanding-in-Chief of RAF Bomber Command, wrote to the Secretary of State for Air arguing 'that the time has arrived when we should make arrangements for the destruction of the Möhne Dam'.[56] Later that year Portal became Chief of the Air Staff – the overall head of the RAF

---

56 John Sweetman, *The Dambusters Raid* (Cassell, 2002), p.26. This chapter
    owes much to the first three chapters of Sweetman's book.

– and it was in this position he was later able to give support for the Dams Raid at a number of crucial points.

Independently of the Air Ministry and its committees, the assistant chief designer of the aircraft manufacturer Vickers-Armstrongs, Barnes Wallis, had taken an interest in methods for attacking German dams from the beginning of the war. Wallis started his own research and devised a much larger 22,400lb bomb, but with no aircraft available which could carry such a huge payload, Wallis turned his attention to finding a different method.

By coincidence, a team of engineers from the Building Research Station (BRS) in Garston, near Watford, who had been working on the effects of explosives on structures since before the war, were transferred to the Road Research Laboratory in Harmondsworth. Led by A.R. Collins, they had also identified the Möhne Dam as a possible target.

Wallis and Collins met and discussed how much damage would be caused if a large explosion occurred on the upstream side of the Möhne Dam, very close to the wall. They decided that the most effective way to determine the weight of explosive needed, and the optimum location to detonate it to breach the dam, was to construct a scale model and then blow it up. Dr Norman Davey agreed to build this at the BRS site at Garston, and so work began in November 1940 in a secluded corner of the site. Some 2 million miniature concrete blocks were made, and the construction took about six weeks. The model was completed on 21 January 1941 and the area behind filled with water. The first explosive test took place the following day, the first of ten tests. The model – which can still be seen at Garston – was badly damaged.

Wallis took all the information from the tests and combined it with his own research, and wrote a massive 117-page paper. It described the current bombing campaigns as 'puny efforts' and proposed a different strategy, involving much bigger 4,000 and 10,000lb bombs, and a much larger aircraft in order to deliver them. In March 1941, he circulated more than 100 copies all over Whitehall.

The note was eventually considered by various Whitehall committees and sub-committees. Unfortunately for Wallis, the final answer to his proposals was 'no'. As Wallis knew, at that point four-engine heavy bombers were only just becoming available, and there was no enthusiasm for diverting resources into developing an even bigger one.

But at least Wallis's ideas had been considered, and he had got an audience interested. Although disheartened, Wallis went back to his research and gave the matter further thought. Then came his brainwave. 'Early in 1942,' he later wrote, 'I had the idea of a missile, which if dropped on the water at a considerable distance upstream of the dam would reach the dam in a series of ricochets, and after impact against the crest of the dam would sink in close contact with the upstream face of the masonry.'

Then began Wallis's famous experiments in his garden in Effingham using his children's marbles, firing them from a catapult across the surface of a tub of water, on which they bounced. They landed second bounce on a table, where the fall was marked in chalk by one of his children. He also modified the shape of his bomb, believing that a spherical shape would work better.

At this stage, thinking that the weapon would be most useful for the Fleet Air Arm, he wrote another paper and sent it to another of his circle of friends, Professor P.M.S. Blackett, the scientific adviser to the Admiralty. Blackett could also see its relevance for the RAF, and informed Sir Henry Tizard at the Ministry of Aircraft Production. Tizard had been consulted before about Wallis's earlier paper, but this time he saw merit in the idea and travelled to Burhill Golf Club to meet Wallis again. Wallis found him 'kindly and very knowledgeable' and through him secured permission to use the large water tanks at the National Physical Laboratories in Teddington for further research. Work began there on 9 June 1942 and continued until September. [57] At some point, Wallis decided to introduce back

---

[57] Sweetman, *Dambusters Raid*, p.39.

spin to the projectile. A succession of research grandees came to see the tests in action, and Wallis was given permission for a Wellington to be used for test drops.

Meanwhile, Collins and his colleagues at the Road Research Laboratory had been given permission to scale up their dam experiments on the disused Nant-y-Gro Dam in the Elan Valley in Powys. Early tests were unsuccessful. Then it was decided to place an explosive charge in contact with the base of the dam. On 24 July a mine with 279lb of explosive was placed in at the centre of the dam, 7ft 6in below its crest, and detonated. The result was so spectacular – a huge waterspout and the centre of the dam punched out – that Collins, who was recording events on a ciné camera, temporarily stopped filming. Extrapolation of the results showed that a similar result could be achieved on a larger dam with a 7,500lb bomb. Crucially, a single bomb of this weight could be carried by the new four-engine Avro Lancaster, which had been in service with the RAF since January that year.

The development of four-engine heavy bombers can be argued as being one of the most crucial pre-war decisions taken by the UK Government, contrasting with Germany's perseverance with the medium two-engine bomber throughout the war. And the delay in starting rearmament, caused by the vacillation of the Stanley Baldwin Government before 1936, in fact proved to be a benefit since commissioning of new aircraft at this time would have left the RAF beginning the war with a fleet of immediately outdated aircraft.

Heavy bomber production contracts were given to Short Brothers to build the Stirling aircraft, to A.V. Roe (Avro) and to Handley Page. Avro first developed the Manchester bomber, which used two large Rolls-Royce Vulture engines, but this proved unsatisfactory and it was superseded by the four-engine Lancaster, using the smaller but more efficient Rolls-Royce Merlin engine. Handley Page's Halifax was also designed with four Merlin engines.

Of these three, the Lancaster quickly became the most potent striking force. It had a massive uninterrupted bomb bay (something which would prove important later in the war when the Barnes Wallis-designed Tallboy and Grand Slam bombs became available) and large fuel tanks, and these put targets in both the east of Germany and Italy in range. By the end of 1942 most of the squadrons in Bomber Command's 5 Group had been equipped with Lancasters, and it would be from this group that the aircrew who would make up the Dams Raid strike force would eventually be selected.

Meanwhile, Wallis was busy building a prototype spinning device, and its first airborne trial took place on 4 December. A modified Wellington with Wallis himself as bomb aimer dropped a spherical dummy on the test range at Chesil Beach on the Dorset coast, but it shattered on impact with the water. It wasn't until the fourth trial on 23 January, when a wooden sphere was used for the first time, that a successful series of thirteen bounces occurred.

Several more were dropped successfully over the following days. Then Wallis set about trying to get agreement to develop two separate versions of the weapon: a large version, called Upkeep, for use in a Lancaster against the dams, and a smaller version, Highball, which could be dropped by a Mosquito against shipping, and he began the process of hawking film footage from Chesil Beach and Teddington around Whitehall. To go with this, he had written another paper, 'Air Attack on Dams'. This was accompanied by a covering letter which claimed Mosquitoes would be ready to test the Highball weapon in six to eight weeks but 'unfortunately have overshadowed the question of the major German dams'. Wallis went on: 'if a high-level decision' were taken to give equal priority to both weapons 'we could develop the large sphere to be dropped from a Lancaster bomber within a period of two months'.[58]

The one senior RAF officer who was not convinced was the man who commanded the aircrew who would be needed to drop the weapon, Air Marshal Sir Arthur Harris, now the Air Officer Commanding-in-Chief of Bomber Command. His Senior Air

---

58 Sweetman, *Dambusters Raid*, pp.49–50.

Staff Officer, Air Vice Marshal Robert Saundby, sent him a lengthy minute on 14 February, outlining the research and testing of Highball and considering the possibility of a 'similar weapon' for the special purpose of destroying dams, in particular the Möhne. A specially modified Lancaster would be needed and the attack would need to be made when the dam was full or nearly full. One squadron would have to be nominated, depriving Bomber Command of its strength for 'two or three weeks' for training. The tactics would not be difficult, Saundby concluded, somewhat optimistically.

Harris was not at all convinced. He handwrote a scathing note on Saundby's minute:

> This is tripe of the wildest description … there is not the small-est chance of it working. To begin with the bomb would have to be perfectly balanced around it's [sic] axis otherwise vibration at 500RPM would wreck the aircraft or tear the bomb loose. I don't believe a word of it's [sic] supposed ballistics on the surface … At all costs stop them putting aside Lancs & reducing our bombing effort on this wild goose chase … The war will be over before it works – & it never will.[59]

Harris had been in charge of Bomber Command for just over a year, and was busy implementing his strategy of area bombing. Ultimately, he was most concerned that a squadron of his most effective bombers was not going to be available for this task. Although the production of Lancasters was now running at full tilt, only about 120 new ones emerged from the factories every month.

However, Harris was now in a minority in the senior ranks of the RAF. A few days later, on 19 February at Vickers House in London, Wallis got to show his films to the two of the Joint Chiefs of Staff, the heads of both the navy and the air force, Admiral Sir Dudley Pound and Air Chief Marshal Sir Charles Portal.

---

59 TNA, AIR 14/595.

Harris was still not appeased. Nor was he impressed with the films when Wallis went to visit him at Bomber Command HQ in High Wycombe on 22 February. Portal tried to smooth Harris's feathers. He accepted that the weapon might come to nothing, but it was worth conducting a trial in a Lancaster to see if it could work. 'I can assure you that I will not allow more than three of your precious Lancasters to be diverted for this purpose until the full-scale experiments have shown that the bomb will do what is claimed for it,' he wrote. 'I shall ask for the necessary conversion sets to be manufactured but there will be no further interruption of supply of Lancasters to you until it is known that the difficulties to which you refer have actually been overcome.'[60] Reluctantly Harris accepted the decision.

The crucial meeting took place in the Air Ministry in Millbank on Friday, 26 February 1943. It set in motion what would soon become known as Operation Chastise. The meeting's participants were told that Portal wanted 'every endeavour' to prepare aircraft and weapons for use in the late spring of 1943, and that both Avro and Vickers-Armstrongs should give the work the highest priority. Three Lancasters were to be prepared for trials as soon as possible, with another twenty-seven to be similarly modified. The best possible date for an attack on the dams would be 26 May, so all aircraft and mines should be delivered by 1 May to allow for training and experiments. Wallis pointed out that 'no detailed scheme' for preparing the modified Lancasters had yet been agreed, but the demarcation between Avro and Vickers-Armstrongs was settled, with the latter handling the attachment arms and driving mechanism and the mine itself. Wallis revealed that no detailed drawings for Upkeep yet existed, but that he hoped to be able to get them ready in 'ten days to a fortnight'.

Everything was very tight, and Wallis's often-repeated assertion that the whole process could be done in eight weeks would be tested

---

60 'Harris Papers H82', RAF Museum, cited in Leo McKinstry, *Lancaster: The Second World War's Greatest Bomber* (John Murray, 2009), p.266.

to the limit. That was almost exactly the timescale now proposed. He recalled later that, as he left, he felt 'physically sick' because his bluff had been called and that he realised the 'terrible responsibility of making good all my claims'.

On the evening of this day, Guy Gibson flew from RAF Syerston on his second-last operation as Commanding Officer of 106 Squadron. It was an attack on Cologne, which he recorded in his logbook as a 'wizard prang'. Thirteen days later, he would fly on his last 106 Squadron trip. Thirteen days later still, he would walk into Barnes Wallis's office at Burhill, and the lives of both men would change forever.

11

Training for Operation Chastise

Central to the organisation of training for the new squadron was the allocation of the crews into two flights and the appointment of an officer to command each of them. Contrary to popular myth, Gibson had never previously met either of the two men who were appointed as flight commanders and did not personally select them.

Like most RAF stations at this time, Scampton had been built to accommodate two bomber squadrons. Already present when 617 Squadron was formed were the officers, airmen and ground crew of 57 Squadron, calmly going about their business. It had recently been decided to establish a third flight in the squadron, a procedure sometimes used as the precursor to it being spun off into a new squadron. Brought in to head this new C Flight was an experienced pilot, Sqn Ldr Melvin Young DFC and Bar. Young was not long back in the UK after being away from operations in northern Europe for almost two years. Although Young had completed two operational tours, these had all been on medium bombers. He was sent to 1660 Conversion Unit to learn how to fly a four-engine Lancaster, and while there was allocated a crew who had been through training together, but whose Canadian pilot had gone on sick leave. Young and his crew had joined 57 Squadron on 13 March but were yet to fly on an operation together.

There were four other crews in the nascent 57 Squadron C Flight. One was headed by Flt Lt Bill Astell DFC who, like Young, had only previously flown on medium bombers and had also been allocated a crew who had lost their pilot while in the last stage of training. The second was skippered by Plt Off Geoff Rice, who been on operations for three months, flying on nine operations. The other two were Flt Sgt Ray Lovell and Flt Sgt George Lancaster and their crews. Rice and his crew had gone on leave on 24 March. When they got back on 1 April, they found that they had been moved across the Scampton station, into a new squadron which had only just been given a number.

The transfer occurred on 25 March, the day after Gibson had first met Barnes Wallis at Burhill. The five pilots and crews were simply transferred to 617 Squadron, where they became part of A Flight, under the command of Young. The driving force in this transfer may have been Gp Capt Charles Whitworth, who commanded the Scampton station. He had known Young for a number of years, having taught him to fly while Young was a student at Oxford before the war.

Nineteen ground crew were also transferred from 57 Squadron on the same day as the aircrew. These included one of the new squadron's administrative lynchpins, Sgt Jim Heveron. His colleague, Flt Sgt George ('Chiefy') Powell, and ten more ground crew made the same administrative journey the following day, Friday, 26 March.

Melvin Young (known widely as 'Dinghy', because twice in the early part of the war he had been rescued from the sea after ditching an aircraft) would prove to be not only an effective deputy to Gibson on his many absences but also a crucial and effective organiser of the training schedule. The commander of B Flight, Sqn Ldr Henry Maudslay DFC, still only 21, didn't have Young's breadth of experience, although he had completed a full tour in 50 Squadron and been decorated. He had followed this up with a long spell testing the early Lancaster prototypes before embarking on a second tour, which he was about halfway through. Too often characterised as an old Etonian patrician and athlete, Robert Owen has noted when writing his biography that this description is wide of the mark. Maudslay did go to Eton and his family were well off having made money in industry, but he would be better characterised as a thorough planner, not especially gifted but hard working and determined to make the most of his abilities.[61]

Gibson then held a meeting to discuss the training programme with Young and Maudslay, along with the Navigation and Bombing Leaders, Jack Leggo and Bob Hay. He wasn't able to tell them the secret details of the weapon they would be using, nor did he yet know the targets, but he was able to tell the attendees that the operation would involve low flying, at night and over water. A tough assignment, everyone agreed.

On Saturday, 27 March, things became a little clearer when Gibson received instructions from Gp Capt Harold Satterley, the Senior Administrative Staff Officer at 5 Group, which detailed the type of training which the squadron should follow. The squadron would be attacking a number of lightly defended targets in moonlight with a final approach at 100ft at a speed of about 240mph. The orders stated that, in preparation for the attack, it would be 'convenient to practise this over water' and crews should be able to release their 'mine' within 40 yards of a specified release point. Various lakes and reservoirs were listed as being suitable for this. Night flying would be simulated by making the pilot and bomb aimer wear amber-coloured goggles with blue Perspex screens fitted to the windows. Armed with this information, Young and Maudslay were asked to draw up a training programme for the crews who were now present, and Bill Astell and his crew were sent off to photograph the lakes and reservoirs which Satterley had identified, on the pretext that they were needed for training crews at conversion units.

On Monday, 29 March, Gibson was called over to Grantham to meet Cochrane again. There in his office were two packing cases containing scale models of the Möhne and Sorpe Dams, and he was thereby let into the secret of the targets. In *Enemy Coast Ahead*, Gibson says that

61   Owen, *Henry Maudslay: Dam Buster*, pp.xii–xiii.

his first feeling was 'Thank God it's not the Tirpitz'. (He actually wrote that there were three packing cases, the third containing a model of the Eder Dam, but that is not the case. The Eder model wasn't finished until after the raid had taken place.) Now that he knew the targets, he went to visit Wallis again and was given a much fuller briefing.

Back at Scampton, a number of different training routes had been devised, taking the crews up to the north of Scotland, out over the Irish Sea or to the western tip of Wales. Bombing was carried out over the range at Wainfleet on the northern side of the Wash, dropping smoke bombs as markers. The special Lancasters which were being adapted for use in the operation were not yet available, so about a dozen Lancasters were borrowed from other squadrons, and rotas were constructed giving each crew their chances to practise both flying and dropping bombs at very low altitude.

The Commanding Officer's crew weren't part of either flight, and with their own skipper often tied up in his other duties, they trained on fewer occasions than some of their counterparts. Their training started in earnest on 5 April when Gibson records them as going on a Scottish cross-country/lakes trip, taking four hours five minutes. Hutchison and Taerum concur with this. Further cross-country trips followed in the month, the longest taking more than five hours. One of these was flown with the synthetic Perspex screens, another was a genuine night cross-country on 20 April, when WAAF officer Fay Gillon was brought along as a passenger. There wasn't as much late-night flying as Gibson implies in *Enemy Coast Ahead*, but logbook analysis shows that there was some. The 20 April trip may well have been the day when Trevor-Roper remarked that night flying had an advantage: 'It's a good thing flying with the Wingco, it keeps us off the booze.'

The length of the test flights and the results on the bombing ranges were closely monitored and reports sent back to Satterley at 5 Group HQ. Flt Sgt Clifford, the bomb aimer in George Lancaster's crew, was one of the stars and was singled out by Gibson in *Enemy Coast Ahead* as getting free beer for his prowess. However, his crew did not stay much longer in 617 Squadron, leaving because they objected to a plan to replace Flg Off Cleveland, their navigator. In a case of 'one out, all out', they went as a unit to 61 Squadron. Lancaster's removal followed that of Sgt Ray Lovell and his crew, who were returned to 57 Squadron on 9 April on the grounds that they 'did not come up to the standards necessary'.

Two of the most difficult technical problems – how to drop the mine at the correct distance from the target and how to maintain the correct altitude – were in fact solved quite early in the training process. Wg Cdr Charles Dann from the Royal Aircraft Establishment at Farnborough devised a simple wooden range finder which bomb aimers could use to line up with the towers on the target dams. Some bomb aimers used this, while others devised their own methods by making a series of chinagraph marks on the Perspex surface of their blisters, with a piece of string keeping their eyes at the right distance.

The Deputy Director of Scientific Research at the Ministry of Aircraft Production, Benjamin Lockspeiser, came up with an idea to check the aircraft's height. He suggested using spotlights fixed so that their beams would converge at a specified height, a technique which had been developed in the First World War. Despite some initial scepticism (including some from Air Chief Marshal Harris), it was decided to try this out and Maudslay and three of his crew flew to Farnborough on 4 April to have lamps fitted. The beams were adjusted to form a figure of eight (two touching circles) at the required height, and could be seen just forward of the leading edge of the starboard wing. The navigator could clearly see the circles through the window on the starboard side, and could advise the pilot to adjust his height. On their return to Scampton on 8 April, test flights showed they could successfully keep to the required height.

Meanwhile, although the crews were training in low flying from their base in Lincolnshire, testing of the weapon that they would eventually use had moved to Reculver on the Kent coast, close to RAF Manston where the aircraft could be bombed up and then kept securely. On 12 April, Gibson and Bombing Leader Bob Hay went down to Kent to watch the first test runs, which occurred the next day. They saw the first test Upkeep weapon dropped successfully by a Wellington, but then the second, dropped by a Lancaster, broke up. Flying over the range in a small Magister, Gibson and Hay had a lucky escape when its single engine failed. Gibson managed to crash-land in a field near Birchington, which was full of devices designed to stop enemy gliders landing. Further tests of Upkeep followed, and Plt Off Henry Watson, 617 Squadron's Armaments Officer, was despatched to Manston to observe the tests.

While Gibson was away over this period, Harlo Taerum got some extra training in with his old pilot Mick Martin. He clocked up two full-length cross-country routes on 11 and 12 April (the first at night) and a shorter trip to Uppingham reservoir and the Wainfleet bombing range on 15 April. On 20 April, the whole Gibson crew did a full night flight.

On 22 April the first of the modified 'Type 464' Lancasters arrived at Scampton. All the crews took the opportunity to inspect the new arrivals, which must have given them an inkling as to how special the operation was going to be. It was a strange-looking machine, compared with the sleek lines of the normal production Lancasters. Both the bomb bay doors and the mid-upper turret had been removed, and beneath the bomb bay hung a pair of callipers with discs at the end of the arms, specially designed to hold some sort of weapon, as yet unseen. This was obviously going to be rotated as one of the discs was connected to a drive belt.

The absence of a mid-upper turret confirmed what the crews already knew, that one gunner would have to fly in the usually unused Lancaster front turret. There was obviously not much debate in the Gibson crew. The slightly built George Deering, who stood 5ft 9in, would take this position, complete with stirrups to keep his feet out of the way of the bomb aimer lying prone below him. The rather larger Richard Trevor-Roper would be in his accustomed turret in the rear of the aircraft.

On 1 May, Gibson and his crew flew a Type 464 Lancaster for the first time. They left for Manston at 0800, returning in the afternoon.

Melvin Young was a passenger. The following day, Armaments Officer Henry Watson returned from his three-week attachment to Manston and was called into Gibson's office to report on progress. Gibson was very perturbed by some of what Watson told him and sat down immediately to write a report of the conversation for Gp Capt Harold Satterly at 5 Group Headquarters. He was obviously angry and frustrated, and also so concerned to maintain the utmost secrecy that he wrote most of the memo by hand, not even trusting the details to be given to a typist. He wrote:

(1) Within three days of arriving at Manston, P/O Watson was shown a file which I think you have seen. This contained:
  a. Sectional drawings of certain objectives.
  b. A map of the Ruhr showing these objectives.
  c. Various secret details in connection with Upkeep.
(2) That P/O Watson, an armament officer in this squadron, thus knows more about this operation than either of my Flight Commanders and at the time, more than I did myself.
  I have had a long talk with this officer and am satisfied that he understands the vital need for security, and the disregard of security will lead to most distressing results. But I consider that there is no need for a squadron armaments officer to be given such information.[62]

At the bottom of the page there appears in Gibson's handwriting the phrase 'seen by me', and below is Watson's own signature. Gibson apparently wanted to ensure that Watson knew the importance of keeping the secret by getting him to countersign the memorandum.

Shortly after this, on 6 May, Gibson called a training conference in his office. All the Captains were present, along with Watson and the Engineering Officer, Plt Off Cliff Caple. Of the men in the room, only Gibson and Watson knew the targets, and Gibson still didn't divulge it to the wider meeting. He did, however, indicate that the operation would take place within the next fortnight and that the

---

62 TNA, AIR 14/595.

squadron would now move from individual training flights to flying in formation. The groups of three would fly on a new route and would carry out simulated attacks on both the Eyebrook and Abberton reservoirs, while another six would use the Derwent Dam as a target. The remainder would carry out bombing over the Wash. On all these, the aircraft would fly at the maximum all-up weight, to simulate the load needed for the operation itself. Young was given the task of calculating this and told to get his figures checked by a flight engineer.

The meeting also decided one other important matter. VHF radio telephony sets, which would allow direct aircraft-to-aircraft communication, would be installed in all the new Lancasters. (The Dams Raid would in fact become the first time this was used in Bomber Command.)

More round-the-clock work was required for this, and in advance and on the evening of 8 May Maudslay and Young took off in two separate aircraft to test the communication systems out. Bob Hutchison, as Signals Leader, flew in AJ-X with Maudslay, who set off in a straight line from Scampton, while Young flew AJ-A in a circuit round the airfield. The system was found to work up to about 50 miles at 500ft, and a little less at 200ft.

Having proved the system worked, VHF sets were installed in all the remaining aircraft, and special work benches and booths were set up in the crew room where Hutchison trained all the wireless operators in how to use the sets and the code words they would deploy.

Gibson must, however, have had some time off at around this time because one evening in early May, he phoned Margaret North, now married, and they arranged to meet up. They had a drink in a pub and asked each other whether they were happy and how their respective wife and husband were. Both just said, 'All right,' and then the pair laughed, diffusing the tension. Then they went to the cinema in Grantham to see *Casablanca*, which had just arrived in British cinemas. Its theme tune, 'As Time Goes By', much impressed Gibson, North recalled.[63]

---

63 Morris, *Guy Gibson*, p.159.

Also in the first week in May, down in Kent, the two Vickers test pilots, Sqn Ldr M.V. 'Shorty' Longbottom, an RAF pilot seconded to Vickers, and the civilian Richard Handasyde, began testing dummy Upkeeps at Reculver under the supervision of Barnes Wallis. Screens were erected on the beach to simulate dam towers, and for the first time the aircraft flew in at right angles to the shoreline, so that a series of successful bounces would leave the mine on the beach. By 7 May, Wallis had made various adjustments to the calliper arms which held the mine in position, and he recorded in his diary that 'Shorty did two good drops – direct hits'. Frustratingly, the weather then closed in for three days so it wasn't until Tuesday, 11 May that more tests were possible.

Meanwhile, back in Scampton John Pulford had received bad news. On 7 May, his father George Pulford had died of a cardiac arrest at home in Hull, aged just 57. His mother had been present at the time. It's not known how the information was sent to John, but he must have requested permission to attend the funeral, which was granted. George Pulford had stopped working as a dock labourer at the time of his death, so his occupation was recorded as a fire watcher.

By that time, the draft operation order had arrived at Scampton. This had been handwritten by Harold Satterley at Group HQ, pulling together information from a number of sources. Satterley asked Whitworth and Gibson for their comments and amendments, and both men sent back their observations. Gibson also added a provisional order of battle to his copy. Nine pilots, in three groups of three aircraft, were listed in the First Wave, scheduled to attack the Möhne and Eder Dams, and they included both Joe McCarthy and Les Munro.

In this note, which is undated but which was probably written on 11 or 12 May, six aircraft were allocated to the Second Wave, which was going to attack the Sorpe Dam. They would take off singly, at three-minute intervals after the First Wave had departed. There appears to be some mistake in Gibson's handwritten additions to the typing in that he allocated the Third Wave, which was supposed to be a mobile reserve, earlier take-off times than the Second Wave. He also bracketed them together as attacking Target C, the Sorpe. One can only conclude that this indicates some of the pressure he was under.

At this time, four or five days before the operation, all the senior crews had been allocated to the First Wave, so it was perhaps no surprise that changes were made before the final list was drawn up. If breaching the Sorpe Dam was to be treated as a major priority then allocating some of the best crews available would be necessary. This, however, wouldn't be sorted out until the evening before the raid itself.

On 11 May, the day after the draft operation order arrived, the Upkeep mine was tested for the first time by crews who would have to drop it for real. Gibson, Hopgood and Martin, who would make up the first section of three aircraft on the Dams Raid, flew to RAF Manston, each in the aircraft they were scheduled to use. Gibson recorded in his logbook that he was accompanied by his 'usual crew'. Taerum confirms that he was on this flight, and that an Upkeep was dropped. Hutchison was also present but, perhaps more security conscious, just records it as 'Local Flying'.

At Manston, they were loaded with inert mines and then took off for nearby Reculver, where they took turns to fly towards the target screens which had been set up on the beach. Each mine worked perfectly, taking several bounces before running up the beach. Gibson noted in his logbook: 'Low level. Upkeep dropped at 60 feet. Good run of 600 yards.' Hopgood recorded the flight as: 'To and from Manston. Low-level formation with Wing/Co. VHF tests,' followed by a thirty-five-minute flight recorded as 'Store dropping'.

On the following days more crews dropped dummy mines. But it appears that it was recognised that there might not be time for all twenty-one crews still in training to get a chance to do a test drop. So when Henry Maudslay, David Shannon, Les Munro and Les Knight set off from Scampton on Wednesday, 12 May, Norman Barlow and Bill Townsend flew as second pilots in the Shannon and Munro crews respectively.

Maudslay and his crew were in AJ-X (ED933), but flew in at an altitude so low that when the mine was dropped the splash of water and shingle caused such severe damage that it couldn't be repaired in time. Fortunately, a spare Lancaster, ED937, arrived at Scampton the following day, and Maudslay was given it instead. It was given the code name AJ-Z. Munro also flew in too low and damaged his tailplane, but his aircraft was repaired back at Scampton. Time was now so tight that it seems that fewer than half of the squadron had actually dropped an Upkeep by the time they set off on Operation Chastise the following Sunday.

Thursday, 13 May did, however, see what would prove to be the one and only test drop of a live weapon. It was decided to carry this out further out to sea to reduce the risk of it being observed from shore. The mine was dropped by Longbottom, rather than one of the 617 Squadron pilots. He headed to a spot some 5 miles off Broadstairs, and dropped the mine from 75ft. Spinning at 500rpm, it bounced seven times over 'almost 800 yards' without deviation. Handasyde flew the other Lancaster at 1,000ft and 1,000 yards away from Longbottom, with two cameramen and Gibson aboard.

The film of this test showed that the waterspout when the mine exploded rose to about 500ft above Handasyde's aircraft, and the estimated depth of detonation was about 33ft. For all concerned the day was eminently successful.

The following day, Friday, 14 May, what amounted to a full-dress rehearsal took place. Nearly all the crews flew on a four-hour simulated attack on the Uppingham and Colchester reservoirs but David Maltby and Mick Martin both missed out. Gibson wrote a very positive entry in his logbook, noting that 'G/C Whitworth DSO DFC' was on board as a passenger and that the trial was 'completely successfull [*sic*]'.

Friday also saw the final decision to proceed with the operation. The Vice Chiefs of Staff had met in Whitehall on Thursday morning, and had been unable to agree whether to proceed with deploying the Upkeep weapon in the upcoming full moon period, or to wait another month in order for Wallis's smaller Highball weapon to be ready for possible use against shipping. The matter was referred upwards to the Chiefs of Staff, who were in Washington with Churchill. The reply took until Friday afternoon to arrive, but when it did, it was positive: 'Chiefs of Staff agree to immediate use of Upkeep without waiting for Highball.'

If the operation was going to be on Sunday evening this left a little over forty-eight hours to finalise everything. On the Saturday morning, Gp Capt Satterley took the handwritten draft operation order out of his safe and arranged for it to be typed for distribution.

While Satterly was doing this, his boss Cochrane flew to Scampton to tell Whitworth and Gibson that the operation would take place on the Sunday. He arrived early on Saturday afternoon and flew back to Grantham at about 1600, taking Gibson with him. Meanwhile, Barnes Wallis had arrived at Scampton in a Wellington, piloted by Vickers' test pilot Mutt Summers. By 1800, Gibson was back at Scampton and at a meeting in Whitworth's house he and Wallis began the process of briefing the crews by calling in four of the key personnel: Melvin Young and Henry Maudslay, the two flight commanders, John Hopgood, who would act as Gibson's deputy at the Möhne, and Bob Hay, the squadron Bombing Leader.

The meeting went through the operation order in detail. Hopgood noted that the route took the squadron over Hüls, which he knew was heavily defended, and suggested it be changed. Gibson recalls this rather dramatically in *Enemy Coast Ahead* with the remark, 'That night Hoppy saved our lives'.

One of the main topics for conversation was doubtless the attack on the Sorpe, and this may well have been the first time that Wallis told the strike force about the different method needed for attacking it. This led to the decision to beef up the Second Wave who were to be given that task. Both Joe McCarthy and Les Munro had been listed in the First Wave but were now moved to the Sorpe attack, with their places given to Bill Astell and Les Knight. This was not a reflection of the bombing abilities of either crew but rather a late acknowledgement that the Sorpe should be seen as a higher priority.

With hindsight, the lack of a detailed strategy for attacking the Sorpe Dam can be seen as a major failure by Wallis and the operation's planners. Tests had shown that Upkeep had a good chance of working when delivered at right angles to a concrete-walled dam, such as the Möhne and Eder. Over the course of the trials, Wallis had been trying to think of an effective way of delivering the same exploding depth charge against the Sorpe embankment-style dam with its sloping wall, built of earth with a concrete core, but nothing had been decided. Nor had any detailed plan been devised for how the sequence of attack would be mounted, since the five aircraft would not fly in formation but would take off at one-minute intervals. Wallis had in fact previously expressed the view that it might take the successful drop of five or six Upkeeps by this method for the central core of the Sorpe to be breached. It is clear now that insufficient consideration of this took place in the frantic period before the raid.

Harry Humphries was in his office early on the Sunday morning and Gibson arrived at about 0900. He had been up for more than three hours and had already visited the Medical Officer, Flg Off Alan Upton, with pains in his feet. Asked if he was flying, Gibson replied: 'Yes, but if you tell anyone you'll be shot.'[64] Upton, who diagnosed gout, thought about giving him aspirin or codeine but decided against it as he didn't want to dull his patient's reactions.

Meanwhile, Gibson's flight engineer, John Pulford, was on his way to Hull to attend his father's funeral, which had been fixed for the Sunday. He had been given special permission to attend. He was driven there in an RAF car, and was escorted throughout by two RAF policemen in order to ensure he didn't let something slip about the planned operation. They never left him during the funeral service and afterwards they went with him to his mother's house, but only for long enough for him to speak to his mother, not other family members. Then he and the policemen left to return to Scampton. It

---

64 Morris, *Guy Gibson*, pp.163–4.

is not clear whether they got back in time for Pulford to attend the all-crew briefing which took place at 1800 that day.

Gibson told Humphries that at last the squadron was going to war, but he didn't want 'the world' to know about it.[65] He instructed him to make out a battle order but to title it 'Night Flying Programme', and then gave him the crew details and the code orders.

There were nineteen crews on the list as both Bill Divall and Harold Wilson had now reported sickness in their crews. Ken Brown's front gunner Don Buntaine was also sick, so Divall's front gunner, Daniel Allatson, was substituted into the Brown crew. Divall and Wilson's absence also led to the promotion of the Rice and Byers crews to the Second Wave, detailed to attack the Sorpe. Warner Ottley and his crew were moved into the mobile reserve. Several copies of the typed 'Night Flying Programme' were produced, and they show all these late changes.

With the battle order typed up, the eighteen other pilots and nineteen navigators, including Taerum, were called to a briefing at about midday, when they were told their targets by both Gibson and Wallis. The briefing was held in the first-floor room of the Junior Ranks' Mess at Scampton. Around the same time, the wireless operators were called to a separate briefing by Wg Cdr Wally Dunn on code words and protocols. As the Signals Leader, Bob Hutchison would have played a key part in this. At some point in the afternoon, bomb aimers and gunners were brought into the picture, with small groups clustered around the models, noting details which would be relevant.

At 1800 the general briefing began, with everyone brought together in one room. All 133 aircrew sat on benches in front of a dais holding Gibson, other senior officers and Wallis. Gibson spoke first, ending his speech by saying: 'Well, chaps, if you don't do it tonight you will be going back tomorrow night to finish it off.'[66] He then introduced Wallis, who described the weapon, how it had been

65 Morris, *Guy Gibson*, pp.163–4.
66 Morris, *Guy Gibson*, pp.163–4.

developed and the arguments for attacking the German dams. His arguments that the loss of the dams would lead to the curtailment of industrial production for a very long time were well remembered by those who heard him.

Cochrane spoke after Wallis, briefly emphasising the 'historic' nature of the operation. He ended his remarks by saying that the raid might do a lot of damage but that they might never read about it in the news. 'It may be a secret until after the war. So don't think that you are going to get your pictures in the papers.'[67] Cochrane may have thought that there might be little publicity, but some people at the Air Ministry had other ideas. The Director of Bombing Operations, Air Cdre Sydney Bufton, had already devised a plan for press communiqués after the raid and had organised for photographer Flg Off W. Bellamy to be present for take-off.

Cochrane was followed by Gibson again, who repeated the details of the three waves that he had already given to the pilots and navigators. After the briefing, at about 1930, the crews went off for their meal – the traditional eggs and bacon, with an extra egg for anyone on an operation. The WAAFs who worked in the separate messes for the officers and NCOs could not help noticing the extra rations, and were therefore now in on the secret. The squadron was flying that night. Operation Chastise was under way.

---

67 Morris, *Guy Gibson*, pp.163–4.

12

The Dams Raid:
History is Written

The crews started milling around the dispersal points where their bombed-up aircraft waited an hour or so before take-off. There was not much they could do but wait, and some began their familiar pre-match rituals. Gibson and his crew had, of course, never flown together on an operation, so they wouldn't have had any of the male bonding sessions that many long-established crews had built up.

Adjutant Harry Humphries was also there, and thought that he had better check whether Gibson had anything he wanted done back at Scampton while he was away on the raid. He set off for Gibson's Lancaster but before he could reach the CO, Richard Trevor-Roper intervened. It's fair to say that he and Humphries didn't get on, and this was to prove no exception, as all he said in greeting was 'Hello, short arse'. Flushed, Humphries didn't reply but gave him what he thought was a withering glance. In response, Trevor-Roper gave him a silent smile: grinning from ear to ear he resembled a sinister stage villain, Humphries thought. Moving on, he managed to have a word with Gibson, but his only request was for him to make sure that there was plenty of beer in the mess for the post-op party.[68]

---

68 Humphries, *Living with Heroes*, p.10.

The First Wave consisted of three groups of three aircraft, taking off at ten-minute intervals. The trio who were due to lead Operation Chastise's First Wave were scheduled to leave the ground at 2139. Gibson and crew were in AJ-G, and the other two aircraft were AJ-M and AJ-P, piloted by John Hopgood and Mick Martin respectively. Four of the aircraft from the Second Wave, with further to fly, were already airborne by this stage. The fifth, Joe McCarthy, had been delayed: with a mechanical problem in AJ-Q, he and his crew had transferred to the reserve aircraft, AJ-T, which had only arrived at the station that afternoon.

As Gibson and his crew climbed aboard their Lancaster, they were photographed together as a complete crew for the first and only time. Their rather self-conscious pose, with Gibson paused on the top step, was later recreated in the 1955 film. In his account in *Enemy Coast Ahead*, Gibson made it sound as though it were a surprise: 'An RAF photographer came running up and asked to take a picture – these men certainly choose the queerest times,' he wrote.[69] The man who approached them was photographer Flg Off W. Bellamy, who stayed on duty all night. He took several other pictures before the raid, including one of a single Lancaster taking off, which was probably AJ-E, piloted by Norman Barlow. He would later cover the debriefing session after the operation.

In the crew photograph, only Hutchison is looking at the camera with the rest all facing left. All are wearing life jackets. Bellamy had taken an earlier picture of Gibson and Hutchison helping each other out with their life jackets, checking they had been fitted correctly. Gibson is wearing a much-prized German *Schwimmweste*, which he acquired as a souvenir from a crashed enemy aircraft while serving in 29 Squadron in 1941. Spafford and Gibson are carrying parachutes, and Spafford has a bundle of maps under his arm, anticipating that he will have to spend quite a lot of time map-reading for Taerum. Pulford has a canvas tool bag, which probably also contained the

---

69   Gibson, *Enemy Coast Ahead*, p.280.

Gibson and his crew pose for a picture as they set off on Operation Chastise.
(© IWM CH 18005)

various log sheets he would be required to fill in during the flight. Gibson is in shirtsleeves, anticipating the strenuous effort needed to fly for six or more hours at low altitude. The rest are in battledress jackets, the weather had been fine and was expected to remain so, there would be no need for flying jackets. All of them except Pulford and Trevor-Roper are wearing ordinary shoes, for the same reason.[70]

As Gibson wrote *Enemy Coast Ahead* less than a year after the Dams Raid, we can probably assume that the first and last chapters are a fairly reliable account. Certainly, it is a book which historians have used as a source ever since it first appeared in 1946. It does, however, suffer from one enormous defect – Gibson was not permitted to divulge the details of how the Upkeep mine was delivered,

---

70 Robert Owen, 'Lasting Images', Appendix in Guy Gibson, *Enemy Coast Ahead* (Greenhill Books/RAF Museum edition, 2019), pp.361.

specifically that it was spinning when it was dropped and therefore bounced after it hit the water, propelled by its own momentum up to the dam wall. This crucial fact doesn't appear anywhere in the text. Nor does it in Paul Brickhill's 1951 book, *The Dam Busters*.

As we have seen, Gibson uses the first chapter of *Enemy Coast Ahead* to introduce his crew to us. For his account of the rest of the Dams Raid we have to jump to the very last chapter, which takes up the story seventy minutes into the flight, as the three crews leading the First Wave are almost at the Dutch coast. The trio had a quiet flight across the North Sea but experienced stronger winds than forecast, so they made landfall on the enemy coast late and some distance off course. They had reached Walcheren Island rather than the nearby mouth of the Scheldt river. Fortunately, the land-based anti-aircraft gunners failed to pick them up and they were able to alter course. Again, they were not threatened as they crossed Holland and reached the Rhine. Once more they found themselves off course, 6 miles too far south. Gibson turned and flew up the Rhine towards the intended turning point, a bend in the river near Rees. It was on this short section that they encountered their first flak, being fired on by guns positioned on barges on the river and its banks.

Gibson describes the way they threaded a path through the enemy defences, correcting their course occasionally and skipping over high-tension wires. There were in fact several bouts of anti-aircraft fire through which Gibson and Martin brought their aircraft without damage, but at Dülmen it seems that Hopgood in AJ-M was quite badly damaged, although he never reported this to his leader. Hopgood himself was bleeding from the scalp and his front gunner George Gregory suffered near-fatal wounds and was not able to fire.

Finally, they reached the Möhne lake and saw the dam for the first time. Martin arrived first and Gibson and Hopgood were not far behind. All three took a few minutes to assess it in real life. 'It looked grey and solid in the moonlight as though it were part of the countryside itself and just as immovable,' Gibson wrote. The guns on the two sluice towers were already active, and there were further emplacements on the nearby banks. They took up position flying circuits over the Arnsberg Forest to the south of the dam, out of range of the guns. The direction of attack was to fly straight at the dam from there, hopping over a small spit of land (the Heve promontory) and quickly getting down to the right height for the last stretch of about a mile.

In that last mile the pilot would have to get down to exactly 60ft and stay level, the flight engineer would use the throttles to maintain the approach speed at 230mph, and the wireless operator would ensure that the mine was spinning backwards at 500rpm. Meanwhile the navigator would switch on the spotlights and check that the beams were touching. Flying at 230mph, the aircraft would cover the 1-mile stretch in about fifteen seconds.

In order to assess the defences at close range, Gibson decided to do a dummy run over the dam. He chose a different angle of approach so not to give too much away to the defences. As he rejoined the waiting aircraft, he announced that he 'liked the look of it'. At that point, the first group of three were joined by Melvin Young, David Maltby and David Shannon.

Gibson then prepared to launch the first attack. As he did so, he reminded Hopgood that he should take charge of the operation should anything happen to AJ-G. Brave man that he was, Hopgood still did not tell Gibson the extent of the damage he and his crew had already suffered.

Gibson then set off towards the target. After AJ-G had crested the Heve spit, Taerum switched on the spotlights and stood by the blister, calling out instructions in order to maintain the height at 60ft. Hutchison checked that the mine was rotating, and Pulford kept his hand on the throttles to control the speed. In the front turret, Deering began firing at the defences while Spafford, in the bomb aimer's position below him, prepared to press the bomb release switch which would drop the spinning mine:

The gunners had seen us coming. They could see us coming with our spotlights on for over two miles away. Now they opened up and their tracers began swirling towards us. This was a horrible moment: we were being dragged along at four miles a minute, almost against our will, towards the things we were going to destroy ... By now we were a few hundred yards away and I said quickly to Pulford, under my breath, 'Better leave the throttles open and stand by to pull me out of the seat if I get hit.' As I glanced at him I thought he looked a little glum on hearing this.[71]

Spafford dropped the mine at 0028 at the correct distance, 400 yards from the dam wall. In the rear turret Trevor-Roper saw it bounce three times and then sink, short of the dam. As AJ-G passed over the dam wall, Hutchison, positioned in the astrodome, fired a red cartridge from his Very signal gun to blind the flak gunners. Some ten seconds later, as Gibson turned the Lancaster back towards the holding position, a huge column of water flew up into the air and great sheets of water surged high over the wall. However, when this subsided the dam was seen to be still intact.

The group had to wait about five minutes for the water to settle, whereupon Gibson ordered Hopgood into the attack. As he prepared to do so, Maudslay and Knight from the third group arrived. Astell was gone, he had hit a high-tension electricity line en route. Hopgood set off, 'casual, but very efficient', but the gunners on the dam now knew from which direction the attack would come and were waiting for him. The damage which AJ-M had already suffered made it even more vulnerable, as its front gunner George Gregory was almost certainly not firing, having been severely wounded. Both port and starboard wings were hit during the attack and in the confusion bomb aimer John Fraser was late releasing the mine. It bounced over the dam wall and landed near the power station on the other side. A Very cartridge was fired, lighting up the stricken aircraft, which was seen to be engulfed in flames. Hopgood managed to lift it up to about 500ft and shouted over the intercom, 'For Christ's sake,

---

71   Gibson, *Enemy Coast Ahead*, p.288.

get out of here!' Somehow, the wounded John Minchin managed to drag himself towards the rear escape hatch, with one leg almost severed. Burcher bravely pushed his colleague out of the hatch first, pulling his parachute ripcord as he did so, and then followed him. Sadly, Minchin did not survive the drop, but Burcher did, although he was captured and taken prisoner. Fraser escaped from the front hatch. The aircraft exploded and crashed near the village of Ostonnen, some 6km from the dam. Minchin's body was found about a kilometre away. The mine also exploded, severely damaging the power station.

Things were not going well. Gibson had six bombed-up aircraft left, but their crews had just seen how simple a target Hopgood had presented to the dam's gunners, although they did not know that the explosion of Hopgood's mine had actually put the left-hand gun tower out of action. In John Sweetman's authoritative account of the raid this was where 'Gibson's leadership and Martin's courage ensured that the operation would not disintegrate' and the next few minutes were what earned Gibson his Victoria Cross. Martin attacked and, in the hope that the gunners would be distracted, Gibson flew on his starboard side, slightly ahead of him. Martin's mine was dropped in the right place, but something went wrong with it: the weapon veered left and exploded near the southern shore of the lake. Its casing may have been damaged when the unfused mine had been dropped accidentally onto the hardstanding at Scampton after being loaded that morning, or perhaps Martin hadn't got the aircraft exactly level as it was released.

By this time a certain amount of desperation must have been creeping in. Gibson and Martin's mines had not been successful and Hopgood had been shot down. Melvin Young in AJ-A was next and Gibson decided to vary his diversion tactics, and brought Martin in to act as another decoy. This time, Gibson flew across the defences on the far side of the dam wall, while Martin came in on Young's starboard side. Young was accurate in his approach, and his bomb aimer, Vincent MacCausland, dropped the mine accurately. It bounced three times, hit the dam and seemed to explode while it was in contact with it, but, as the tumult subsided, there was no obvious breach.

A few minutes later, it was the turn of AJ-J, piloted by David Maltby. As he launched his attack Gibson again varied the decoy operation. This time, Gibson flew on Maltby's starboard side, Martin on the port. As he approached the dam wall, Maltby suddenly realised that from this close he could see that a small breach had occurred in the centre and that there was crumbling along the crown. Young's mine had been successful after all! He steered slightly to port but stayed dead level as his bomb aimer John Fort steadied himself to press the release. The mine bounced four times and struck the wall. Maltby said afterwards: 'our load sent up water and mud to a height of 1,000ft. The spout of water was silhouetted against the moon. It rose with tremendous speed and then gently fell back. You could see the shock wave at the base of the jet.'[72] His navigator, Vivian Nicholson, wrote a briefer account in his log, just three words long: 'Bomb dropped. Wizard.'

However, it was still not apparent that a further breach had occurred. AJ-J sent a standard 'Goner' message back to base, and Gibson carried on watching. But then, as David Shannon in AJ-L was called in to deliver a sixth mine, Gibson realised that the dam was broken, and Bob Hutchison transmitted the code message for a successful attack. Elation followed, and all seven Lancasters present took turns to fly over the dam to observe the results of their work. Gibson wrote:

> It was the most amazing sight. The whole valley was beginning to fill with fog from the steam of the gushing water and down in the foggy valley we saw cars speeding along the roads in front of this great wave of water which was chasing them and going faster than they could ever hope to go ... I felt a little remote and unreal sitting up there in the warm cockpit of my Lancaster, watching

---

72 Sweetman, *Dambusters Raid*, p.166.

this mighty power we had unleashed; then glad because I knew this was the heart of Germany, and the heart of her industries, the place which had unleashed so much misery upon the whole world.

To remind them of the human cost the attackers had themselves suffered, they saw the remains of Hopgood's aircraft still burning gently, 'a dull red glow on the ground'.

After a few minutes, Gibson called for order, and set about the second phase of his night's work. He told Martin and Maltby to make their way home, and ordered Shannon, Maudslay and Knight, who still had mines on board, to proceed with him to the Eder Dam. Young was also told to accompany the party, to act as deputy leader if anything should befall Gibson.

The Eder lake was difficult to locate and Shannon found himself circling over another patch of water nearby. Hutchison guided him to the correct location by a firing a flare. The attacking force quickly realised that the dam presented a much more difficult target than the Möhne. The lake is smaller and set in a deep valley, meaning that there is a much shorter approach which starts with a very tricky steep dive from over the Waldeck Castle. This is followed by a sharp turn to port. Given the geography, the Germans had obviously discounted the idea of an aerial attack, since there were no gun batteries in the vicinity.

Shannon was the first to try an attack, and made three or four passes without releasing his mine. It was very difficult to get down to the right height after the dive, and then turn. Gibson told Maudslay to try, and he found it just as hard, so Shannon had another go. Two more dummy runs followed until, at last, he got the angle and speed right and dropped his mine. It bounced twice, hit the dam wall and exploded, sending up a huge waterspout. At the later debriefing his effort is reported as 'no result was seen' but Shannon in fact felt that he had made a small breach.

Maudslay had another attempt but then something went wrong. His mine was released too late, hit the parapet and exploded. Although his aircraft was beyond the dam by the time this occurred, it may have been damaged, since his progress home was slower than would be expected. Some reports say that something was seen hanging down below the aircraft, perhaps caused by hitting trees on the run in.

Gibson saw that AJ-Z had fired a red Very light signal after passing over the dam wall and called Maudslay on the radio: 'Henry – Henry. Z-Zebra – Z-Zebra. Are you OK?' Nothing was heard, so he repeated the call. This time Maudslay's voice could be heard, although the signal was faint: 'I think so. Stand by …' This signal – confirmed by members of Shannon's and Knight's crews – was the last voice contact anyone made with AJ-Z.

It was now down to Les Knight in AJ-N, who was carrying the only mine left. Shannon advised him on the direction and speed. After a dummy run, which was dangerous enough for rear gunner Harry O'Brien to record afterwards that he 'never thought they would get over the mountain' on the other side of the dam, Knight switched his radio off so that he could concentrate. With a bright moon on the starboard beam, he brought AJ-N into attack. The mine was released, bounced three times and hit the dam wall. Knight climbed steeply and, as the aircraft reached a safe height, saw an explosion which caused a 'large breach in wall of dam almost 30ft below top of dam, leaving top of dam intact'.

Wireless operator Bob Kellow had his head up in the astrodome, looking backwards. It seemed, he said, 'as if some huge fist had been jabbed at the wall, a large almost round black hole appeared and water gushed as from a large hose'. It took a while for Kellow to send a message confirming the drop, and in fact it was sent six minutes after the official code message denoting a breach of the Eder had been transmitted from AJ-G by Bob Hutchison.

Gibson, Young and Shannon and their crews were elated, and more congratulations ensued when Group HQ at Grantham received the signal. Air Chief Marshal Harris rang Air Chief Marshal Sir Charles Portal, the Chief of the Air Staff, who was in Washington DC with the Prime Minister. Portal sent congratulations to all the civilian and service personnel responsible and said he would inform Churchill without delay.

Group HQ then asked Gibson if he had any aircraft left that might be sent on to attack the Sorpe Dam. Gibson answered that he had none and ordered the three aircraft with him to set off home. He was not able to reach Henry Maudslay and assumed the worst for him. In fact, at this stage Maudslay was still trying to limp home in his damaged AJ-Z, and would stay airborne for a further fifty minutes. However, he and his crew were all killed when they were shot down approaching Emmerich, which was defended by several Heimat light flak anti-aircraft batteries, largely manned by non-military personnel. Some of the outbound force had in fact passed over the town a few hours earlier so the batteries were on alert for the opportunity to fire on any returning crews.

The squadron's other flight commander, Melvin Young, and his crew were desperately unlucky. Young had piloted AJ-A from the Eder Dam on the same route as Maudslay as far as the Dutch coast, which he reached just before 0300. Then, out over the sea and only a few hundred yards from safety, he hit disaster when the gun battery at Wijk-aan-Zee hit his rapidly disappearing Lancaster.

When he left the Eder, Gibson flew back past the Möhne, noting that for 3 miles below the dam, the river had swollen to 'several times its normal size'. After a warning of a possible night fighter in pursuit, he dropped down to the lowest level possible. On their port side, the crew also saw an aircraft shot down near Hamm. This was probably Ottley from the mobile reserve. Gibson followed the third of the prescribed exit routes, crossing the Helder peninsula north of Haarlem, deviating to pass through a known gap in the coastal defences near Egmond. At this point he climbed slightly beforehand in order to go over the coast in a fast dive. Having achieved this successfully, the rest of the flight was uneventful and AJ-G landed at Scampton at 0415, the only damage from the night's work being three small holes in the tail.

13

Fame and Glory:
After the Dams Raid

The two aircraft that returned early from the Dams Raid, those of Munro and Rice, touched down at Scampton before one in the morning. Those who had reached their targets began arriving back some two and a half hours later – David Maltby in AJ-J was the first to land at 0311. The three who came from the Eder Dam landed about an hour later: AJ-L with Shannon and crew at 0410, AJ-G with Gibson and crew at 0415 and Les Knight and crew in AJ-N at 0420.

The same Flg Off Bellamy who had pictured the crew climbing into AJ-G a few hours earlier was ready to take their photograph as they were debriefed. This was taken in the briefing room in the Other Ranks' Mess, the room into which all nineteen crews had crammed fewer than twelve hours previously. In it Air Chief Marshal Harris and Air Vice Marshal Cochrane watch on as Scampton's Intelligence Officer, Sqn Ldr Townson leafs through his notes. Sheets from the Eder Dam briefing are clearly visible, including a pre-war German photograph of the dam itself. An animated Fred Spafford is next to Townson, with Taerum alongside him looking pensive and perched on the edge of the table. On the other side in the foreground, we see Trevor-Roper, hair brushed back. The hand with the cigarette is probably that of Hutchison, sitting on Trevor-Roper's right. All we can see of him is his officer's peaked cap. Next, in shadow but still

Debriefing after the raid. (Bomber Command Museum of Canada)

distinguishable, are the sunken eyes of Gibson, also deep in thought and looking strained. The ridged hair beyond him is that of Deering. Pulford is not to be seen.[73]

Townson would have gone through a specially compiled questionnaire with all the crews, which has been preserved. In answer to the questions as to what could be seen of the objective and at what distance, the answers from the AJ-G crew were 'Saw the whole thing' at '3–4 miles'. The Upkeep weapon is said to have been spun at 500rpm and bounced three times. There was an 'enormous column of water' after its explosion. Two holes were made in the dam by the overall attack and they reported that the river below the dam to a distance of about 3 miles was several times its normal size. The gunners said that the '100% night tracer' had a

---

73 Owen, 'Lasting Images', pp.366–9.

very satisfactory effect against enemy gun positions, and they had experienced no dazzle.

Once they were released from their official duties, most of the crew got involved in the two impromptu parties which took over in the Officers' and Sergeants' Messes, where the bars were reopened and much beer was consumed. The squadron adjutant, Harry Humphries, met Gibson in the Officers' Mess anteroom, and congratulated him on the attack's success. Gibson asked him of the latest news of the late-comers, and Humphries told him there were eight still missing:

'Humph, bad show.' He was downcast for a moment, then brightened visibly. 'Still we've done as much damage as a thousand-bomber raid. Perhaps shortened the war, so Bomber Harris says. I understand that Churchill is pleased with the result.'[74]

Sometime after breakfast time a series of photographs were taken. Many of the men posing had not yet been to bed, so some rather dopey and tired expressions can be seen in the pictures. Two images captured for posterity were taken outside the Officers' Mess. One shows the eleven pilots who took part in the raid and survived, plus Flt Lt Harold Wilson, who had withdrawn late through illness. The second shows twenty-one men: eleven pilots plus ten aircrew, all in No. 1 uniform. Four are from the Gibson crew: Harlo Taerum, Fred Spafford, Richard Trevor-Roper and Bob Hutchison.

Three more well-known pictures were probably taken shortly after. These were photographs taken for the press in Canada, Australia and New Zealand, and show most of the personnel from those countries who returned from the raid. These were taken on the hardstandings next to a parked-up Lancaster. All the men who were in No. 1 uniform in the earlier shots are still wearing them, but the rest are in battle-dress. Rather bizarrely, many men are holding random pieces of flying equipment – mainly Mae West lifejackets or helmets, but in the case of

---

74 Humphries, *Living with Heroes*, p.38.

Australians, Bob Hay and Lance Howard, a map and a binocular case – presumably in order to look as though they have just returned from the mission. All fifteen Canadians who returned from the raid are present, including Harlo Taerum and George Deering, plus the American Joe McCarthy. Fred Spafford is in the Australian picture.

The airfield seemed a lot quieter that morning. A Tannoy announcement told everyone on the base what had occurred, but many were more aware of the scale of the losses. Wallis stayed for the morning, mingling with survivors, and very upset with the losses. Harry Humphries and Sgt Heveron spent much of the morning sending telegrams to the next of kin of those who were missing. In the afternoon, they were interrupted by Gibson, bearing the news that all 900 aircrew and ground crew were to be given leave, starting the next day. The administrative work needed for this meant that the process of sending letters to the next of kin didn't begin until later, and most weren't sent until after the leave period had started.

By lunchtime, the world had been informed of the scale of the achievement. The Air Ministry communiqué had been released to the press, and was broadcast by the BBC:

The Air Ministry has just issued the following communiqué. In the early hours of this morning, a force of Lancasters of Bomber Command led by Wing Cdr G.P. Gibson DSO DFC attacked with mines the dams of the Möhne and Sorpe reservoirs. These control over two-thirds of the water storage capacity of the Ruhr basin. Reconnaissance later established that the Möhne dam had been breached over a length of one hundred yards, and that the power station below had been swept away. The Eder dam, which controls the headwaters of the Weser and Fulde valleys and operates several power stations, was also attacked and reported as breached. Photographs show the river below the dam in full flood. The attacks were pressed home from a very low level with great determination and coolness in the face of fierce resistance. Eight of the Lancasters are missing.

Gibson called Eve in London, hardly mentioning the raid, perhaps because he was conscious that the Scampton phones were still being tapped. He and others then went to a party at Woodhall Spa, forty-five minutes away by bus, where he behaved with his usual combination of intensity and blatant attempts at seduction. Meanwhile, Sgt Heveron, stuck in his office typing sympathy letters, was surprised to be interrupted by a mess waiter carrying a bottle of beer. 'With the Wing Commander's compliments', he was told.

On Tuesday, 18 May, every newspaper carried the story of the raid as its lead. Coming as it did only a day or two after news had reached Britain of the final Allied victory in Tunisia, which meant that plans for the invasion of Sicily and Italy could go ahead, it was a major boost to public morale.

Some of the details were either wrong or based on speculation. *The Daily Telegraph*, for instance, informed its readers that 'three key dams' had been blown up, while the *Daily Mirror* was more sensationalist, with a headline reading 'Huns get a flood blitz: torrent rages along Ruhr'. The *Daily Mail* ran a headline over its photographs: 'The Smash-Up: RAF Picture Testifies to Perfect Bombing'. Its story went on: 'Two mighty walls of water were last night rolling irresistibly down the Ruhr and Eder valleys. Railway bridges, power stations, factories, whole villages and built-up areas were being swept away.'

The coverage lasted for days, fed by further information coming from the Air Ministry, as the floods spread further and further down the valleys. 'Havoc spreads hour by hour', one paper recorded, and there was speculation that the third dam might burst at any moment. Even the foreign press got in the act. The unnamed journalist writing for the American magazine *TIME* spun a wonderfully fanciful account:

Now the planes were roaring 50 feet above the water; now the target was dead ahead. Now the bombardiers pushed their buttons, and now the big, dark mines, each weighing 1,500 pounds, tumbled from the planes. Some landed with a splash in the water; some hit the dams fair & square. When the roar of their explosions had subsided, the sustained, deeper roar of pent-up waters, suddenly released, struck terror into the hearts of those below.

By lunchtime on Tuesday the whole squadron had gone on leave, after they had been called together to hear speeches from Cochrane, who had come over from Grantham for the occasion, and Gibson. Presumably Pulford, Hutchison and Trevor-Roper travelled to their home towns, Taerum, Spafford and Deering to wherever they normally spent their leave periods. An old crewmate from 50 Squadron, Gordon Cruickshank, bumped into Taerum in a Lincoln pub the day after the raid. The navigator was understandably elated and told Cruickshank how successful the operation had been and that their aircraft had returned with just one hole in it.[75]

It must have been a bittersweet return to Hull for John Pulford. On the Sunday morning he had been present at his father's funeral. Accompanied as he was then by two RAF policemen, others at the interment must have wondered whether he was in some sort of trouble. Now, less than seventy-two hours later he was back in the city, allowed to speak, and the reason for his previous silence now emblazoned on the front page of every newspaper in the country.

Gibson meanwhile stayed at Scampton until all the letters had been despatched. Although the letters were all typed and contained several chunks of standard text about getting news from the Red Cross and what was going to happen to the man's personal effects, some of them had paragraphs written especially for the particular family receiving them. The one sent to the Hopgood family is especially poignant. After the salutation and expression of regrets, Gibson goes on:

John has been with me for over a year and we have done many operations together, and it is with the deepest regret that I now say I am alone. He was a great personal friend and was quite the finest pilot I have ever known.

---

75 Cruickshank, 'Memoir'.

The circumstances which led to his not coming back are most unlucky. When attacking the Möhne Dam, his aircraft was subject to intense light flak fire and his port outer engine caught fire. I watched him climb to 1000 ft to enable his crew to bale out, and although I am quite certain that some got away I would not like to raise your hopes too high until we know for certain. John would always be the last to leave his aircraft, and this is but one of the many small things that made him one of the finest pilots in Bomber Command.[76]

Hopgood's loss seems to have hit him the hardest. Gibson knew that he had asked him personally to join the squadron and had also placed huge responsibility on him, effectively making him his deputy. The accolade of being called a 'fine pilot' by your peers was only bestowed occasionally in wartime, but there is no doubt that, for Gibson, Hopgood fell into that category.

News of the Dams Raid success reached the media of the Commonwealth countries involved in the war almost as quickly as it did that at home – an assiduous press office campaign run by their own air forces saw to that. So it was that later in the week readers of the *Calgary Herald* heard of Harlo Taerum and Revie Walker's exploits. Under the headline 'Alberta Fliers Helped Blast German Dams', the article started, 'When Canadian and RAF planes unleashed several large "packets" of bombs on the Mohne and Eder Dams in Germany several days ago, one Calgary and one Blairmore airmen were included in the 11 [sic] Canadians who took part in the successful foray. The Albertans were Flying Officer Daniel R Walker DFC of Blairmore and Pilot Officer Harlo Taerum of Calgary.' In her Calgary home, Hilda Taerum clipped this article neatly from the newspaper and pasted it into the scrapbook she was keeping about her two sons' service in the RCAF.

Not to be outdone, the unnamed journalist writing for *The Advertiser* in Adelaide, South Australia, secured a series of quotes

---

76 Jenny Elmes, *M-Mother* (The History Press, 2015), p.246.

from Fred Spafford (or perhaps a press officer speaking on his behalf):

> Wg-Cmdr. Gibson is a marvellous pilot, and a marvellous man. I will eat my hat if he doesn't get the Victoria Cross.
>
> Wg-Cmdr. Gibson, after seeing the Mohne dam smashed, flew 50 miles to the Eder dam and gave the course for the attackers, which were led in by 20-year-old Flt-Lt. Shannon. It was a brilliant attack, just as though it had been rehearsed for weeks. Our Lancaster was holed only three times. The Germans obviously were rattled.
>
> Our Lancaster was purposely drawing the enemy's fire at the Mohne and Eder dams, which was not so suicidal as might be imagined, because a fast, low-flying Lancaster must have resembled a giant, swooping eagle.
>
> When the Eder dam burst Wg-Cmdr. Gibson led the formation back to Mohne, where the Germans were so shocked and battered that only one gun was still operating. In the bright moonlight we saw rescue cars and trucks rushing to the stricken villages.
>
> It was hard to tell which was dam and which was floodwater, so many millions of tons of water had already cascaded all over the countryside. Without further event we returned to the base, where Air Chief Marshal Sir Arthur Harris and others were waiting. Everyone was so elated that celebrations began at 5.30 a.m.[77]

Gibson, meanwhile, headed off on his belated leave. But before he joined Eve in Penarth he fitted in another trip to see Margaret North at her workplace in Rauceby Hospital. Her workmates crowded around to get a first-hand account of the daring raid they had read about in their papers. He was quite circumspect, saying only that it had been a 'bit of a do'. He told Margaret that David Shannon and Ann Fowler had just got engaged. 'You're quite fond of Ann, aren't

---

[77] *The Adelaide Advertiser*, 22 May 1943.

you?' said Margaret. Gibson delayed his reply, and when it came it was telling: 'Ann is a really good mate.' Margaret was becoming an astute judge of the Gibson character.[78]

On the following Sunday, Gibson was staying with Eve in her parents' house when he received a phone call from Arthur Harris himself, with the news that he had been awarded the Victoria Cross. He seemed almost subdued with the news, telling the assembled relatives that it all seemed a bit unfair, presumably thinking again of the extent of the losses. 'I'm afraid they've given me the Victoria Cross,' was all he could say to his aunt and uncle when he called them with the news.[79]

Gibson's Victoria Cross was top of the list of thirty-four awards to members of the squadron who had returned from the Dams Raid. The names were given to the squadron on Monday, 24 May, and appeared in *The London Gazette* the following day. The squadron was also told that the King and Queen would be visiting Scampton on the Thursday, although this was not announced to the press for security reasons.

The award of thirty-four medals to one squadron for one operation was unprecedented. The list began with an award for every one of the men who had flown in AJ-G, starting with Gibson. Hutchison already had the DFC, so he received a Bar. Taerum, Spafford, Deering and Trevor-Roper all got the DFC. (Both Spafford and Trevor-Roper already had DFMs from their earlier service.) Pulford, the only NCO in the crew, received the DFM. In all the other seven crews who dropped their mines successfully, the pilot, navigator and bomb aimer were decorated as well as another six men across three crews. A strict pecking order was followed: the officer pilots were awarded the Distinguished Service Order (DSO) while Bill Townsend and Ken Brown, the two non-commissioned pilots, got

---

78 Morris, *Guy Gibson*, pp.170–8. This account owes much to these pages of Morris's book.

79 Ottaway, *Dambuster*, pp.136–7.

the equivalent, the Conspicuous Gallantry Medal (Flying) (CGM). In the awards for other aircrew, officers got the DFC while the NCOs got the DFM.

The RAF press operation backed up the awards by sending information to the home town newspapers of all the decorated men. In Hull, the local *Daily Mail* carried two stories about John Pulford on the same day, Friday, 28 May. The first reported on an interview with his mother, Ada Pulford. Her son had been home on leave for six days, but had said little about the raid. He was 'a happy go lucky lad who takes the good with the bad', she told the newspaper. The article explained that his father had died earlier in the month and that he had been allowed to attend the funeral. The reporter also interviewed Charles Norton, the superintendent at Pulford's pre-war employers, Paragon Motor Company, who was very complimentary:

> It has come as no surprise to me that he should be one of the airmen taking part in such an exercise. There was all the enthusiasm of youth in his work for us. We engaged him as a lift attendant but he was bent upon getting into the workshops. Anything mechanical attracted him. We are immensely pleased with the award made to him.[80]

The second article contained news of Pulford's DFM and also how the King and Queen had visited a 'North Lincolnshire aerodrome', and been given details of the raid. Not reported in the local press is an incident during Pulford's leave when one night he went out for a drink with his brother Thomas, also an RAF flight engineer. Both men were in civilian clothes and at some point in the evening someone put white feathers into their pockets.

The King and Queen were due to visit a series of RAF stations 'somewhere in England' on Thursday, 27 May but after the Dams Raid the schedule was revised to add Scampton, where they were due to be given lunch. The visit was organised so quickly that many

---

80 *Hull Daily Mail*, 28 May 1943.

aircrew were still on leave when it was confirmed, and they had to be summoned back to Scampton by telegram.

On the day, the royals were first given lunch, and then there came the inspection. Each crew was lined up behind their Captain, who stood smartly to attention, toecaps touching a white line painted on the grass. Gibson introduced the King and Queen to his crew and to each of the pilots.

An official RAF photographer, Flg Off Henry Hensser, recorded the inspection. Most of the pictures are in black and white but a few are in colour. When you are so used to seeing wartime pictures in black and white the rich Kodachrome process is almost shockingly bright. Most of the shots show the King and Queen talking to the pilots, but they also inspected the WAAF contingent, spoke to the squadron's Armament, Engineering and Electrical Officers and met representatives of 57 Squadron. They looked at the models of the Möhne and Sorpe Dams, and were invited to choose from a selection of possible designs for the squadron crest. Having chosen the one showing a broken dam wall, with the motto 'Après Moi Le Déluge', the King signed the artwork.

Harlo Taerum wrote to his mother about the events of the previous few weeks, and his mother passed the letter on to the *Calgary Herald*. He first described the operation, and then went on to write about what had happened since:

> It was by far the most thrilling trip I have ever been on and I wouldn't have missed it for anything. We all got back in the mess about 5.30 in the morning, and then we really did relax … A couple of days later, five of us went to the factory where they make Lancasters and gave the workers a pep-talk. Can you imagine me making a speech? We were just about mobbed for autographs afterward.
>
> The next thing was five days of leave in London, and all the boys were down there, so we really had a time. One morning they woke me up and told me I had been awarded the DFC. Later I had the ribbon sewn on my tunic.

> At the end of five days we were ordered back to our stations
> to meet the King and Queen ... I was very lucky because I
> was introduced to both of them. The Queen is most charming
> and gracious ...
>
> I then got two weeks leave but it was stretched to 17 days.
> When I told the CO I was going to South Wales he hooked me for
> a Wings for Victory speech at Bridgend and I'm getting good at
> speeches now.[81]

By the time she received the letter from her son, Mrs Taerum had
clipped out the *Calgary Herald*'s photographs of Gibson with the King
and Queen and pasted them into her album. She didn't know at the
time that within four months she would be sitting in her own home
showing Gibson the pictures and asking him to sign them. She also
clipped out a picture of Eve Gibson from a Canadian paper, posing
coyly with a photograph of her husband. The erstwhile actress had
been the subject of several photocalls.

Meanwhile, the Australian press had heard of more celebrations
going on in London. One was attended by a well-known group of
rowdies who had served together in 50 Squadron on their previous
tours of operations. They had been to a dinner at the Savoy Hotel
given for the 'heroes of the raid' on the Möhne and Eder Dams,
where Carol Gibbons and his orchestra played and a Soufflé à la
Möhne made by Chef Santorelli was on the menu. The special guests
included Fred Spafford, Jack Leggo and Toby Foxlee.[82]

Spafford cropped up again shortly afterwards, making a positive impression on *Australian Women's Weekly* London reporter
Anne Matheson, who reported that the lead bomb aimer on the
Dams Raid was a 'good-looking, cheerful South Australian pilot
officer, with laughing hazel eyes, brown skin and regular features'. He had seen it all, the piece said. 'A great jet of water' had

---

81 *Calgary Herald*, June 1943, Bomber Command Museum of Canada.
82 *Northern Star*, 3 June 1943.

The pretty wife of Wing-Cmdr. Guy Penrose Gibson, V.C., D.S.O. and Bar, D.F.C. and Bar, who led the successful raid on the Mohne and Eder Dams and who has been in Canada recently with the Churchill party, is seen above looking at a photograph of her famous husband. Until recently, Mrs. Gibson worked at a camouflage factory. She is the former Evelyn Moore of Penarth, Glam., and was married in November, 1940.

"Dam-Buster" Is Mum

By A. C. CUMMINGS.   I'm going.' I did not know he was wit

Eve Gibson in a photocall in her London flat. (Bomber Command Museum of Canada)

CENTRAL CHANCERY OF
THE ORDERS OF KNIGHTHOOD,
ST JAMES'S PALACE, S.W.1.

21st. June 1943.

CONFIDENTIAL.

Sir,

    The King will hold an Investiture at Buckingham Palace
on Tuesday, the 22nd June, 1943, at which your
attendance is requested.

    It is requested that you should be at the Palace not
later than 10.15 o'clock a.m.

DRESS—Service Dress, Morning Dress, Civil Defence Uniform or
       Dark Lounge Suit.

    This letter should be produced on entering the Palace,
as no further card of admission will be issued.

    Two tickets for relations or friends to witness the
Investiture may be obtained on application to this Office
and you are requested to state your requirements on the
form enclosed.

    Please complete the enclosed form and return immediately
to the Secretary, Central Chancery of the Orders of
Knighthood, St. James's Palace, London, S.W.1.

        I am, Sir,

            Your obedient Servant,

Pilot Officer Harlo T. Taerum,
*   A.X.6. R.C.A.F.*

Secretary.

Instructions for the protocol to be followed for the Buckingham Palace investiture.
(Bomber Command Museum of Canada)

134,000,000 tons of water behind it. 'The weight tore the breach wider as I watched, and the torrent swept down the Ruhr, tumbling everything before it.'[83]

The person most in demand for public events was, of course, Gibson, who spoke at Wings for Victory events in Sheffield, Gloucester and Maidstone. In Sheffield thousands turned out and he had pride of place at a civic lunch beside Mrs Clementine Churchill. In Maidstone on Saturday, 19 June, Gibson took the opportunity to meet local scouts and take part in a celebrity auction. The climax was the arrival of four Lancasters, piloted by David Maltby, David Shannon, Mick Martin and Les Munro, beating up the town.

Three days later, on Tuesday, 22 June, came the investiture in London. John Pulford had been admitted to hospital (the cause isn't known) so wasn't able to attend but Gibson and the rest of his crew all planned to go. For Bob Hutchison and his family, it would be the second trip to Buckingham Palace in four months. But first they had to get to the capital.

Squadron Adjutant Harry Humphries had his legendary administrative skills tested to the limit getting the boisterous aircrew to the railway station, onto the train and up to London without a major incident. The news that Avro had organised a dinner in a West End restaurant for the evening of the investiture added to the determination of many to start the party a day early, so copious amounts of alcohol were brought along to ensure that the trip was well lubricated.

Perhaps he was celebrating the safe arrival of his new son Charles, born on 15 June, because Richard Trevor-Roper was obviously in a party mood when he boarded the train. One of the reserved compartments became a card school in which a considerable amount of drink was consumed. One unfortunate who got caught up in this was Brian Goodale, the wireless operator in David Shannon's crew. He did not have much of a head for drink (he features as the butt of the joke in several episodes in Paul Brickhill's book) but got lured into a session by a group which included Trevor-Roper, pilot David

---

83 *Australian Women's Weekly*, 12 June 1943.

Maltby and his bomb aimer John Fort. At some point Goodale suffered the indignity of having his trousers removed and then confiscated by the card players. He wandered off down the corridor, and into a compartment where Harry Humphries was chatting sedately to two WAAF officers. 'Ladies were present', so modesty had to be preserved. The gallant Humphries pushed Goodale into one of the train lavatories and set off in search of the missing trousers. He entered the drinking den with some trepidation, but succeeded in retrieving the dusty and creased trousers, covered in cigarette ash. He tried to make his departure but could see that Trevor-Roper had an eye on him, and briefly worried that he might be the next victim. Then Trevor-Roper spoke:

'Have a Scotch before you go Adj.' said Trevor-Roper, fumbling in a suitcase.

I didn't really feel like one but thought I had better accept. He handed me the top of a vacuum flask, half full of neat whisky.

'Go on shorty, let's see you knock that back,' he said.

I gulped, my prestige was at stake. Taking a deep breath I took the contents of the cup at one swallow. I nearly went through the roof of the carriage. My throat burned away at the sudden contact with the raw spirit, my head swam and tears came to my eyes as I gasped for breath.

'I'm proud of you Adj.,' said Trevor-Roper. 'Like another?'[84]

When the group got to London, they had been left to sort out their own accommodation, so those without relatives in the city headed to various hotels. Some went to the Savoy, but others settled for the more downmarket Strand Palace. A lot more drinking followed, and this carried on into the night.

Somehow, everyone made it next morning to Buckingham Palace where, to general surprise, the investiture was conducted

---

84 Humphries, *Living with Heroes*, p.46.

Taerum and his fiancée outside Buckingham Palace. (Bomber Command Museum of Canada)

by the Queen, as the King was away in North Africa. All the men receiving decorations had been allowed to bring up to two guests, and these were led in by Eve Gibson, dressed in a pillbox hat and fur stole for the occasion. The delegation from 617 Squadron was first, headed by Gibson, now the most heavily decorated airman in the British Empire. He received not only the Victoria Cross but also the Bar to the DSO he had been awarded in March 1943. Thirty-two other officers and NCOs followed, with John Pulford thought to be the only absentee. The Queen made personal remarks to some of the men as they came forward for their medals. Of Fred Spafford,

Buckingham Palace June 22nd 1943. Guy Gibson (centre) and award winning 'Dam Busters.'

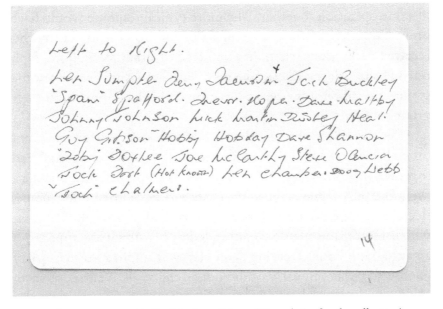

617 Squadron group outside Buckingham Palace. (Humphries family collection)

whom she recalled meeting at Scampton a few weeks earlier, she enquired whether he and his colleagues had recovered from the party they had been planning on the day of that visit. (It had been organised to celebrate the twenty-first birthday of Spafford's fellow South Australian, David Shannon.)[85]

Afterwards, photographers jostled and shouted as different groups were organised for pictures and newsreel film sequences. The largest number photographed together is twenty, caught together in the palace forecourt. Although six of the Gibson crew were present, Bob Hutchison doesn't appear in this or any of the other semi-official shots. Spafford and Deering are also missing from this large group, but they do turn up in their respective Australian and Canadian photographs. Taerum also found the time to be photographed outside the palace with his fiancée Pat, who had worn a smart suit for the occasion.

It's perhaps a shame that no one thought to record the men in Gibson's crew all together, but perhaps this reflects the fact that they weren't really the same as other crews: the seven men who flew on just one operation together. The more typical response would have been that of five of the six members of Bill Townsend's crew who received decorations when they gathered together for a photograph outside the palace. These five men had, however, been on some twenty operations together, a situation which had surely built their group solidarity.

After the investiture, another drinking session started and went on well beyond lunchtime. Gibson and Eve were photographed together with some American air crew they bumped into outside a West End pub. Some grabbed the chance to catch up on a few hours' sleep before the evening dinner party in the Hungaria Restaurant, which Hutchison may have attended as his signature appears in an autograph book. Deering is on Harry Humphries list of 'party guests', so either left early or did not attend at all. Neither of them appears in the later photographs.

---

85 *The Advertiser*, 5 July 1943.

Canadian contingent after the investiture. (Bomber Command Museum of Canada)

Australian 'Dam Busters'
Buckingham Palace June 22
1943.

Australian contingent after the investiture. (Humphries family collection)

A pair of famous misprints on the menu card states that the dinner was in honour of 'The Damn Busters' and congratulates the crews on 'their gallant effort on the Rhur Dams'. Besides the RAF personnel (which included a number of ground crew), there were several other distinguished guests. These included Barnes Wallis as well as Sir Charles Craven and Sir Hew Kilner from Vickers and Roy Chadwick and Sir Roy Dobson from A.V. Roe. The famous aviation pioneer T.O.M. Sopwith was also present, and made a speech before presenting Gibson with a silver model of a Lancaster aircraft. Gibson replied, managing to thank everyone involved, not forgetting the ground crew, the 'back room boys' and the workers at Avro. Then a picture of the breached Möhne Dam, brought by Barnes Wallis to the dinner, was signed by those present who had taken part in the raid and given back to him. He had the 'before' and 'after' photos framed and hung them on his study wall, writing afterwards that

T.O.M. Sopwith presents Gibson with a silver model Lancaster. (Humphries family collection)

they 'formed a historical record of this outstanding accomplishment on the part of the RAF'.

Various well-known entertainers turned up at the end of the dinner and provided an impromptu cabaret. There was a lot of free drink on offer – cocktails, a 1929 'Rizling [*sic*]', a 1930 Burgundy and Commendador port – and therefore there is a certain amount of confusion in the accounts of the night.

Sometime late in the evening, a famous photograph was taken in which a number of people seem pretty worse for wear. Standing rather awkwardly at the back are a number of knighted bigwigs, alongside the newly promoted but always glum-looking Air Cdre Charles Whitworth, whose pyjamas had formed a trophy at the party in Scampton in the early morning after the raid, when a conga line invaded his house. More of the great and the good – including Barnes Wallis – are sitting on the floor at the front, along with the

Party attendees after dinner at the Hungaria Restaurant. (Humphries family collection)

rather younger and more untidy uniformed guests. In the middle of the front row are Mick Martin, David Maltby and Guy Gibson with several members of their crews around them. Fred Spafford's head is poking up behind Martin and further back, with the most raucous grin of all, is squadron debagger-in-chief, Richard Trevor-Roper.

The awards party returned to Scampton in a subdued state. Trevor-Roper must have made a swift recovery, however, because by the following Sunday, 27 June, he was the star speaker at a church parade organised by the Skegness Council of Christian Churches as part of the local Wings for Victory campaign.

A large procession, headed by the police and the RAF but also including 'practically every local organisation' and accompanied by the Skegness Town Band, which 'included a woman instrumental-ist in its ranks', had marched to the cricket ground for a drumhead service. The address was given by the Rev. Sqn Ldr H. Glyn Lewis, an RAF padre. He drew a parallel with the Old Testament's account of Naboth's fight against King Ahab's desire to possess his vineyard. 'We were not fighting for our land, precious as it was, but for some-thing higher. The country would never exchange its ideals for the soul destroying principles of the blood-hungry Nazi savages.'

Following this, Trevor-Roper spoke, as later reported in the *Skegness News*:

> He felt honoured to address a Skegness congregation as ten days ago his son was born in the resort, so he had a personal interest in the town. His hearers should have a personal interest in the battle of the Ruhr. He was in Wg Cdr Gibson's plane which raided the Möhne and Eder dams and he saw the dams breached and he knew if that operation was successful the Nazis had no chance of winning.
>
> Victory in the Battle of the Ruhr would lead to greater and final victory. Battles were not fought without losses in men and machines. It was more important than ever that we should have more and more aircraft than ever before and we could not have

aircraft without money. All should give every penny they could spare and then add a ha'penny to that.[86]

June had indeed been a momentous month for the 28-year-old Flight Lieutenant, having to fit his new family responsibilities into a life of danger.

---

86 *Skegness News*, 30 June 1943.

14

The Handover to Holden
and the Trip to Africa

Gibson was technically still in charge of the squadron, but in the top ranks of the RAF thought was being given as to what to do with him, as well as the squadron he commanded and the weapon it had deployed. Gibson's name was so widely known that, for the moment, he could not be allowed to fly over enemy territory. If he were to be shot down and killed – or captured – it would present a significant propaganda boost to the Germans. As to the squadron, it was not going to be used on run-of-the-mill bombing operations, even on those in which 'maximum effort' was required to deliver hundreds of aircraft on a mass operation. The squadron would continue to trial different ways of using the Upkeep weapon and also prepare itself to use the new 'thin case' 12,000lb High Capacity bomb that was about to be brought into service.

There were more than thirty Upkeep mines in the Scampton armaments store. At this stage the Air Ministry didn't know that its secret was in the hands of the enemy. An unexploded Upkeep had been captured intact by the Germans, after Norman Barlow's AJ-E had crashed near Haldern. The crew had made the mistake of not engaging the self-destruct mechanism, so it had failed to explode. It didn't take the German bomb disposal teams long to work out that this was a *Rollebombe*, and they made their own detailed drawings of the mechanism. But what should the air force do with the stored mines? No decision was made, and it was obviously filed under 'For Another Day'.

As well as the range of social and publicity activities, there were a couple of post-Chastise pieces of work to keep Gibson and some other members of the squadron busy. One such was what Gibson recorded as a 'smoke exercise' on 4 July, which was to test the effectiveness of the defences of Allied dams, in case the Germans sprang a similar attack on them. The second was a flight to Southend by Gibson, David Maltby and Bob Hay to inspect possible practice targets on the beach at Shoebury Sands. Plans were in hand to use Upkeep on real-life shore targets, running the weapon in from the sea.

David Maltby, now a Squadron Leader and very popular with all at Scampton, had taken over as flight commander of A Flight after the Dams Raid, and had been acting Commanding Officer on several occasions when Gibson was absent. But the higher powers had obviously decided that he wasn't experienced enough to take on the mantle full time, and that the squadron needed a new Commanding Officer. Sqn Ldr George Holden was therefore lined up to take over. He was born in 1913 and had been in the Royal Air Force Volunteer Reserve (RAFVR) before the war, which gave him a head start in training immediately hostilities began. After qualifying as a pilot, he had gone on to fly the Halifax heavy bomber, completing a first tour in 4 Group's 35 Squadron. In October 1942, after a period training, he was given command of 102 Squadron when the previous Commanding Officer was killed in a freak accident. He had moved on from this posting in April 1943, with a grand total of forty-five operations, a DSO and a DFC and Bar.

On 2 July Holden was posted into 617 Squadron and became the flight commander of B Flight, on the understanding that he would take charge of the whole squadron when Gibson left. As he had previously only flown Halifaxes, Holden had to become familiarised with Lancasters and he took Taerum, Spafford, Hutchison, Trevor-Roper

Gibson, Spafford, Hutchison, Deering and Taerum at Scampton. (© IWM TR 1127)

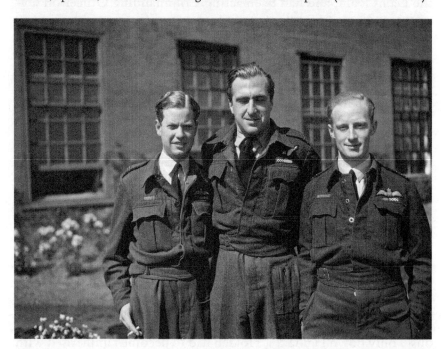

Trevor-Roper (centre) at Scampton with Shannon (left) and Holden (right). (© IWM TR 1129)

and Deering on two long cross-country flights on both 7 and 8 July. He didn't list a flight engineer or second pilot on either trip.

Sometime in the early part of July, an official RAF photographer was at the station and shot a series of colour transparencies. One shows Holden with Richard Trevor-Roper and David Shannon. Another has Gibson with four of his Dams Raid crew, Spafford, Hutchison, Deering and Taerum, with a dark sky looming behind them, threatening a severe storm. Probably taken on the same day was another well-known photograph of Gibson and David Maltby, taken in the squadron CO's office. Gibson has a pipe clenched between his teeth, and both men have a finger on the same page of what looks like an aircraft identification manual. These three photographs, plus others of Joe McCarthy, Harold Wilson, Les Knight and their respective crews are currently (in 2023) listed by the Imperial War Museum as being taken on 22 July. However, this cannot be the case as most of the personnel in them were at RAF Blida in Algeria on that date.

Just to add confusion to the date, another photograph often thought to be taken at the same time is of Gibson sitting in a field of poppies, reading a copy of the *Morte D'Arthur*. However, the Imperial War Museum dope sheet shows that this was actually shot on 26 May by the same Flg Off Bellamy who had been on duty on the night of the raid. This photograph had been released to the press on the day of the announcement of the decorations list.

At about the same time, on 9 July, two panorama pictures, one of the aircrew and one of the complete squadron, were taken by Bassano's, the London portrait photographers, who also specialised in large-format photography. The aircrew picture shows fifty-seven of the seventy-seven men who had landed back at Scampton on 17 May. Six of the AJ-G crew are in the picture, but Fred Spafford is missing. He may have been on leave.

A curious anomaly occurs here. Bob Hutchison recorded flights to and from West Malling in Lancaster ED735 at 1045 and 1510 on 9 July, with Gibson back on the scene as pilot. For this period,

Gibson's logbook records are very poor, and he failed to note this flight, although he does mention an earlier low-level flight to Cornwall and a 'smoke exercise'. This was probably the day when Gibson was filmed at the house of his friend Glad Bincham, in a separate visit from the one made at the time of the Maidstone event a few weeks earlier. The film sequence is in colour, and shows him talking about the Dams Raid to some teenage boys, showing them the silver-model Lancaster he received at the Hungaria and also his medals. He is then seen posing in a garden with Eve and three others.

The following day, Saturday, 10 July, Gibson was in Nottingham, presenting the Albert Ball VC Memorial Sword to the best local Air Training Corps (ATC) cadet as well as other merit prizes. Local dignitary and sometime Mayor of Nottingham Sir Albert Ball had presented the Sword of Honour in memory of his late son, also called Albert Ball, a First World War Royal Flying Corps (RFC) pilot who won the Victoria Cross after his fatal last flight in 1917, when he was shot down, possibly by the younger brother of the Red Baron, Lothar von Richthofen.

George Holden, meanwhile, was getting his Lancaster practice in. On 12 and 13 July he took Gibson's erstwhile crew out on four separate training flights, three at low level. Then, on Thursday, 15 July, 617 Squadron finally went back on operations, and he led the detachment of ten crews who took part. The mission was to bomb two Italian electricity transformer and switching stations, at Aquata Scrivia and San Polo d'Enza. Because these were beyond the 'out and back' flying range of the Lancaster it was necessary to fly on to another airfield to refuel and reload. Blida, some 30 miles from Algiers, now in Allied hands after the victories in North Africa and used as a launch pad for operations in the Mediterranean, was the obvious choice.

George Holden took charge of one section of five aircraft, while David Maltby led the other section. Holden flew in ED931, a Lancaster borrowed from 57 Squadron, with all six members of Gibson's Dams Raid crew on board: Pulford, Taerum, Hutchison,

Spafford, Deering and Trevor-Roper. A lot had happened in the two months since Operation Chastise, and this is the only other time all six would fly into conflict together. Gibson saw them off, watching from the marshalling point with Harry Humphries. For many of the other men from the squadron who flew that day, it would be the last time they saw him.

Everyone was delighted with the chance of getting their knees brown, so they packed sunglasses and tropical kit into their service-issue suitcases and kitbags and stowed them in the body of their aircraft. It was a long flight but largely without incident, and with very little opposition en route or over the target. Holden's crew reported some flak damage but they all arrived safely at Blida, although Les Munro's aircraft had a dodgy landing caused by a burst tyre.

Blida was fun at first. For many of the aircrew this was the first time they had set foot outside Britain. There was wine to drink, exotic fruit and food to enjoy, sunshine to bask in. Lots of photographs were taken, although sadly there doesn't seem to be one of the ex-Gibson crew together.

Bob Hutchison described the trip in a letter to his family on his return. He seems to have bonded with Holden, even if others had not:

We were some thirty-odd miles from Algiers which town we visited to gain my first impression of life out of England. Naturally I was pleased to get back here again but it was an experience I wouldn't have missed for the world ...

We went swimming in the Med at Sidi Ferruch twice a day and thus got quite a tan. It is the most lovely beach I have yet to see ... I swam for nearly an hour each time after first getting in without stopping and then sat around or dived for shells etc for the rest of the time. Taken all in all an almost perfect holiday.

Even the language wasn't really a bother. French is the spoken word and mine improved out of all recognition ... In the very short time I was there I began remembering things all over again and it was great fun, too.

One afternoon the Group Captain i/c us took George Holden (my new skipper) and myself to Chrea a winter sports village eighteen miles behind the camp but perched 5,090 feet up in the mountains. That was a hair raising incident. The G.C.'s driver knew the road well but it was still a thrill as he averaged 30 mph up 18 kmtrs of steady climb on a twisting switchback of a road with blind corners and 1500 foot drop over the edge if you missed it. We didn't.[87]

But then the weather closed in, which meant the 617 Squadron contingent had to stay for a total of nine days. Some people got bored, including Holden, who appalled other members of the squadron by gleefully driving a jeep straight into a flock of goats and goatherds.

Eventually the crews were able to set off for home, and were instructed to bomb the docks at Leghorn (Livorno) on the way back to England. However, something had happened in the relationships between the men in the skipper's crew in the nine days they were in Africa, as Pulford swapped over to Ken Brown's crew for the return leg. The reason why isn't known, but it was obviously a permanent rift as Pulford never flew with Holden again. Whether Basil Feneron, Brown's usual engineer, flew back with the Holden crew isn't known. The Operations Record Book doesn't list any engineer as fulfilling this duty, but as Feneron isn't listed anywhere else in the detachment and he wasn't left behind in Algeria, it's likely to be the case.

Again, it was a long flight, taking off from Blida at about 2100 on Saturday, 24 July and landing after 0500 the next day. The bombing was uneventful, done on a time-and-distance run from Corsica, and everyone got home safely. In anticipation of this, the crews had loaded up the aircraft with souvenirs, crates of fresh fruit and vegetables (Hutchison brought back grapes and

---

87 Robert Hutchison, letter to family, dated 'Monday' (probably 26 July 1943). Spelling and punctuation as in original. (Hutchison family collection)

lemons for his family), as well as bottles of Benedictine and wine. Martin was wearing a red fez when Harry Humphries met him at the dispersal point.

Round about the same time that the Blida contingent landed, some seventeen Lancasters from 57 Squadron also touched down at Scampton. They had been part of the contingent of 779 RAF bombers who had taken part in a massive attack on Hamburg. This was the first of four devastating attacks in the next ten days on the north German city. For the first time, the crews dropped 'Window' – strips of tinfoil designed to confuse the German radar – as they flew over enemy territory. It worked well; so well, indeed, that on the night of the second attack on 27–28 July, a firestorm was created in the densely built-up residential district of Hammerbrook when all the fires joined together and started sucking the oxygen out of the surrounding air. The firestorm lasted three hours and only sub-sided when all the burnable material in the area was consumed. It is estimated that 40,000 people died. The name given by Bomber Command to the series of raids – Operation Gomorrah – with its connotation of a city being destroyed by the wrath of God, was aptly chosen. Here was Harris's 'area bombing' strategy realised to its full potential.

Doubtless there was discussion in the Scampton messes between the 57 Squadron contingent, who participated in the Hamburg raids, and the 617 Squadron aircrew, who did not. There was certainly resentment that 617 Squadron was not being sent out on routine operations, a feeling that must have intensified on one side when on Thursday, 29 July, nine aircraft led by Holden were despatched on a really soft trip, on the same night as a force of 777 other Bomber Command aircraft were despatched on the third trip to Hamburg. The 617 Squadron detachment went on a 'nickel run', dropping leaf-lets on cities in northern Italy, and going on to Blida again. Neither John Pulford nor Richard Trevor-Roper were in the Holden crew, being replaced by Sgt Allan Hill and Sgt Doug Webb, from the crews of 'Bunny' Clayton and Bill Townsend respectively. They flew back two days later, with no operational duty required on the return trip, landing at Scampton in the early hours of Sunday, 1 August.

On Saturday, 24 July, while his sometime crew were away on the first Italian operation, Guy and Eve Gibson were among the guests at a small lunch party at Chequers with Winston and Clementine Churchill. A car picked them up outside the Dorchester Hotel in London (Eve in a borrowed hat) and drove them to Buckinghamshire. After lunch the couple sat with Churchill to watch a film – not a feature, but a specially compiled edit of snippets about the Holocaust which had been smuggled out of occupied Europe. Gibson was appalled at the subject matter.

The couple then took a stroll in the gardens, and Churchill apparently broached the subject of Gibson making a trip to North America. He didn't discuss the purpose in front of Eve, but in effect there were two reasons. One was to bolster American support for the bombing campaign in Europe, which Harris, among others, believed was flagging. The second was for Gibson to be part of the British party, led by Churchill, which would take part in the forthcoming Quadrant Conference in Québec, hosted by the Canadians, where the British and Americans would discuss a range of forthcoming military initiatives.

The Gibsons left in time for Guy to attend an already arranged meeting with Air Chief Marshal Sir Charles Portal, the Chief of the Air Staff. Portal was likely to be intrigued as to what the young Wing Commander had discussed with the rather older Prime Minister, but the main purpose was probably to brief him on his forthcoming North American tour, and to emphasise the political importance of enthusing about the role of the United States Army Air Forces (USAAF) in the European theatre of war.

Gibson travelled back to Scampton and his logbook and the A Flight authorisation book records a couple more trips in the following week. On 27 July (recorded in his logbook as the day before) one took him to Northolt near London, from where he went to the Ministry of Information to receive a briefing on his forthcoming trip. He also fitted in a visit to Margaret North. He had heard a rumour that she might be leaving the WAAF, and he wanted to hear this first hand. She told him that this was indeed the case and, when he asked her directly, that she was pregnant. She asked him if he wanted to be the godfather, and he said yes.

By now, his old crew were back at Scampton, and Gibson met up with them to say his goodbyes, and complete the handover to George Holden. The two pilots took five of them (Taerum, Hutchison, Spafford, Deering and Trevor-Roper) on a final flight at 1150 on Monday, 2 August. They flew in ED933, one of the Lancasters converted for Operation Chastise. This had been allocated to Henry Maudslay but had been damaged before the raid, so was not used. Gibson recorded this as an 'Attack on Special Objectives' while Hutchison recorded it as 'Local Flying'.

After the flight, the air crew posed for a photograph with some of the ground crew who had worked on Gibson's aircraft during his time with the squadron. Gibson had prints made immediately and signed each one himself on the front. He then had the reverse sides signed by all the aircrew, and presented the prints to everyone who was in the shot. He left the next morning, Tuesday, 3 August, so this was the final farewell to five of the men who had met together for the first time just four months previously. We don't know whether he sought out Pulford, who was probably somewhere else on the station, to speak to him, but it's unlikely.

When he arrived in London in the afternoon, he told Eve that he would be leaving for 'overseas' the next day, which meant catching a train north after midnight that night. They went out for dinner, and then he set off for the Dorchester (again) from where the transport was leaving. More than 200 people boarded the train, which arrived on the Clyde the following afternoon. The party was taken out to the *Queen Mary*, which set sail for Canada at about 0530 on 5 August.

Gibson and crew in handover to Holden. (Hutchison family collection)

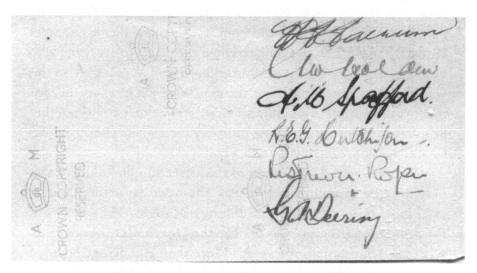

Reverse of the handover print, signed by all aircrew. (Hutchison family collection)

Richard Trevor-Roper also left the squadron at about the same time. He is recorded as being posted to the Central Gunnery School at RAF Sutton Bridge on 24 August. The school had been established to give more junior gunnery instructors advanced skills in aerial gunnery, so that they could better train the air gunners passing through Operational Training Units.

Gibson had been in command of 617 Squadron for just nineteen weeks. At the end of August, the squadron would be transferred to RAF Coningsby so that concrete runways could be installed at Scampton. The Dambusters legend was literally being set in stone.

15

Gibson's Trip to North America and Operation Garlic

The passengers in the *Queen Mary* who crossed the Atlantic with Gibson in August 1943 provided very distinguished company. Besides Winston and Clementine Churchill and their daughter Mary, who acted as the Prime Minister's aide-de-camp, there were also Lord Louis Mountbatten, Air Chief Marshal Portal and the other service Chiefs of Staff, Lt General Ismay (Churchill's Chief Staff Officer), Averell Harriman (President Franklin D. Roosevelt's special envoy to the UK) and assorted senior officers, diplomats and political staff.

Gibson's youth must have marked him out among this rather mature crowd. Mary Churchill, one of the few on board of a similar age, found him debonair and having '"school boy" cherry cheeked fair good looks'. On the last night at sea, he was asked to make a speech on the subject of the Dams Raid, and many found it impressive. Afterwards, however, Churchill instructed him to tone down the more forthright of his remarks when speaking to the public.[88]

The *Queen Mary* docked at Halifax, Nova Scotia, on 9 August and it was then an overnight rail journey to Québec. Thereafter, Gibson participated in some of the social activities around the

---

88 Ottaway, *Dambuster*, p.151.

Quadrant Conference but was soon being taken on a series of press activities, where he made a big impact. On his twenty-fifth birthday, 12 August, he attended a press conference in Québec City chaired by the Canadian Air Minister C.G. Power, a notoriously heavy drinker who was forced to stay off alcohol for the day by his Prime Minister. Gibson charmed his way through the event and was greeted by ecstatic reports the following day. He remained in Québec for a few days, visiting various training schools, and then it was on to other parts of eastern Canada, including Toronto, before travelling to New York City on 3 September.

While in New York, he recorded a radio interview and also met Flt Lt Roald Dahl, who had travelled up from his job as Assistant Air Attaché at the British Embassy in Washington DC. Dahl had been a fighter pilot earlier in the war and would, of course, later become a world-famous author. He had been in the USA since April 1942, and had already achieved a reputation for his active official security work and his vigorous social life.

Dahl already had one eye on his post-war career, wanting to break into the writing and film business. By the time he met Gibson, he had been in Washington for some sixteen months, making contacts with the movie scene over in Hollywood. He had also developed a career as a writer, with several short stories published and film treatments drafted. Feted as a great new talent, he had also become heavily involved in the Washington social scene.

Earlier in the year, on 31 May 1943, Dahl had sent a proposition to the Air Ministry in London for a film on the effects of bombing. This didn't specifically involve the Dams Raid, but given that this had taken place only two weeks previously it was doubtless on his mind. He had already been introduced to the American film director Howard Hawks, and he must have also contacted him at this time because, at the end of July 1943, Dahl's superior in the Air Attaché's office, Sqn Ldr G. Allen Morris, wrote to Arthur Harris, asking for 'every possible releasable detail' about the Dams Raid. Hawks, he said, had asked Dahl to write a script about it.

Gibson, who was doing a lot of the flying between venues himself, moved on to Winnipeg from New York on 6 September. There he met the parents of Harvey Glinz, the sole Canadian in the crew of Aussie pilot Norman Barlow on the Dams Raid. He went on to more training establishments in Manitoba, Saskatchewan and Alberta, until on 11 September he set out for Calgary, the headquarters of No. 4 Training Command of the British Commonwealth Air Training Plan and then, as now, Alberta's largest city. This was building up to be a major event: the local radio station carried live reports from the countdown to his arrival, which was scheduled for 6 p.m.[89]

The dignitaries were lined up on a podium equipped with a PA system so that the many members of the public could hear the speeches. Accompanying them was a middle-aged bespectacled woman in a smart victory suit and homburg hat, Mrs Hilda Taerum, Harlo's mother. Gibson greeted her with a handshake: 'You are the living image of him, you know,' he said, 'or should I say, he is the living image of you?'

Getting the formal speeches under way, Air Vice Marshal G.R. Howsam welcomed their guest: 'You have come here to tell our instructors and air crews things which they are very anxious to know. These are the things they are going to do in the future, like dam-busting, Cologne-busting, Hamburg-busting and finally busting Hitler's phoney fortress of Europe.'

Responding, Gibson spoke quite candidly of the feelings he had experienced on the Dams Raid: 'We knew we were going to die, or not die, as the case may be.' He had 'a funny empty feeling in the stomach, but not frightened'. He went on: 'The creed of the bomber command is to hit Germany hard and thereby shorten the war. There is no difference between a Canadian, an Englishman, a New Zealander or anyone else. We are all … fighting under the same flag, against the same enemy and with the same planes. We're all damn good. That's why we're winning this war.'

---

89 Barris, *Dam Busters*, pp.269–76. This section owes much to Barris's account.

Gibson speaking at Calgary airfield. (Bomber Command Museum of Canada)

Then Gibson turned to Hilda Taerum and introduced her to the audience. She was the mother of the man he knew as 'Terry', he said. 'Terry is a great boy. And a great navigator. He got the whole squadron to the dam.'

Hilda Taerum beamed proudly, and then opened up the notes she was carrying, which someone had typed up for her (misspelling her son's name as 'Harlow'). 'I am really very thrilled,' she said. 'I have been looking forward to meeting you. I feel as though I have known you for some time. Harlo has said so much about you in letters. When you go back to England, Wing Commander Gibson, tell Harlo we are all well at home. This has been a real privilege, and one I will never forget.'

The next day, the local press went ecstatic, with headlines reading 'Terry Got Dam Busters to the Job W/C Gibson Tells His Mother Here' and 'Modest Dam Buster Hero Gets Enthusiastic Welcome'. Gibson's modesty was noted as he 'spoke little of the escapades

THE CALGARY

CALGARY, ALBERTA, THURSDAY, JUNE 24, 1943

EXAMINING PHOTOGRAPHS of the havoc caused by the breaching of the Mohne and Eder dams in Germany are King George (centre) and Wing Commander Guy Penrose Gibson (left) who led the raid. For this brilliant feat he was awarded the Victoria Cross by His Majesty. Previously he had been awarded the D.S.O. and bar and the D.F.C. and bar, and is Britain's most decorated man in the present war.

Photograph in Taerum family album, signed by Gibson. (Bomber Command Museum of Canada)

which won for him the Victoria Cross, DSO and Bar, and DFC and Bar. Rather, this young airman, probably the most famous hero yet to emerge from the present war, led the conversation to the splendid job Canadian fliers are doing and to his "great pal" Flying Officer Harlo "Terry" Taerum DFC, of Calgary.'[90]

The next day Gibson spent several hours at the Taerum residence. Mrs Taerum showed him her treasured album, full of photographs,

---

90 Quotations taken from Taerum family album, now in the Bomber Command Museum of Canada collection.

press cuttings and photographs and asked Gibson to autograph it. She summed up her experience by saying that it was one of the proudest and happiest times of her life.

★ ★ ★

Meanwhile, back in England 617 Squadron was preparing for a very difficult new challenge, the first in its new role as a specialised bombing unit. It would be asked to deploy the biggest bomb the RAF had yet carried in an attempt to breach another German key industrial target, the Dortmund–Ems Canal.

The bomb was a new 12,000lb thin-cased weapon, essentially three 4,000lb bombs bolted together, with a six-finned tail unit on the end. It was fitted with a delayed action fuse, so that the bomber which released it would be away from the dropping zone before the explosion. The bomb was so big that it needed special trolleys to move it from the store and took thirty-five minutes to be winched up into the Lancaster's bomb bay.

The Dortmund–Ems Canal stretches over 150 miles, linking the Ruhr valley to the sea. At Ladbergen, near Greven, just south of the junction with the Mittelland Canal, there is a raised section where aqueducts carry the canal over a culverted river. This had long been an important target for Bomber Command and had been attacked several times without success. Now, with a new much bigger bomb, the plan was to drop it from very low height into the soft earth embankments of the raised waterways.

The plan, given the name Operation Garlic, was drawn up in great detail by Air Cdre Harold Satterly, the Senior Air Staff Officer at 5 Group, and the man who had earlier drawn up the final orders for Operation Chastise.[91] The eight Lancasters detailed for the operation were to be accompanied by six Mosquitoes, specially brought in from

---

91 TNA, AIR 14/2038, No. 5 Group Operation Order No. B66, 10 September 1943.

418 and 605 Squadrons. Their role was to deal with searchlights, flak and any fighter opposition met along the way or over the target. The force was to be divided into two sections of four Lancasters and three Mosquitoes each, with the force leader commanding the first section and the deputy force leader commanding the second. The two sections would fly out by separate routes, maintaining formation if possible, crossing the English coast at 1,500ft and then dropping to 100ft over the North Sea. The deputy force leader would arrive first, and mark the area with three special parachute beacons dropped on an exact grid reference. If they didn't work, incendiaries were to be used instead. When all the Lancasters had arrived at the target, they would come under the control of the force leader, who would attack first. They were expected to drop their bombs in turn at a precise point within 40ft of the western bank of the canal. The bombing height was to be 150ft above the ground, at a speed of 180mph. Once a breach had been caused, the aircraft were to drop their remaining bombs on alternate banks of the canal 50 yards further north each time until all the bombs were used up. The bomb fuses gave a delay of between twenty-six and ninety seconds, which was supposed to leave sufficient time for aircraft to get clear. The force leader was therefore supposed to ensure that at least two minutes were left between each aircraft's attack.

The 12,000lb bomb they were going to drop was designed to take advantage of the Lancaster's bomb-carrying capacity. As with the Dams Raid, the Lancasters had to be specially modified for the operation, this time with special larger bomb bay doors, making the bay big enough to hold the enormous weapon. In this case, however, the mid-upper turret that had been removed for the Dams Raid was still available. Because the canal was known to be heavily defended, it was decided to carry a full-time front gunner on this trip, so an extra gunner was brought in for each aircraft to ensure that all three gun positions were filled.

The six Mosquitoes arrived on 5 September. Nearly every day afterwards they practised on co-operation flights with the Lancasters, which were still being modified.

The raid was important enough to be given its own code name, Operation Garlic, and was scheduled for Tuesday, 15 September. That morning George Holden asked Harry Humphries to draw up the battle order. Holden was to lead the first section of four, with Les Knight, Ralf Allsebrook and Harold Wilson. David Maltby would lead the second group: David Shannon, Geoff Rice and Bill Divall. Six Mosquitoes would fly with each section, three each from 605 and 418 Squadrons. As deputy force leader, David Maltby was due to drop the special parachute beacons which would mark the target.

Four of Gibson's Dams Raid crew – Harlo Taerum, Bob Hutchison, Fred Spafford and George Deering – were in Holden's Lancaster EE144 on this operation. George Deering took the front turret, the same position he had occupied on the Dams Raid, and there were three more crew members aboard: Sgt Dennis Powell (flight engineer), Flg Off Henry Pringle (mid-upper gunner) and Plt Off Thomas Meikle (rear gunner).

Less than an hour into the flight, word was received at base that the weather conditions at the target had deteriorated. The aircraft, which were then over the North Sea, were recalled. Then came disaster: as it turned, Maltby's Lancaster suddenly exploded. One of the accompanying Mosquitoes saw the aircraft in flames before it hit the sea. David Shannon stayed with the wreckage, sending fixes and circling above until air sea rescue launches arrived. It's not clear what caused the explosion. It could have been pilot error, or something may have gone wrong with the bomb. But there is also some evidence that it may have collided with a 139 Squadron Mosquito, returning from a raid on Berlin but out of radio contact.[92]

The seven remaining aircraft landed back at Coningsby in a state of shock. However, it was decided to go ahead with the raid the following day, Wednesday, 16 September, with Mick Martin and his crew replacing Maltby. Ralf Allsebrook took over as deputy force leader.

---

92 dambustersblog.com/2021/09/14/the-final-flight-of-david-maltby-and-his-crew-14-september-1943/ [accessed 1 November 2022].

This was to be an even more catastrophic night for the squadron, and Holden's was the first of five aircraft to be lost. He led his section of four across Holland flying in a diamond formation, Martin on his starboard side, Knight on port and Wilson at the rear. Tom Simpson, Martin's rear gunner, could hear Martin and Hay complain on the intercom that Holden was flying too high, allowing searchlights to pick them up. 'We seemed to be getting into a lot of trouble and I had never experienced such intense ground fire.' Just before they reached the small German town of Nordhorn, Martin was still keeping low, squeezing between factory chimney stacks where Simpson noted that the top of the stacks was higher than they were, while Holden, flying much higher, was drawing heavy anti-aircraft fire.[93] Some sources reckon that Holden rose to about 300ft in order to fly above a white-painted church with a high steeple in the town centre. Sutherland reckons that he was much higher:

> We had this new guy, Sqn Ldr Holden. He just came off high level. He had never flown low-level. So the first thing we did was we crossed into Germany and went over a small town. Instead of staying down and going around the church steeple, he went up to about a thousand feet. The story is that Martin and everybody else stayed down low but that's not true. When Holden went up, we all went up. Holden was in front of us and he got hit and he made a flamer. He went in front of us. We were on the port side and a guy called Wilson was behind us and Martin was on our starboard side. There were four in the formation. When they shot Holden down he just went like a torch. He went right in front of us. You could see the flames coming up between the ailerons.[94]

When Holden's Lancaster was hit, it went out of control, veering to port, and Knight himself had to swerve hard to avoid a collision.

---

93 Simpson, *Lower than Low*, p.107.
94 Dave Birrell, *Big Joe McCarthy* (Wing Leader Publishing, 2012), pp.153–4.

Within seconds, they had hit the ground and exploded with the loss of everyone on board. 'It was some sight – eight guys just dying in front of my eyes,' said Sutherland. 'They didn't have a hope. It was so close I could almost reach out and touch it. Your friends are getting killed in front of your eyes and you are scared as hell but you can't let it bother you. If you did, you could never do your job. You just think: "Thank God it wasn't us."'[95]

When considering these accounts, it is difficult to avoid the conclusion that a more cautious pilot – perhaps someone who had flown on the Dams Raid – would probably have changed course to go around the spire.

Holden's Lancaster had crashed but its 12,000lb bomb had a delay fuse fitted, and it didn't explode immediately. If it had the aircraft of Martin, Knight and Wilson would probably have also been destroyed. The Lancaster had crashed onto the farm of a German family called Hood, who were sheltering in a cellar beneath their farmhouse when the crash occurred. A few minutes later, realising that the remaining aircraft had gone, the parents went above ground to get warm clothing for the children. While they were doing this the huge bomb exploded, demolishing every building on the farm, killing Frau Teupe Hood immediately. Her husband Jan survived, shielded by what remained of a wall he was fortunately behind, but was in hospital for a month.

The other seven aircraft continued towards the canal but ended in failure, with the loss of three more complete crews – those of Ralf Allsebrook, Bill Divall and Harold Wilson – and the pilot Les Knight, whose heroic sacrifice of his own life allowed the seven men in his crew to bail out successfully. Such a catastrophic result meant that the squadron had to be almost completely rebuilt, and it became the task of the new Commanding Officer, Leonard Cheshire, to restore morale and focus on a new role.

---

95 John Nichol, *After the Flood* (William Collins, 2015), pp.40–1.

That was all a few months in the future. When Martin, Shannon and Rice, the only survivors, landed back at Coningsby, the mood was desperate. 'It was the blackest day in the history of the squadron,' wrote Harry Humphries. Bob Hutchison was a good friend of his, and he was gone, and he couldn't help thinking about how Hutchison had called into his office that afternoon to leave some keys behind with him for safekeeping. Hutchison had given him his customary greeting of a 'peculiar little salute', a habit (or perhaps a superstition) that he always carried out when he saw Humphries, even though they were both Flight Lieutenants. They talked for a few minutes, and then he left. '"Well, must be going, see you tomorrow, Humph." Again, that funny little salute, and so went Bob. I never saw him again.'

A little later, Humphries watched the eight aircraft take off and then went back to his office. Waiting for him were Joe McCarthy and Les Munro, who had both been left off the night's roster. McCarthy then announced that he would rather wait in the watch office and the others accompanied him. A couple of hours passed, and Humphries was on the balcony staring forlornly into the night sky when McCarthy came up:

> 'We've lost George Holden, Adj,' he said. 'Shot down just over the German border, a place called Nordhorn.'
>
> I just said, 'Good God,' and added 'that takes care of most of Gibby's crew, Mac.' 'Yeah, I know,' said the big American, 'poor old Spam.' He said 'poor old Spam,' because in all instances like this one thought of one's personal friends first.
>
> I thought 'poor old Hutch.' No more salutes, no more tennis, no more stage shows. The night suddenly became cold and chilly.[96]

The next day Humphries's job was to organise the telegrams and letters for the men who were missing. There were forty of these to do: five crews each containing eight men, as at this stage no one knew

---

96 Humphries, *Living with Heroes*, pp.67–8.

that the Knight crew had survived. Mick Martin was the acting Commanding Officer, so the letters went out under his signature.

The telegram would have arrived at the Hutchison house in Liverpool in the afternoon of Thursday, 16 September, and sometime later at the Taerum and Deering residences in Canada and the Spafford house in Adelaide, South Australia. All four families must have been dreading that this moment would arrive, probably ever since their bright-eyed sons had come home one day a few years before and said that they were joining the air force. The letter, with its well-meant personal touches, must have been scant consolation, but more heart-felt communication would arrive, at least for the Hutchisons.

Revie Walker had been navigating David Shannon's Lancaster on the same night. He was in a different section, so hadn't seen Holden's crash, but he had seen the appalling conditions the crews had faced when they eventually arrived at the Dortmund–Ems Canal. He gleaned what information he could from Martin and his crew about how Holden had been shot down and then the following day, Friday, 17 September 1943, he sat down in the mess and wrote to the family of his best friend Bob. It was almost exactly two years previously that the pair had met, both trainee aircrew in 25 Operational Training Unit at RAF Finningley, and Walker had been to the family home in Liverpool on several occasions. The emotion rings out from his handwritten page:

Dear Folks

It is with a heavy heart that I sit down to write this letter seeing as to how Bob failed to come home from a raid last evening …

My two year friendship with Bob have convinced me that he is the finest lad I've ever had the pleasure of meeting. His happy and steady ways won everyone. I'm positive Folks that although you will not hear from many of the squadron lads they all will want me to offer their condolences. Bob was well known not only as a airman but on the ground for his organizing of sports and plays. In whatever he tackled he soon made many friends.

One of the boys has already called to see Twink. He told me
that she is doing her very best to be brave. Expect you will by this
time have heard from Twink yourself Folks.

Before I close Folks please remember that if there is anything
I can do or look into from this side for you please do not hesitate
in writing.[97]

A few days later Harry Humphries also wrote to Robert Hutchison
Snr, saying that he had 'reliable information' that the 'aircraft in
which Bob was flying was seen to be shot down over enemy territory. I hate to have to tell you this, but I think that you would rather
know than have any false hopes.'[98]

Humphries had heard enough, and knew that it was better to be
direct about matters like these. But it must have been hard reading in
the Liverpool suburb of Allerton.

★ ★ ★

On the previous Sunday afternoon Hilda Taerum had been sitting in
her family home in Calgary with Guy Gibson as her guest, showing
him her album filled with neatly clipped press cuttings and photographs. 'Meeting Wing Commander Gibson was one of the proudest
and happiest moments of my life,' she told the *Calgary Star*. 'He is
one of the nicest persons I have ever met.'

On the following Friday, Mick Martin's telegram arrived and
her world changed. The Canadian press were on to the story very
quickly, with Monday's *Calgary Herald* running a double column
photograph of Taerum and a story underneath.

---

97 Revie Walker, letter to Hutchison family, 17 September 1943. Spelling and
punctuation as in original. (Hutchison family collection)
98 Harry Humphries, letter to Hutchison family, 23 September 1943. Spelling
and punctuation as in original. (Hutchison family collection)

CALGARY'S DAM BUSTER IS REPORTED MISSING
Survivor of the famous Mohne and Eder raids and described as
the navigator who 'got the dam busters to the job,' FO. Harlo
Taerum DFC has been reported missing as a result of air operations overseas.

Official word that her son was missing was received Saturday by
Mrs. H. Taerum, 334 15th Ave. W. The operation from which he
failed to return occurred on Sept. 15.

FO. Taerum was decorated by the Queen for the part he played
in assisting to destroy the Mohne and Elder dams in Germany.

He was navigator on the plane of Wing Commander Guy P.
Gibson V.C., D.F.C and Bar, D.S.O. and Bar, who led the dam-
busting raid.

On a visit to Calgary a little over a week ago, Wing Commander
met Mrs. Taerum and described Terry as a 'great boy and a great
navigator ... he got the whole squadron to the dam.'[99]

Gibson had travelled to Vancouver after his time in Calgary, and had
proceeded from there to Montreal. It was there that he heard of the
loss of Holden and his crew on the Dortmund–Ems Canal operation.
In the course of a press interview which took place at yet another
training establishment, he said:

'Every man in the crew must depend on the skill and loyalty of the
others, and all are equally important. When a job has been done
well it means that all have contributed an equal share.'

When told that a report had just arrived to the effect that F/O
Taerum D.F.C., 23 year old Calgary airman was missing overseas,
Wing Commander Gibson expressed deep regret. 'He was my
navigator on the raid, and a first-class man,' he said.

The young hero was enthusiastic about his crew, and pointed
out it was almost completely an Empire selection. The bomber

---

99 *Calgary Herald*, 20 September 1943.

was an Australian, Pilot Officer Spafford, the navigator and the front gunner were both Canadians, Flying Officer Taerum and Pilot Officer Deering, the latter of Toronto; and the rest of the crew were Flight-Lieutenant Hutchison, an Englishman; Flight-Lieutenant Trevor-Roper, a Welshman; and Sergeant Bulford [*sic*], an Englishman, who was flight engineer.[100]

Gibson's remarks were repeated by other Canadian newspapers, while he himself carried on with his tour, taking in various other units before reaching Halifax on 24 September. It is worth noting that he met the relatives of both Melvin Young and Harvey Glinz, a Canadian air gunner in Norman Barlow's Dams Raid crew, but he doesn't seem to have contacted George Deering's family. Rather surprisingly Canada's biggest city, where the Deering family had made their home, was never on his schedule.

The Australian press does not seem to have picked up the news for a few more days, and it provided much briefer coverage. On 1 October, *The Advertiser* informed the people of South Australia that its Director of Agriculture, W.J. Spafford, had distressing news. He had 'received advice' that Plt Off F.M. Spafford DFC DFM had been reported missing on 15 September, 'following an operational flight'.

Meanwhile, Gibson carried on with his tour. By early October, he was back in Washington DC, and stayed with Roald Dahl. Dahl obviously recognised a kindred spirit in his new companion and wrote about him in a letter to his mother dated 12 October 1943:

I've had Guy Gibson of Möhne Dam fame staying with me for the last few days and we've had quite a time. I threw a bridge cocktail party for him at which there were 2 Air Marshals & I don't know how many Generals and all the pretty girls I could think of in town, just so that he could take his pick. He is the hell of a

---

100 *Montreal Star*, 20 September 1943.

good type. He is in my care here and today I sent him off across the country on a lecture tour ...[101]

In the month since their first meeting Dahl had been working hard on his film project. He wrote an earlier letter to his mother that Gibson was coming 'to see me about the "Bombing of the Dams" script which I am trying to do for Hollywood in my spare time. I've got all the material now and all the photos I want. I've got everything, in fact, except the time in which to do it.' By 21 September, he had completed the script, calling it 'The Dam', and sent it to London for vetting.

However, it was not well received. Some readers raised security concerns, but others, such as Harris, thought it unrealistic. It isn't known how Howard Hawks reacted but it is clear that he soon became involved in other projects, so 'The Dam' was quietly shelved. However, parts of the script also appear almost verbatim in an article called 'Cracking the German Dams' published in the December number of *The Atlantic Monthly* with Gibson's name on the by-line. So it's likely that Dahl was involved in writing this article and getting it published, perhaps with the assistance of Gibson. Several months later Gibson apologised to Barnes Wallis for the article's inaccuracies, excusing it as propaganda written by someone else.

After his bonding session with Dahl in Washington, Gibson set off on the next phase of his tour. Hollywood beckoned, but he had to get through a series of cocktail parties, presentations and award ceremonies in cities all over the USA – New York, Chicago, Minneapolis, Pittsburgh, Miami – before reaching Los Angeles on 1 November. Here he stayed with Howard Hawks for about a week and was introduced to people with connections in the film industry. The research suggests that there were not many official engagements in these weeks, but plenty of opportunity for socialising.

---

101 Richard Morris, 'Roald Dahl and the Dam', in Richard Morris & Robert Owen (eds), *Breaching the German Dams* (RAF Museum, 2008), p.60.

Finally, it was back to Montreal, and on 1 December a seat in a Liberator which was being ferried to Prestwick in Scotland. Of the people he had come across in his three months in North America, there would be a tragic postscript for Hilda Taerum and her family, living out their lives in Calgary without their oldest son and brother. Harlo's brother Lorne, an air gunner just 18 years old, was also killed while serving in the RCAF. His 550 Squadron Lancaster was shot down by a fighter on just his sixth operation in February 1945.[102]

Within a short time of arriving back in London, Gibson set off for Lincolnshire. Without checking where 617 Squadron was now, he marched into the mess at Scampton. When he discovered that they had moved a month after his departure he then had to ask for a car to take him to Coningsby, forty-five minutes away. There, at least, he was in the presence of old comrades but, apart from Martin, Shannon, McCarthy and a handful of others, they were few and far between. The new CO, Leonard Cheshire, was also present, but he tactfully withdrew.

On the Sunday after his return, 5 December, an article had appeared in the *Sunday Express*. Entitled 'How we smashed the German dams', it purported to be written by Gibson, but in fact he had nothing to do with it. Some have speculated that it was the same as *The Atlantic Monthly* article published a few weeks before in the USA, but the two pieces are completely different. Some of the phrasing and a few paragraphs of text from both articles – particularly about the selection of the crews – would eventually appear in *Enemy Coast Ahead* but there is a lot of material in both which is pure fiction. The *Sunday Express* article had, of course, been widely read in the 617 Squadron mess, and Gibson was roundly teased by Martin and others for its wide deviation from the truth.

---

102 It is sometimes erroneously reported that Lorne Taerum was killed on his first operation. He had completed five operations in 550 Squadron, the first in December 1944. He was killed on his sixth. Information from Wg Cdr Jack Harris OBE DFC, via Rob Taerum.

Article in *Sunday Express*, 5 December 1943.

Gibson also called over to 5 Group headquarters, presumably lobbying for a return to operational flying, but instead was sent for a medical examination. He was discovered to be sick with a serious throat infection. He spent some time in Rauceby Hospital, the place where he had first met Margaret North a little more than a year previously. This was followed by a period of recuperation leave, with his planned place on a course at the RAF Staff College in Gerrards Cross being deferred to a later date.

16

Back to Work for Pulford and Trevor-Roper

September's loss of Taerum, Hutchison, Spafford and Deering on the Dortmund–Ems Canal operation left John Pulford as the only man from the Gibson crew still serving in 617 Squadron. Operation Garlic had been a disaster for the whole squadron, with six crews lost over two days, which meant that the squadron had to be completely reset before activity could continue. New crews began to arrive, led by the charismatic new squadron CO, Leonard Cheshire, whose management style would prove to be markedly different from that of Gibson. The squadron would not be used as part of the main bombing force but was to be allowed to develop as a special skills unit.

Before he would undertake his next operational activity, John Pulford had a date in London as the only man not yet officially invested with his medal after the Dams Raid. He travelled to Buckingham Palace on 16 November, accompanied by his sister Ivy and his fiancée, whose name sadly seems to have been lost.

One of the new pilots to join the squadron was the Canadian Sqn Ldr Bill Suggitt DFC. The Canadian had two countrymen and two Australians in his crew. Suggitt was recognised as an excellent pilot, but didn't socialise much, so was not always popular. However, Pulford seemed to have got on with him, and became his flight engineer. He and the rest of his crew mostly stayed together for the nine difficult operations they would fly over the following two months.

The arrival of Cheshire brought a new focus on bombing techniques, a subject on which he and Mick Martin were always trying out new innovations. The pair developed new ways of marking targets with flares, some of which were very successful, and this led to the selection of several very secret targets, principally the sites in northern France where the Germans were developing the V1 'flying bomb' with which to attack Britain. The squadron would also carry on using the 12,000lb bomb first deployed on the Dortmund–Ems raid in September.

The Suggitt crew first flew on an operation together on 16 December, attacking the V1 site at Flixecourt. The target was marked for the first time by an 'Oboe'-equipped Mosquito, which was supposed to pinpoint the target by way of intersecting radar beams. The crew was Sqn Ldr Bill Suggitt RCAF (pilot), Flt Sgt John Pulford (flight engineer), Wrt Off John Gordon RAAF (navigator), Flg Off Norman Davidson RCAF (wireless operator), Plt Off Stanley Hall RAAF (bomb aimer), Flt Sgt John Riches (mid-upper gunner) and Flg Off John Dempster RCAF (rear gunner).

Two more operations followed, on 20 and 22 December, the targets being an armaments factory at Liège and the V1 site at Abbeville. On both, the navigator was Flt Lt Revie Walker, Bob Hutchison's Canadian friend who normally flew in David Shannon's crew. The operation to Abbeville on 22 December was abandoned on Cheshire's orders when he circled the target for fifteen minutes but couldn't identify the marker flares. The Suggitt crew touched down shortly before midnight, which is what John Pulford is probably referring to when he wrote to his mother at around this time:

Dear Mother
    Heres a few lines to let you know I'm safe and sound, received both registered letter and parcel. I really want to thank you for

the parcel especially the cigars I really go for those at Christmas time. I've been very busy here lately and couldn't find time to do any shopping, even the Christmas card have been sold out, so if you don't get one from me please don't think your forgotten, and next time I'm on leave I'll be home to see you. The 10/- is for you to get yourself a good drop of short the postal order is for Douglas and give him my Best Wishes for a white Christmas. Well I'm signing off now give all at home my Best Wishes too hope to see them soon.

Cheerio Happy Christmas

Johnny[103]

Pulford was able to get home for a few days in February, but the exact date isn't known. The squadron moved to a new station at RAF Woodhall Spa, a few miles from Coningsby. As this was a single squadron station, it suited Bomber Command better to have 617 Squadron based there as it diminished the chances of information about its specialised work being transmitted inadvertently.

Pulford flew on four more successful operations with Suggitt, three attacking 'special targets'. The fourth was the attack on the Gnome et Rhône aircraft engine factory at Limoges in occupied France on 8 February. This had previously been vetoed as a target since it employed 300 French women, and it was lightly defended because it was in a civilian area. Cheshire proposed flying over the factory several times in order to give the workers time to leave, and this is what he did. The detachment then dropped a mixture of 1,000 and 12,000lb bombs with devastating accuracy, completely obliterating the site. There were no French civilian casualties.

Four days later, on 12 February, Suggitt and his crew were among a detachment of ten aircraft led by Cheshire which attacked the Anthéor Railway Viaduct in southern France. This had been a target

---

103 John Pulford, letter to Ada Pulford, ND ? December 1943. Spelling and punctuation as in original. (Pulford family, via Malcolm Bellamy)

on several previous occasions, but this was the first time it would be attacked with the 12,000lb bomb. Because of the distance and the weight of the bomb, the detachment used RAF Ford airfield in Sussex to refuel before the attack.

The operation was not successful. All the aircraft found the target very hard to approach, let alone drop their bombs. Mick Martin's aircraft was badly damaged by flak, and his bomb aimer Bob Hay was killed. Martin landed in Sardinia, where Hay was buried while the aircraft was being repaired. They flew home several days later. Meanwhile, Suggitt and crew landed back at Ford at 0504 on 13 February, reporting that they had made a bombing run but dropped their 12,000lb bomb before the viaduct was in its sights. Also at Ford that night was Sqn Ldr Tommy Lloyd, a very popular figure at 617 Squadron. Aged 52, he had served in the army in the First World War, and won the DSO. Re-enlisting in the RAF at the beginning of the Second World War, he had become an Intelligence Officer and was at Scampton on the night of the Dams Raid. For the attack on the Anthéor Railway Viaduct he had flown to Ford in order to debrief the crews as they landed. When dawn broke, the weather conditions could be seen to be foggy, and so most of the crews decided to wait a while for the situation to improve. Suggitt, however, decided to set off for Woodhall Spa as soon as possible and offered Lloyd a lift. Lloyd accepted, went for a shave to spruce himself up and climbed aboard. Within five minutes of take-off, he was dead, as their Lancaster crashed into a cloud-shrouded Littleton Down, a few miles from the airfield. John Pulford and the rest of the crew were also killed, although Suggitt himself was dragged from the wreckage badly injured and taken to hospital in Chichester. He died two days later.

The bodies of all the crew were placed in coffins and taken first to Coningsby. That of Pulford was then transported by train to Hull, where the *Hull Daily Mail* reported the news on Wednesday, 16 February. Under the headline 'Raided Italy and Germany: Distinguished Hull Airman Killed', the newspaper wrote that 'a young Hull flyer, who in May last year was awarded the DFM' had met his death on active service. 'His award was in recognition of the part he had played in the destructive raid on the great Mohne and Eder dams in the Ruhr, when he was a flight engineer ... It will be remembered that the men who took part in the daring raids were presented to the King and Queen when their Majesties visited various aerodromes.'

On the same day, Cheshire sent a warm personal letter to Ada Pulford, noting that her son had a very distinguished operational record, showing 'great courage and determination in action, and proved himself to be very capable as a Flight Engineer'. This was followed by a letter from Harry Humphries about the casualty arrangements but adding that he had known her son 'very well and can assure you that he fulfilled his duties very capably'.

On 18 February John Pulford was buried in the city's Northern Cemetery, in a plot next to his father. The inscription on his gravestone reads, 'Until memory fails and life departs you are ever in our hearts. Your loving family'.

★ ★ ★

Meanwhile, Richard Trevor-Roper was back on active service. By coincidence, at the time of Pulford's death Trevor-Roper was about to be posted to the squadron from which Pulford had moved to 617 Squadron almost exactly a year previously. This was 97 Squadron, which was now a Pathfinder unit and was based at RAF Bourn, a few miles from Cambridge. Trevor-Roper had finished his period instructing first in the Central Gunnery School and then the Pathfinders Navigation Training Unit (PNTU) and on 5 March 1944 took up his new posting. His wife Patricia and their son Charles, now 9 months old, remained nearly 50 miles away in Skegness. Trevor-Roper was accompanied by another experienced air gunner, Flg Off Fred Colville, who had also been at the PNTU at nearby RAF Upwood.

Trevor-Roper would see a difference in the size of the force deployed in the year since he had flown on general operations. In the early spring of 1944 Bomber Command regularly sent out more than 500 aircraft on an operation, nearly all heavy bombers. The use of Pathfinder squadrons had improved marking techniques, even though sometimes there was tension at the top level between their commanders and those of the main force.

When they arrived at Bourn, Trevor-Roper and Colville joined a new crew of experienced men, skippered by pilot Flt Lt Desmond Rowlands DFC, who had also just joined the squadron. He was a 97 Squadron veteran, having been one of the men who helped re-establish the squadron in 1941. The Rowlands crew's first outing was a raid on Stuttgart on 15 March, which was completed successfully. The pair of experienced gunners were then asked to fill in on a trip to Frankfurt on 22 March in an aircraft piloted by Wg Cdr E.J. Carter.

The last day of the month, 31 March, brought plans for another mass raid. A force of 795 aircraft was prepared for an attack on Nuremberg. Fourteen of these would come from 97 Squadron, with Rowlands taking off at 2210. The full list of the other men in his crew was Sgt Robert Lane (flight engineer), Flt Lt Arthur Cadman DFM (navigator), Flg Off Edgar Currie (wireless operator), Flt Lt Albert McFadden (bomb aimer), Flg Off Fred Colville (mid-upper gunner) and Flt Lt Richard Trevor-Roper DFC DFM (rear gunner).

It was the period of a full moon which under normal circumstances meant that bombing raids were curtailed. However, the planners decided that a mass attack on Nuremberg could go ahead that night, apparently on the basis that the weather forecast indicated there would be a layer of cloud on the outward route to protect the bomber stream from German night fighters and that the cloud would clear at around the time the bombers reached Nuremberg. However, the weather failed to co-operate. The cloud failed to materialise on the outward route and enemy fighters were therefore able to take a heavy toll of the bombers in the clear and bright conditions.

The danger they were all in must have become startlingly obvious to those who flew on the operation. Two members of another 97 Squadron crew wrote a devastating account of why the operation became such a disaster. The pilot, Flt Lt Charles Owen, wrote a contemporary diary entry: 'Moon far too bright for comfort, and the sky swarming with fighters. Saw combats all over the sky, right from the coast to the target, and a very large number of aircraft shot down. I weaved a lot more than usual and was not attacked.' His navigator, Flg Off Bill Shires, was interviewed in 2004 and recalled: 'I had an idea that travelling at 20,000ft with the rest of them was not a very good idea, so we did it at 15,000ft. All those damned aircraft were just like moths against a cinema screen, whereas we were down below watching all these things. We actually counted seventy aircraft shot down that night.'[104] Shires himself counted seventy losses, out of a total of ninety-six. It was Bomber Command's worst night of the whole war: a total of 540 men were killed – more aircrew lost their lives on this one operation than in all the weeks taken up by the whole Battle of Britain.

The first German fighters appeared just before the bombers reached the Belgian border and a fierce battle in the moonlight lasted for the next hour. Many of them were equipped with the upward-firing Schräge Musik cannon, and it was one of these Messerschmitt 110 aircraft, flown by Major Martin Drewes, which accounted for Rowlands and his crew. They had just reached a turning point and had set course for the last leg of the route towards Nuremberg when Drewes approached. He positioned himself below the aircraft and fired one burst of cannon fire into the starboard wing. There was no return fire, the bomber went straight down and burst apart as its bombs and target indicators exploded. Six bodies were found near the edge of a wood near Ahorn. The seventh was

104 Diary of Flt Lt Charles Owen, IWM Collections and interview with
   Flg Off Bill Shires, May 2004, both in Bending, *Achieve Your Aim*, p.112.

that of Trevor-Roper, found still in his turret, which had been separated by the force of the crash from the rest of the fuselage and some distance away.[105]

Back at Bourn, Trevor-Roper was listed as missing. Telegrams and letters were sent to his family but confirmation of his death didn't reach the public until November 1944, when many tributes were paid to him.

Trevor-Roper's death meant that all of Gibson's Dams Raid crew had been killed on active service within eleven months of Operation Chastise. By this time, Gibson himself was in Whitehall and presumably noted who was on the missing list. He was employed in a desk job, but his real task was to write his book, *Enemy Coast Ahead*.

---

105 Martin Middlebrook, *The Nuremberg Raid* (Penguin, 1986), p.177.

17

The Man in the Ministry: Gibson Grounded

After his month on sick leave, Gibson took up a posting to the Directorate for the Protection of Accidents in the Air Ministry in central London on 6 January 1944. He moved into the flat in Aberdeen Terrace, St John's Wood, which Eve had previously been sharing with a girlfriend.

He also took the opportunity to catch up with things that had occurred while he was away. One of these was to write a letter to the Hutchison family, expressing his condolences for the loss of Bob in September. He is a little disingenuous in implying that he had only just got the news. The letter is dated 19 February 1944:

My dear Mr Hutchison

I was deeply upset on my return from America to hear that Hutch has been posted missing. Squadron Leader Holden was not a bad pilot and it was sheer bad luck that an unlucky cannon shell blew up one of the petrol tanks of the Lancaster which was only flying at 50 feet and went straight into the ground. In view of this evidence I am afraid we must accept the fact that Hutch is dead. There can be no way out, unless a complete miracle saved him. Moreover the position of the Wireless Operator in a Lancaster is not one from which it is easy to escape. As far as obtaining some definite news I am afraid that this is just not possible. I know well the great sorrow and sadness that these things give us and this is just one more which have been my lot for the last four years.

Please accept my most profound sympathy.

Yours sincerely

Guy Gibson[106]

The phrase 'damning with faint praise' might have been coined to describe Gibson's expressed view that Holden was 'not a bad pilot'. Such frankness might not get into a tribute letter these days. It's also worth noting that this letter doesn't contain any tribute to Hutchison himself, other than saying how upset Gibson felt. However, it does seem that this is the only letter he wrote to the families of the six men whom he would call 'My Crew' a few months later.

Despite his job title, it doesn't seem as though Gibson did much work investigating what was the cause of an aircraft having an accident. Instead, he began the project which had been suggested to him at the time of leaving 106 Squadron some nine months previously: the book about his RAF experiences. It is not clear exactly who suggested that he revive this idea, or at what level he was granted the time, the dictaphone and the typist which made it all possible, but he went ahead. The literary agents Pearn, Pollinger and Higham, and three publishers, Hutchinson, Hamish Hamilton and Michael Joseph, were all contacted, but in what order and who made the approach to whom isn't clear. In the end, Michael Joseph was chosen to publish the book.

He must have worked hard, because he produced most of the text over a period of about four months. According to Eve, Gibson spent many evenings and weekends in March and April working on it, which suggests he spent most of the daytime dictating material,

---

106 Guy Gibson, letter to Robert Hutchison, 19 February 1944. Spelling and punctuation as in original. (Hutchison family collection)

Tel. No. HOLBORN 3434.

EXT.

AIR MINISTRY,

ADASTRAL HOUSE,

KINGSWAY, W.C.2.

19th February, 1944.

My dear Mr. Hutchison,

I was deeply upset on my return from America to hear that Hutch had been posted missing. Squadron Leader Holden was not a bad pilot and it was sheer bad luck that an unlucky cannon shell blew up one of the petrol tanks of the Lancaster which was only flying at 50 feet and went straight into the ground. In view of this evidence I am afraid we must accept the fact that Hutch is dead. There can be no way out, unless a complete miracle saved him. Moreover the position of the Wireless Operator in a Lancaster is not one from which it is easy to escape. As far as obtaining some definite news I am afraid that this is just not possible. I know well the great sorrow and sadness that these things give us and this is just one more which have been my lot for the last four years.

Please accept my most profound sympathy.

Yours sincerely,

Guy Gibson

R.G. Hutchison, Esq.,
    Ellerman's City and Hall Lines,
      Tower Building,
        Water Street,
          Liverpool.

Gibson letter to Hutchison family, February 1944. (Hutchison family collection) and then brought the typescript home to read through and correct outside office hours. He had his logbook as source material for the early years and for the 617 Squadron period he asked Sgt Jim Heveron for help. He also wrote to Barnes Wallis. Heveron travelled to London with some files to help his research and thought that he seemed depressed. Later in the year, on 14 April, Gibson would write to Harry Humphries looking for a specific file, a report he had once written on the Le Creusot raid.[107]

At the same time, Gibson's public profile was getting more attention. In early February he was approached by Garfield Weston, the industrialist who was also the Conservative MP for Macclesfield. In order to concentrate on his business interests (he owned the big Allied Bakeries firm, as well as other food businesses in his native Canada) Weston had decided that he would not contest the next general election, and he had also spoken to Churchill about finding a replacement. The Prime Minister told him he was impressed with Gibson, so Weston hatched a plan to introduce Gibson to the Macclesfield Conservative Association, the body who would make the final choice of candidate. He first invited Guy and Eve to spend the weekend with him in his impressive house in Henley, and then asked them to accompany him on a trip to Macclesfield itself. There, they conducted a tour of the constituency, which conveniently included the Avro plant at Woodford, thereby enabling Gibson to take Weston on a brief flight in a Lancaster.

Gibson went straight back to London from this first visit to Macclesfield to meet Roy Plomley at Broadcasting House. His growing fame had led him to be invited onto the BBC's new 'Desert Island Discs' radio programme, the youngest person and the first serving officer to be the guest. The programme, hosted by Plomley, was recorded on Friday, 11 February, and broadcast eight days later on 19 February. The recording wasn't kept after broadcast (standard practice in those days) but the pre-scripted exchanges between

---

107 Humphries, *Living with Heroes*, p.98.

Plomley and Gibson and the list of music chosen were preserved. Among Gibson's choices were the *Warsaw Concerto* because it reminded him of life in the mess at the beginning of the war. 'If I Had My Way' by Bing Crosby had been sung over the intercom many times when he was flying; it would be a treat to hear the original. Wagner's 'Ride of the Valkyries' reminded him of a bombing raid (ironic when you think of how it was used by Francis Ford Coppola thirty years later in the soundtrack of his film, *Apocalypse Now*). And 'Where or When', a 'cracking good dance tune' by Adelaide Hall took him back to the time that he and Eve became engaged.

The next day he had another public engagement, a visit to Bristol, organised by the Ministry of Information, keen to promote a wide range of public service announcements. There he spoke to workers at the Bristol Aeroplane Company, inspected the local ATC and launched the local blood donor campaign. At all of these he had large crowds, all wanting to see the 'Airman VC', as he was frequently billed. Other similar tours followed.

A few weeks later, up in Macclesfield, the local Conservative Association drew up the shortlist for its selection conference. None of the other four men who made it through had anything like the name recognition of the youthful air force officer, a fact alluded to by the local newspaper with the headline, 'Airman VC on short list of five'. Three weeks after this he won the nomination, but the vote proved surprisingly close, with Gibson only winning in the final round by seventeen votes to thirteen. In his statement afterwards he made what sounds like a typical political acceptance speech. He wanted 'to lend a humble hand in shaping the new Britain. Whatever the planners may decide, youth will inherit the legacy. I speak for youth. We have a right, and demand a right, to have some say in moulding the country and the Empire for which youth has fought so hard.'[108]

---

108 Morris, *Guy Gibson*, p.238.

In mid-March, Gibson was posted onto the postponed course at the RAF Staff College, Gerrards Cross, but living in a Nissen hut rather than the smart surroundings of the college itself. At weekends he was still working on the typescript of *Enemy Coast Ahead*, as well as fitting in trips to Macclesfield.

On Friday, 18 May, an all ranks dance was held in a hangar at RAF Woodhall Spa to mark the one-year anniversary of the Dams Raid. Many of those who had taken part were present, although such had been the rate of attrition at this stage of the war that another thirty-one men who had flown on Operation Chastise had died since, including all six of Gibson's crew. Gibson and Cheshire were both present, standing on a pair of tables covered in cloths to make their speeches, and Cheshire paid his predecessor a generous tribute. Gibson spoke in reply and then contrived to step on a space between the tables, falling into a cake and spattering those nearby with icing.

The staff college course finished at the end of May, and he and Eve went on a week's leave to North Wales. It wasn't a pleasant holiday: it rained most of the time, and it seemed more and more inevitable that they would eventually split up. Then came the news of D-Day. His immediate reaction was to cut his leave short and demand to be put back on operations. Eve resisted this, but as soon as he was back, he went straight to see Arthur Harris. Four days later, he was posted to 55 Base at RAF East Kirkby as Deputy Base Operations Officer.

He found this new job frustrating. He was in touch with operational airmen – going to the mess, to briefings, to pubs – but he wasn't one himself. He had no real friends on the base, which may be why he got back in touch with Margaret North. They had exchanged letters in the year since he saw her, so he knew that she was now living in her mother's house in Bognor Regis, with a baby son. He drove down to pay a visit. Even though it was July, it was dark and cold and pouring with rain. They talked for hours, discussing the unhappy state of both of their marriages and Gibson's future, about which he was confused. But sensing that the war might be over sometime soon, he said, 'Afterwards, I'm coming to find you.' He left and a few days later wrote her a note: 'The day was perfect. I love you now and forever.' She never heard from him again.[109]

Meanwhile, at the end of July he completed work on a further draft of *Enemy Coast Ahead*, going through the corrections and amendments proposed by various people in the Air Ministry and writing a series of handwritten notes which were pinned to the final version. It is notable that the final version was composed on at least two typewriters. On 1 August, he sent the entire typescript by registered post to Nancy Pearn at the literary agent Pearn, Pollinger and Higham, who then forwarded it to Michael Joseph. He couldn't think of a good title, he wrote in an accompanying letter, but he did have a few suggestions. They were handwritten on a separate sheet of paper and included *The Boys Die Young* and *Eight Are Missing* as well as *Enemy Coast Ahead*. The typescript was returned to him sometime in early September, and he worked on it over the next two weeks. The bundle of papers, now in several cardboard folders, is held at the RAF Museum. It was not easy, at nearly eighty years' distance, for me to tell exactly when each correction was made.

Back at East Kirkby, he continued to be frustrated. Mick Martin flew in, piloting a Mosquito, and he and Gibson went up in the air for a jaunt. They talked for a while, Gibson saying how frustrated he felt, and confiding doubts about the Macclesfield nomination. He also cultivated a relationship with Sqn Ldr Drew Wyness, who had previously flown in 50 Squadron at the same time as several of his Dams Raid crew. He would later join 617 Squadron and be killed on operations. Wyness invited him aboard his Lancaster when undertaking some local flying tests, and Gibson took the controls for a while. Then, on 19 July, in circumstances that aren't clear he managed to get himself onto an operational flight, piloting a 630 Squadron Lancaster on a daylight attack on a V1 site near Criel in France. The aircraft was normally flown by another pilot and Gibson's name does not appear in the squadron Operations

---

109 Morris, *Guy Gibson*, pp.250–1.

Record Book. However, there is no doubt that it occurred as Gibson's name appears on the aiming point photograph. He was so pleased with being back on operations (after fourteen months) that he pasted the print into his logbook.

On 4 August, Gibson was posted from East Kirkby to a new job as Air Staff Officer at No. 54 Base Headquarters at RAF Coningsby. No. 54 Base had been set up to provide target marking and illumination for 5 Group operations, the work being done by 'controllers' who flew from the station. Coningsby itself was, of course, an old Gibson hunting ground, his home for the first part of his 106 Squadron career. Even more evocative of the past was the presence of his old squadrons nearby: 106 Squadron at RAF Metheringham, 10 miles away, and 617 Squadron even closer at RAF Woodhall Spa.

Also at Woodhall Spa was the only unit in 5 Group which flew Mosquitoes, 627 Squadron, whose job was to supply low-level marking for the bombers. The officers in 617 Squadron messed in the comfortable surroundings of the Petwood Hotel in the town, but those in 627 Squadron had to put up with more modest hutted accommodation near the airfield. Gibson decided to pay them a visit, and his behaviour had echoes of his previous early encounter with his men when he assumed command of 106 Squadron. He walked unannounced into the bar where a large group were socialising. Many recognised him of course – a Wing Commander with a Victoria Cross was not a common sight – but for few moments no one acknowledged his presence. Irritatingly asking, 'Do you know who I am?' was hardly going to help and when the response from an Australian came back, 'So bloody what', the situation escalated. There was an attempt to debag him and a junior officer ended up being disciplined.

Eve Gibson came up to stay with her husband in Skegness in early August, but they ended up only spending a very short time together. They had dinner together on his birthday, 12 August, and he stayed the night. When Gibson left in the morning it was the last time they saw each other.[110] One thing they probably discussed was his change of heart about standing for election. He had already told Garfield Weston that he wanted to withdraw his candidacy, and he confirmed this the following week in a letter to the Macclesfield Conservative Association. He wrote:

> [T]he demands of my service career are so exacting that I could not combine them with a political career and do full justice to both. The European war commands all my present time and energies and when it is won I shall not be satisfied until I have played what part I can in bringing the Japanese war to a victorious conclusion.[111]

At work, he was getting more experienced in flying the twin-engine fighter-bombers commonly used by Bomber Command's in-flight controllers, principally the American-made Lockheed Lightning but also the Mosquito. He flew a Lightning when he clocked up two more operations, on 18 and 22 August, observing how a controller worked. In both he had an experienced observer as his crew (Sqn Ldr Ciano on the first, Sqn Ldr Howard on the second) following attacks on targets in Holland and France. On these operations he was able to see how a controller dropped flares on an agreed position to indicate a marking point. This was then used by the main force bombers who would proceed from it to an aiming point, at which they should drop their bombs. Both these trips fell into the category which Cochrane seems to have agreed to allow him: a non-participatory role on a target in areas where there was reduced danger of him falling into German hands if he was shot down.

The outcome of these two outings, of course, just increased Gibson's desire to get more actively involved. He lobbied Cochrane hard, who made it clear that if this was to be sanctioned Gibson should undergo serious training. As if to demonstrate that he would

---

110 Van den Driesschen, *We Will Remember Them*, p.103.
111 Morris, *Guy Gibson*, p.255.

do so, on 2 September Gibson took a Mosquito on his longest trip yet in one: a five-hour flight to the Shetlands, where he had difficulty landing at a tricky small airstrip, and back. His navigator was Flg Off A.E. Boase, a navigator who had previously served in 49 Squadron.

On 10 September, Gibson flew a Mosquito for the first time on an operation with Wg Cdr John Woodroffe, one of 627 Squadron's most experienced pilots, as his navigator. Their target was Le Havre, again well away from German airspace, and their job was to shoot ciné film of the raid, rather than act as a controller.

Just over a week later, on Monday, 18 September, his sometime 106 Squadron colleague John Searby, now working at Bomber Command HQ in High Wycombe, arrived at Coningsby and talked to Gibson for a while. They looked at a Mosquito parked up in a hangar, and Gibson told him that he had plans to use this particular aircraft when doing the 'odd sortie'. In writing up this account after the war, Searby singled out Gibson: 'Of all the war-time airmen, he stands out the best,' he wrote, singling out his boyishness, liking for fun and having his men around him, and his humanity. Not everyone wrote about Gibson the same way, but plainly Searby was one who admired him.[112]

On the same day, Gibson also found time to write and post a letter to his brother. It is very brief:

> My Dear Old Alick
>
> I haven't heard from you for ages now and think it is about time we knocked back a can of beer together.
>
> If you could give me the name of your nearest airfield I would try to get down.
>
> I'm pretty busy at the moment doing the odd op – and planning others but wish to hell I were in France.
>
> Are you a Lt. Col. yet?

---

112 John Searby, *The Everlasting Arms* (William Kimber, 1988), pp.185–6.

Drop me a line old timer.
Yours Aye
Guy[113]

What prompted him to catch up with family that day we don't know. However, the very next afternoon the pressure he had been exerting to go back on operations would pay off.

113 Guy Gibson, letter to Alick Gibson, 18 September 1944. (Gibson family)

18

Back on Operations:
Gibson's Final Trip

The decision to use Gibson as the controller and marker leader for a 5 Group attack on the towns of Mönchengladbach and Rheydt on 19 September 1944 was probably taken by Air Cdre Alfred Sharp, the Commanding Officer of 54 Base. Whether he was influenced by Gibson's lobbying of Cochrane or Harris is a matter of conjecture. As frequently happened in the run up to any raid, both target and tactics changed in the hours before take-off. Finally, it was settled that the railway network linking the two towns was the destination. There was then a surprise in the briefing room at Coningsby when it was announced that Gibson would perform that role. An overall co-ordinator was needed for the markers as they would be split into three groups of three, one for each of the marking points, red, green and yellow, which led to the targets for the main bombing force, also divided into three sections. The leader for the red marking point trio was a man known to Gibson, in the shape of an old 106 Squadron colleague Sqn Ldr Ronnie Churcher, in whose crew Bob Hutchison had flown briefly. The briefing itself was delivered by another man, Wg Cdr Charles Owen, who had a connection to the Gibson crew, though they may not have known it. He had been a pilot in 97 Squadron on the night of the Nuremberg Raid, 31 March 1944, when Richard Trevor-Roper was among the 540 men who died.

Gibson might have got himself onto the flying roster for that evening, but the navigator he had been planning to use was now sick. Searching around, he found that Sqn Ldr James Warwick, a Belfast man who had recently taken over as Coningsby's station Navigation Officer was free, and Gibson asked him to take on the role. Warwick was an affable man and an experienced navigator but, it would turn out, had not performed this task in a Mosquito very frequently.

There was also the question of which aircraft the pair should use. The 5 Group controllers normally flew from Coningsby, but there wasn't a serviceable Mosquito there, so he would need to use one belonging to 627 Squadron at Woodhall Spa, 3 miles away. He would therefore take off on the operation from there, along with the nine crews from the squadron who were providing the markers. A car was ordered to take Gibson over to Woodhall Spa, and he set off at about 1830. Shortly before he left, Eve telephoned from London, apparently just on impulse. 'Is anything wrong?' he asked. 'No,' she replied, 'I just wanted to talk to you, that's all.'[114] Sounding irritated and busy, he promised to call her the next day and rang off.

When Gibson got to Woodhall, he was shown to Mosquito KB213, the same aircraft he had flown to the Shetlands three weeks before. It had already been loaded with the target indicators (TIs) and flares needed by the operations controller. He argued with this decision, saying he would prefer to fly KB267, a newer aircraft, but which had been prepared for another pilot and therefore had a different load of TIs. The change was resented but Gibson had his way, and the armourers had to rush to change the loads.

While this was going on, Gibson bumped into Douglas Garton, the 83 Squadron fitter who had invented the 'Admiral' naming convention which had proved so popular.[115] They exchanged a few friendly words before it was time for Gibson and Warwick to clamber on board KB267 and join the other nine Mosquitoes preparing

---

114 Morris, *Guy Gibson*, p.272.
115 Ottaway, *Dambuster*, p.186.

to leave Woodhall Spa at one-minute intervals. Gibson took off first and the last was airborne at 2005.

The best that can probably be said about the raid itself was that the results were satisfactory. However, the complicated procedures, the technical problems and the inexperience of the controller did not help. The various contemporary reports and post-war accounts have been synthesised by Richard Morris into a compelling account of Gibson and Warwick's last, fatal, operation. He counters Arthur Harris's account that the raid was 'of course a complete success', with the verdicts of those who took part, which run from modest success to partial failure. He also raises the possibility that the decision to appoint Gibson as the controller was not taken by Air Cdre Alfred Sharp, but that Gibson appointed himself.[116]

The records show that Gibson issued the order for aircraft to leave the area and head for home at 2157. He then sent a congratulatory message to the Flare Force. It is thought that he himself circled the target shortly afterwards at about 2,000ft in order to make one final assessment of the results. He then turned KB267 towards home, flying low directly across Holland, rather than the officially designated route.

At around 2230 in the small Dutch town of Steenbergen, 50km south of Rotterdam, several witnesses heard an aircraft flying low, with engines that sounded in trouble. It was heading over the Graaf Hendrik Polder outside the town, near to a farm and a sugar factory. Some of the witnesses were close enough to see the cockpit lit up by intense light. One couple heard a violent explosion and then saw the aircraft dive into the ground.

The aircraft had come down on the farm of the Van der Riet family but it had completely disintegrated. The two men in it were also blown to pieces, which must have been a terrible shock for the farm owner the next morning when he came across various body

---

116 Morris, *Guy Gibson*, pp.263–307. This chapter owes a substantial debt to Morris's account.

parts thrown against his shed and scattered in his field. The area was still under German control, although Allied forces were now not too far away, and so when Mr Van der Riet informed the local Dutch chief of police, he in his turn told the German *Orstkommandant*. Two Dutch auxiliary policemen joined about twelve German soldiers in searching the field. Together they assembled the body parts and determined that there must have been two airmen in the crashed aircraft. A carpenter was summoned to build a coffin and the parts were placed in it. Warwick's ID tag had been recovered and a metal plate was engraved with his name and the words 'unknown soldier' to signify the other man. Then a sock was found with the name Gibson on a laundry tag, so the plate was inverted and re-engraved with the names of both men, Warwick and Gibson.

The German authorities gave permission for a funeral to be held, provided it was done immediately, so the local Lutheran pastor, Rev. Van den Brink, and his Catholic equivalent Fr Verhoeven agreed to hold a joint service. The bodies were taken to the Catholic cemetery in Steenbergen and placed in a grave. Prayers and a psalm were read and the burial was over very quickly. Curiously, Gibson and Warwick are the only Allied aircrew buried in this cemetery. Most of the bodies of other airmen who died in this part of the Netherlands were transferred after the war to the large Commonwealth War Cemetery at nearby Bergen-op-Zoom. Those buried there included the 617 Squadron crew of Lewis Burpee and his crew who died on the Dams Raid, and who had also served under Gibson at 106 Squadron.

The town of Steenbergen was not itself liberated until 4 November 1944. Soon afterwards, an Identification Squad moved in, under the command of Captain S.T. Watson. Local people informed them of the grave and handed over some other material including engine parts from the Mosquito. A wooden cross with both men's names, ranks and numbers was erected in February 1945.[117]

---

117 Van den Driesschen, *We Will Remember Them*, pp.106–14.

What led to Gibson and Warwick's crash has been the subject of much speculation, not to mention conspiracy theories. There are thought to be three possible causes. The first (and most likely) is that the Mosquito simply ran out of fuel because neither Gibson nor Warwick were very familiar with the aircraft and didn't know how to switch to the reserve fuel tank. The second scenario is that they were shot down, either by ground-based anti-aircraft fire or a German night fighter. A third possible account, that they were shot down in a 'friendly fire' episode by a main force bomber, has been put forward by some, but there is doubt about both the veracity of the 'confession' of the rear gunner allegedly involved and the exact position of a two-engined aircraft which attacked the bomber in question.

The loss of fuel theory is given weight by both Gibson and Warwick's lack of experience flying in a Mosquito. Gibson had not had any formal 'type' training, where he would have learnt cockpit drills, although he did undertake a ninety-minute flight with Wg Cdr John Woodroffe on 31 August where they practised dive-bombing. He had also, as has been noted above, taken Mosquito KB213, which he later rejected for the operation, on a five-hour flight to and from the Shetlands.

Whatever was the cause of the crash, Gibson and Warwick were both described as 'missing' in the early hours of the morning of 20 September 1944 and telegrams were sent to their families. Eve was at home, waiting for the phone call that her husband had promised the day before. Warwick's mother was doing her ironing in her house in Belfast. It was common for the RAF to publicise lists of those who were officially listed as 'Missing', but in the case of Gibson and Warwick it does not seem to have done so. Gibson's death was finally reported officially in Britain on 8 January 1945 but in Canada it appears to have been announced at the end of November 1944.[118] Many of course found out unofficially, including the Macclesfield Conservative Association, whose current MP Garfield Weston

---

118 'VC Dam Buster Missing', *Calgary Herald*, 30 November 1944.

probably heard House of Commons gossip. Churchill wrote to Eve Gibson in December 1944, calling him 'the glorious Dam-buster' and expressing his great admiration. Further tributes followed the official announcement, with Ralph Cochrane and Henry Kendall of St Edward's School having signed tributes published in *The Times*.

It's not clear exactly how far along the path to a published book *Enemy Coast Ahead* had reached at the time of Gibson's death. However, eventually the whole bundle, with Gibson's handwritten corrections and the amendments made by the editor and censor, was sent back to Michael Joseph at the end of December, then in February 1945 to the Ministry of Information for final approval, before returning to Michael Joseph to handle the typesetting and printing. The typescript was later returned to Eve Gibson, who donated it to the RAF Museum after the war.

But while this was going on, a series of six articles based on the draft were published in the *Sunday Express*, all credited to Gibson. The first appeared on 3 December 1944. Nowhere in the text is his status as 'missing' mentioned, so the general public must have thought that there was nothing amiss. The last of the six articles appeared in the newspaper published on 7 January 1945, the day before the official announcement, which might make one wonder whether this had been co-ordinated.

The book itself wasn't published for another year, in January 1946. There are many errors in the text which survived the copyediting and proofreading supposedly done by the Michael Joseph production department. As well as the errors in the listing of his own crew, there are several misspellings of names in the first few pages – Foxley, Hevron and Humphrey for Foxlee, Heveron and Humphries, to name a few. Also, events are wrongly dated and wartime censorship means many details are omitted. Exact sales figures weren't published in those days, but the edition was quickly reprinted and has been in print almost continuously ever since. However, the various editions produced by different publishers over the years have not helped clear up its faults. Most have been just straight reprints, reproducing the original text. One from 2003 is described as being 'uncensored' but, as it doesn't show what exactly was changed by the censor, it is not very helpful. Sadly, this has not prevented many people citing *Enemy Coast Ahead* as an accurate account of events and this in its turn has helped to perpetuate many of the incorrect myths which surround the Dams Raid.

It took until 2019 for a publisher to go back to the original text, and then annotate it to flag up Gibson's errors and inconsistencies. This was done in an edition produced by Greenhill Books, in association with the RAF Museum.

Gibson's views as expressed in the book are sometimes criticised for their fervent anti-German voice, but he was capable of distinguishing between the German people themselves and their Nazi-led prosecution of the war. In May 1940, he had gone to a chapel service at his old school, St Edward's, where the sermon had been delivered by a young priest, Rev. Stephan Hopkinson, also an old boy of the school. The subject had been that while Fascism was an evil ideology to be utterly resisted, there was no reason for unthinking hatred of the German people. The Christian should hate the sin but love the sinner. As they left the chapel, Warden Kendall expressed his disapproval to the preacher, blaming the German people, not Fascism, for the havoc they had caused. A young man in civilian clothes then introduced himself to Hopkinson, thanking him for the sermon and the sentiments. It was the then unknown Gibson.[119]

But that is to detract from the book's qualities. Gibson had many faults, and was not a natural writer, but it has a candour and freshness which could probably only have been supplied by someone who did so much in the four or five years it covers. It is a book of its time, displaying all the certainties and much of the politics of someone who saw himself as a natural officer and leader.

Gibson was admired by many of his peers and associates, but not by all of them. 'Those who liked or loved him did so intensely,' writes his biographer, Richard Morris. 'More looked upon him with a wary respect. Many thought him unpleasantly rebarbative. A few found

---

119 Oxley, *St Edward's School*, p.280.

him insufferable.' But he was a wartime warrior with a formidable record: few matched his two tours of bomber operations in either two- or four-engined bombers and ninety patrols in night fighters.[120] It was this record that undoubtedly impressed his superiors, such as Arthur Harris, who famously reserved for him a place in Valhalla, 'as great a warrior as these Islands ever bred'.[121]

On public occasions, Gibson was certainly capable of completely failing to read a room. This has been demonstrated in a couple of instances in this book: bawling out the ground crew on his arrival at 106 Squadron and behaving much the same in the Officers' Mess at 627 Squadron a few weeks before he was killed. There are other examples which could have been cited. However, among those who served with him, there were some who admired him greatly, such as David Shannon, who described him as a fantastic leader. Ken Brown, another Dams Raid pilot, also changed his views over the months he served under Gibson and ended up with more than a modicum of respect. Brown had joined the squadron as a Flight Sergeant but was then commissioned, and Gibson is sometimes described as having less time for NCOs as a group. However, that wasn't the view of one Sergeant who got to know him very well, Sgt Richard James, who flew as his observer for eleven months in 29 Squadron. They flew together on nearly eighty operations, and James said that Gibson always treated him well and was a delight to fly with.[122]

To quote Morris again: 'He achieved greatness because his combat experience was backed by a practical application of rules of leadership which he had learnt: the need to unify his squadrons behind clear aims, to communicate his aims with confidence and to balance discipline with the enlistment of hearts.'[123]

---

120 Morris, *Gibson*, p.321.
121 A. Harris, 'Foreword', in *Enemy Coast Ahead* (Michael Joseph, 1946), p.5.
122 Van den Driessschen, *We Will Remember Them*, p.153.
123 Morris, *Gibson*, p.xxvii.

19

The Dam Busters:
The Book and the Film

Because Gibson wasn't there to promote his book *Enemy Coast Ahead*, the Dams Raid might have stayed in the collective consciousness as just one of the war's many daring true stories but for the intervention of Air Marshal Sir Ralph Cochrane. In February 1945 he had been promoted from Bomber Command 5 Group to become the head of Transport Command. However, he retained a paternal interest in 617 Squadron and was convinced that it needed a special history of its own. He identified the Air Ministry librarian John Nerney as the key civil servant who would need to be involved in the decision, and wrote to him on 4 December 1946:

> I have always felt that No. 617 Squadron deserved a special history. Not only did its first two Commanding Officers receive the VC but it probably inflicted more damage on Germany than any other unit of comparable size in any of the Services.[124]

In this letter, Cochrane also wrote that he had asked Leonard Cheshire to take on the task of writing this account, and that he had initially consented but had changed his mind. Cheshire had himself

---

124 TNA, AIR 2/10147.

nominated W. McGowan Gradon, now a civilian, but who in wartime had been an Intelligence Officer at RAF Woodall Spa. Cochrane asked Nerney if there would be any objection to a civilian writing such a history, and would he be able to see official records.

Gradon was approached and he accepted the opportunity. However, he was then turned down by Cochrane and Nerney in favour of a rather better-known author, John Pudney. He was a poet and a novelist, with many connections with the RAF, having edited several collections of war poetry and serving in the Air Ministry's public relations department with a number of other writers. (This outfit was also closely associated with Nerney and nicknamed 'Writer Command'.) Pudney approached the publishers The Bodley Head, and then spent the best part of eighteen months trying to work out a way of telling the story. However, in January 1948, he gave up, telling Nerney that he had made three separate attempts, each of several thousand words, but had discarded them all.

All went quiet for a while, but in November Cochrane made another attempt to kick-start the history, visiting Nerney and threatening 'blood' if progress wasn't made. Nerney went back to Pudney and eventually the pair settled on approaching someone completely different, the author of a well-received book about RAF prisoners of war.

This was Paul Brickhill, an Australian pilot who had been shot down during the war, and who had stayed on in London after being released from a prisoner-of-war camp. He returned to work in his old profession as a journalist, writing for his previous newspaper in Sydney and on various freelance projects in the UK. In his possession were the notes he had made in the camp, which he had managed to conceal from his captors, and which he would later turn into his bestselling memoir of the escape from Stalag Luft III.

Journalism was in Brickhill's blood. His father had a long experience in the trade and had risen to reach the editor's chair on newspapers in both Adelaide and Sydney. In the late 1930s Paul Brickhill had started at the *Sydney Sun* as a copy boy and worked his way up to a reporter. When the war came, he joined the RAAF and trained as a pilot, serving in fighter squadrons in both Britain and the Middle East. He became a prisoner of war in 1943 after being shot down in Tunisia. In prison camp he was involved in planning what became called the 'Great Escape', but did not take part in it because, apparently, he suffered from claustrophobia. After the war, he had gone back into journalism, but, when a book he co-authored in 1946 with fellow prisoner of war Conrad Norton, *Escape to Danger*, was a modest success, he decided to try full-time writing. By coincidence he became a client of the literary agent Pearn, Pollinger and Higham, who also represented the Guy Gibson estate.

Brickhill and Norton's book had contained first-hand accounts by some of the men who had taken part in the Great Escape, and Brickhill decided to write a full-length book on this one story, thinking that this would be a much better seller. But before he could begin work on this, he travelled back to Australia in autumn 1947 to sort out his parents' financial situation, pooling the advance he had received from Faber and Faber for *Escape to Danger* and his wartime back pay. He took on a job at his old newspaper, the *Sydney Sun*, to live off now he was at home, and stayed there throughout 1948.

Late in the year, he heard from David Higham in London that John Pudney had been in touch, keen to turn *Escape to Danger* into a series for the newly established BBC TV. Norton and Brickhill were, of course, enthusiastic about the prospect of getting into this new broadcast medium, but in the end, nothing came of it. However, the relationship with Pudney had been established and would later become very productive because soon afterwards Brickhill was contacted by John Nerney.

Nerney had a proposition: would Brickhill be interested in writing an official wartime history of the RAF's 617 Squadron? He envisaged this as a government-produced publication and could only pay a small honorarium. The Air Ministry would facilitate his research but in order to undertake this work, he would need to be based in the UK. Brickhill was tempted, but decided that he couldn't afford to go back to the UK, so turned the offer down. However, Higham then approached him again: John Pudney had taken up a new job as an editor at the London publisher, Evans Brothers. He had approached Higham with a proposition for Brickhill: write an extended version of the Stalag Luft III mass escape section from *Escape to Danger* as a new book, to be called *The Great Escape*. Brickhill was quick to agree to this, providing the publisher's advance would cover his passage back to Southampton. All was agreed in May 1949, and Brickhill booked his ticket.

Also on board the ship was a 20-year-old art student, Margot Slater, travelling to the UK with her younger sister for an extended holiday. Despite their twelve-year age difference the pair began a relationship which would culminate in a stormy marriage and it was on the voyage that Margot persuaded Brickhill to think again about the 617 Squadron history. When they reached London, Brickhill made contact first with Pudney and then Nerney, saying he was prepared to 'have a go' at the squadron history.[125]

On 29 July 1949, Nerney wrote to Cochrane to tell him the news:

> The question of No. 617's History has again been raised by John Pudney in a letter which I enclose. As you will see, he suggests that this History might now be undertaken by Paul Brickhill – who, as you may remember, wrote an excellent book on his escape from Germany 'Escape to Danger'.
>
> I have had a talk with Brickhill on this subject and, as a result, I have received a letter from him (enclosed) in which he states that he is willing to undertake this work and suggests a general treatment ...
>
> Brickhill is an Australian (he has just returned from that country) and is a Journalist by profession. He has a very forthright manner and may be considered by many people as having a somewhat

---

125 Stephen Dando-Collins, *The Hero Maker* (Vintage Australia, 2016), pp.193–202.

rough personality. However, in view of the fact that he is willing to undertake this task and has two publishers extremely interested, it may be worth serious consideration.[126]

But first, he had to write *The Great Escape* and his research for both this and the 617 Squadron project necessitated trips to Germany and beyond. He delivered the manuscript for the first book in the early part of 1950, and turned his attention to work on 617 Squadron almost immediately, pausing only in April to get married to Margot.

The title of *The Dam Busters* was chosen quickly, formalising an unofficial name which had come into popular use soon after the raid itself. But getting a structure for the book was a bigger problem. For *The Great Escape*, it had been easier because of his personal involvement in the events it described and knowledge of the man Roger Bushell, who was its principal character. Wading through the official squadron information which the RAF had provided for the new job was a harder task.

Brickhill started his research with a letter to Harry Humphries, whom Nerney had suggested as a source. He told Humphries what he was planning to write and that what he wanted was 'human details, anecdotes, little sidelights':

With the warm support of Air Chief Marshal Sir Ralph Cochrane I am preparing to write the history of 617 squadron, and he, Micky Martin, and others have given me your name as a man who knows most of the gen.

It is not to be a formal history, but more of the human story of the squadron. Sir Ralph is very keen that it should be a story of the RAF spirit, and I quite agree.

At first, Humphries was extremely annoyed by this approach. When the squadron had first been formed, he replied, Gibson had asked

---

126 TNA, AIR 2/10147.

him to keep notes with a view to someday writing its story. He had compiled over 100 pages of typescript, along with a host of other information. This put Cochrane and Brickhill in a difficult position, and they had to wheel out Leonard Cheshire, who wrote to Humphries 'in the name of the Squadron and with the purpose of ensuring that the history shall be as full as possible'. Humphries obviously idolised Cheshire and he then agreed to co-operate.[127]

With Humphries on board Brickhill set about the task, but it wasn't until he hit on the idea of using Barnes Wallis as the central character that he was able to work out a structure for the book. For security reasons, in *Enemy Coast Ahead* Wallis had been given the code name 'Jeff', but the authorities now consented to his real name and occupation being used, and Brickhill conducted a series of interviews with him. He devoted the first three chapters almost exclusively to Wallis, and his struggles to design and then build a weapon which could attack massive structures like a dam. Brickhill's gift for explaining the complex engineering principles involved is displayed well here as he boils the theory down into a few sentences, which he enlivens with little human touches. However, the details of how the weapon worked – and specifically that it 'bounced' off the water – were still a secret, so similar circumlocutions to those that appear in *Enemy Coast Ahead* were also used in the first hardback and paperback editions.

Gibson's life and career pre-617 Squadron were not relevant to Brickhill but he did use the parts of the book which dealt with the Dams Raid itself and the period immediately before it as part of his narrative. By the time he came to interview the men who took part in the raid, only seven pilots were still alive and Martin and Shannon were the only ones who had flown in the First Wave, so his account has a distinctly Australian tinge. Wallis, Cochrane and Whitworth provided much of the detail for the build-up to the raid and what happened on the ground but much of the dialogue spoken in the

---

127 Humphries, *Living with Heroes*, p.107.

air, particularly that heard inside AJ-G's fuselage, is taken directly from Gibson.

He was still writing the new book in August 1950, when *The Great Escape* was published to excellent reviews, and sold very well. It was praised not only for the story itself, but for the quality of the writing, something about which Brickhill was very pleased. Money was still tight, however, as royalties would take six months to arrive and he wouldn't get an advance on *The Dam Busters* until he finished the manuscript. This he did by the end of the year, and a handsome five-figure sum was handed over.

There is a central theme in *The Dam Busters* of the main protagonists struggling to achieve an unlikely victory not only against the Germans but also against a certain sort of obstructive stuffiness in the upper reaches of Whitehall. It is a pacy, gripping narrative, peppered with dialogue which sounds authentic, but was sometimes recreated by the author himself, since he put it into the mouths of people long dead. ('Someone said' is a frequently used construction.) As an Australian, Brickhill didn't need any prompting to pay due respect to the men from the Commonwealth who added a breath of irreverence to the proceedings, but he was also very keen on a certain type of Britishness, what he calls in the introduction 'the British synthesis of talents' where 'exceptional skills or ingenuity can give one man or one unit the effectiveness of ten'.

The Dam Busters was published in the summer of 1951, and again the reviews were excellent. And it wasn't long before David Higham was approached about the film rights. In the early 1950s Associated British Pictures Corporation (ABPC) was the largest of the British film production companies, owning Elstree Studios, Pathé News and other parts of the industry. Soon after Brickhill's book came out, in October 1951, ABPC's Director of Production, Robert Clark, bought the film rights for £7,500, giving Brickhill half and allocating the rest for a screenwriter.[128] Clark was looking for a vehicle for

---

128 John Ramsden, *The Dam Busters* (Tauris, 2003), p.35.

one of the studio's contract stars, Richard Todd, but whether he had noticed the physical resemblance of Todd to Gibson is not certain.

Clark started work on the project almost immediately, setting up a meeting which was recorded in production supervisor Bill Whittaker's diary as being with 'high officials of the Air Ministry for general discussion about projected film'.[129] Whittaker and script editor Walter Mycroft then produced a suggested 'treatment' in order to brief possible scriptwriters. Various names were put forward, including Terence Rattigan, Emlyn Williams and C.S. Forester, but in January 1952, Clark settled on R.C. Sherriff.

Robert Cedric (Bob) Sherriff had shot to stardom as a writer in the 1920s with his play *Journey's End*, the story of a group of First World War infantry officers and the pressures they were under in the trenches before a major attack. He had served on the Western Front himself and had been shipped home after being wounded, and it was the authenticity which he brought to the stage which made it such a hit. (It ran for more than two years.) What Sherriff captured beautifully in *Journey's End* was the way in which British officers of the period spoke. In fact, he could almost be said to have invented the genre of film in which laconic understated dialogue is the order of the day, since after the play's success he had spent a number of years in Hollywood. Recruited by Sam Goldwyn as a scriptwriter and editor just at the time, in the early 1930s, that 'talkies' were taking off, he wrote films like *The Invisible Man*, *Goodbye Mr Chips* and *The Four Feathers*. He even worked as an unaccredited script editor, on one of the doyens of the genre, the wartime weepie *Mrs Miniver*. Although set in England, this film was actually produced in Hollywood and must have needed the touch of a real-life Brit on the script.

Before Sherriff began work, he travelled to Effingham with Brickhill and Whittaker and Mycroft from ABPC to meet Wallis, who proudly demonstrated the catapult and water tub on which

---

129 Roland Wales, *From Journey's End to The Dam Busters* (Pen and Sword, 2016), p.277.

he had conducted his original experiments. 'It's just as it was at the time. Now I'll show you how it works,' he said. Somewhat embarrassingly, it didn't. But it did give Sherriff the opening scene of the film. Wallis also gave him a copy of one of his wartime papers on the principles behind the Upkeep weapon, an indication that the security measures had been relaxed. Sherriff was going to be allowed to reveal to the general public exactly how the weapon had been delivered.[130] ABPC was also permitted to use the original film shot by Wallis's team, the reels of which he had hawked around the corridors of power in 1942 and 1943.

Although Sherriff hardly mentioned the script for *The Dam Busters* in his own autobiography it is now widely acknowledged as one of his best pieces of work. As a keen oarsman himself, he must also have been delighted to find that he was able to work in several references to rowing in the text. His style, updated with RAF slang and ways of speaking from the Second World War, has many touches that show a master craftsman was at work. For instance, there is a great line given to Wallis, confronted by a bureaucrat telling him how difficult it would be to get him use of a Wellington bomber for test drops. 'What possible argument could I put forward to get you a Wellington?' Wallis replies, 'Well, if you told them I designed it, do you think that might help?' In the next scene, we see the Wellington in the air, with Wallis on board.

There are other lines which have echoes to his most famous creation. In *Journey's End*, when told about an upcoming attack on the opposing trenches, one character remarks, 'What a damn nuisance!' To which comes the phlegmatic reply: 'It is, rather.' Much the same construction is employed when Wallis and Gibson are watching the unsuccessful test drop at Reculver. Gibson: 'It's the devil, isn't it?' Wallis: 'Yes. It is rather.'

Clark did not find it difficult to find a suitable director. Michael Anderson was under contract as a director to ABPC and had already

---

130 Wales, *Journey's End to The Dam Busters*, p.279.

made a number of features. He was born in London in 1920, and started work before the war as a runner and office boy at Elstree Studios. He worked as an assistant director on several films, including Noël Coward's *In Which We Serve*, where he also acted in a small role. He then served in the Royal Signals. When peace came, he returned to the film business and gained a reputation for being able to deal with some of the industry's 'difficult' characters, such as Peter Ustinov and Robert Newton.

Anderson chose to tell the story in a straightforward documentary style, reflecting Sherriff's script, and enabling him to use Wallis's wartime films just as they would have been seen by the original viewers. (When the film finally reached the cinemas there must have been a collective exhalation of 'Wow' in the nation's auditoriums as the general public saw for the first time the big secret behind the successful attacks.)

With a draft script completed, the production team started the process of getting approval from all the people whose real names they were using. More than seventy letters were sent out, mostly via the Air Ministry, some to the principals themselves but mainly, such as had been the rate of attrition, to their relatives. Each one was accompanied by an individually numbered copy of the script, some 120 pages of foolscap bound in a paper cover. The six members of the Gibson crew seem to have received identical letters. The one sent by Bill Whittaker to the Pulford family, dated 13 January 1954, is an example. (Unfortunately, the company did not seem to have been appraised of the fact that George Pulford, John Pulford's father, had died ten days before the Dams Raid took place, and so he was the named recipient.)

Dear Mr Pulford

We have for some time been making preparations for a film of the magnificient [*sic*] operation carried out in 1943 by 617 Squadron, Royal Air Force, in which the Moehne and Eder dams were destroyed and which earned for them the title of

'The Dam Busters'. Our film story, written by R.C. Sherriff, is based mainly on Paul Brickhill's book of the same name, but we have also received considerable information, encouragement and assistance from the Air Ministry, Mr Barnes Wallis, Air Chief Marshal Sir Ralph Cochrane, Group Captain Whitworth, Wing Commander H.B. (Micky) Martin and many others closely connected with the events portrayed, all of whom have now read our script and expressed their approval.

In endeavouring to tell the whole story from the time the idea was first conceived until it was so successfully carried out we are very conscious of the fact that it has not been possible to pay full credit to everyone concerned for their part in the great achievement. Obviously, however, a large part of the story must be centred around Wing Commander Guy Gibson V.C., and those closely associated with him, in the planning and carrying out of the operation. Amongst these his own crew necessarily figure prominently. We are, therefore, sending to you a copy of our script in order that you may see how it is proposed to tell this part of the story. You will see that we have kept very closely to fact and that it is our intention to present a simple, sincere account of achievement and heroism which will bring added prestige to the Royal Air Force, and to 617 Squadron in particular, wherever it is shown.

Wing Commander Gibson's father has read and given his approval to the script. We hope that it will also have your approval. If, however, there is anything which, from your personal point of view, you would wish to have altered please do not hesitate to let us know.[131]

It is interesting that ABPC had gone to A.J. Gibson to get approval for its treatment of his son's character, presumably not knowing of the degree of estrangement between him and Guy. Quite how he

---

131 Bill Whittaker, letter to Mr Pulford [*sic*], 13 January 1954. Spelling and
 punctuation as in original. (Pulford family, via Malcolm Bellamy)

became the family member responsible for script approval is a matter for conjecture.

For once, ABPC allowed the production budget for *The Dam Busters* to go above the £150,000 they normally set as a maximum, which allowed them to use real Lancasters, and real RAF crew to fly them, for the aviation sequences. There were only four serviceable aircraft available, so they had different numbers painted on each side to allow them to look like more. (Real aviation buffs can tell that the Lancasters used in the film were the later models made after the war by the types of guns in the rear turret and the absence of engine exhaust manifolds.)

When it came to selecting the actors, the casting director Robert Leonard looked for physical resemblance to the character each was playing. George Baker, who played David Maltby, described how Leonard and Michael Anderson had a photograph of Maltby on the desk during their casting session with him.[132] It can certainly be said of the six actors who played the members of the Gibson crew that they all resemble their characters. Brewster Mason, the classical actor who later became a pillar of the Royal Shakespeare Company, played Richard Trevor-Roper and probably has the most lines. Nigel Stock and Brian Nissen have a certain physical resemblance to Fred Spafford and Harlo Taerum, and had to use Australian and Canadian accents respectively. Both could probably have benefited from some more work with a dialogue coach. Anthony Doonan played Bob Hutchison and Peter Assinder played George Deering, but the pair have very little to say. The man with the least dialogue is Robert Shaw, as John Pulford, with just one line in the script, in his opening scene sitting next to Gibson in the cockpit. But he is on view in every shot of the interior of the aircraft, checking gauges and pushing levers. Of all the seven men who played the subjects of this book Shaw became the biggest film star, with his most famous roles being in *Jaws* and *The Sting*. He reportedly did not get on well with Todd, a

---

132 George Baker, email to Charles Foster, 2006.

Actors cast in the roles of Gibson and his crew pose with Michael Redgrave, playing Barnes Wallis. (Vintage Press photograph, 1955, via the National Portrait Gallery)

case of art imitating life, reflecting as it did the real-life difficulties in Gibson and Pulford's relationship.

Much of the film was shot at Scampton, with the flying sequences taking place both there and at nearby RAF Hemswell. There was a certain amount of confusion during filming between real RAF personnel and actors, with numerous tales of actors getting salutes to which they weren't entitled, and complaints that actors playing NCOs were allowed to eat in the Officers' Mess.

What is not widely known, however, is that the film was nearly scuppered by a contractual dispute with Guy Gibson's widow, Eve, after the shooting was completed. She maintained that Brickhill had used material sourced from *Enemy Coast Ahead* in his own book *The Dam Busters* without permission. ABPC were furious that their film project was at risk and demanded that Brickhill sort it out, and if he didn't they would sue him for all the production costs.[133]

The production company's correspondence on this matter seems to have been lost, so exactly how the matter was settled is not clear, although it took many weeks' negotiation between teams of lawyers. It appears that Brickhill never paid any money to Eve Gibson but it was agreed that *Enemy Coast Ahead* would be added to the credits in the opening titles. More remarkably, it appears that it was also agreed that two more short sequences would be shot to appear in the final film. These are the cockpit scenes which take place after Gibson's AJ-G has crossed the Dutch coast. In the original edited version of the film, all that Richard Todd as Gibson says here is, 'Stand by front gunner, we're going over'. This is followed by a scene where Wallis, Bomber Harris and others are shown waiting tensely. But in the final cut, instead of going on to show the progress through Holland, two rather odd scenes then follow. The first shows the Lancaster cockpit with the actors playing Melvin Young, his engineer and navigator, leading the second group of three in AJ-A. His navigator then says, 'Enemy Coast Ahead'. An external shot is then followed by a similar cockpit scene, this one showing Henry Maudslay in AJ-Z. This time it's the pilot who says the key phrase 'Enemy Coast Ahead' and then fastens his oxygen mask. This bit of business and the double use of the title of Gibson's book seems to have been enough to placate Eve Gibson, and she called off her legal action. What Bob Sherriff thought of the addition of two rather clunky scenes to his elegant screenplay isn't known.

When the film was finished there was so much interest that it had two royal premieres, on consecutive nights, 16 and 17 May 1955, to coincide with the twelfth anniversary of the raid. Princess Margaret went to the first, the Duke and Duchess of Gloucester to the second. A detailed 'Order of Procedure' was sent to all those who would be

---

133 Dando-Collins, *Hero Maker*, pp.290–7.

presented to the Princess, including the relatives of those who had died on the raid. These included Eve Hyman (Eve Gibson's new name after her second marriage) and A.J. Gibson. Apparently so slight had been their previous acquaintance that the latter wasn't sure who the woman who had once been his daughter-in-law was when they were introduced to each other. But as they may never have previously met, this may not be surprising. Among the others in the line-up were Bob Hutchison's mother Ada and Richard Trevor-Roper's mother, now Mrs Gertrude Poyntz.

The way in which the premieres were set up can be seen as contributing greatly to the mixing of fact and fiction. Surviving members of 617 Squadron, next of kin of those who died, Barnes Wallis and his family and wartime and post-war leaders of the RAF mingled with the cast and crew from the film, with musical accompaniment from the RAF Central Band and a march past by the Air Training Corps band. There was even a model of the Möhne Dam, alongside which Barnes Wallis and Richard Todd posed for pictures.

Although he had become involved in the film project, A.J. Gibson remained aloof from his family into his old age. A few years later he bumped into his older son, Alick, on a street in London, where he learnt about Alick's job and that they in fact lived quite close to each other.[134] He attended a few other events, the unveiling of a memorial window at St Edward's School being one. He died in 1968, at the age of 92.

It seems odd now, but there was a four-month gap after the premiere before the film went on general release. However, this gave ample time for cinemas around the country to stoke up publicity, and they did not fail. Once again, they were encouraged to get the RAF involved in local premieres. ABPC produced a 'publicity book', giving local addresses and phone numbers for RAF Associations (for veterans) and local 'area publicists' in RAF regional offices. Cinemas were encouraged to get an RAF band to play on the opening night

---

134 Morris, *Guy Gibson*, p.317.

and even to let the service have a recruiting stall in the foyer. In fact, the publicity was hardly necessary since *The Dam Busters* proved to be a big success. Even though it had only opened nationwide in September, it was the top-grossing film of 1955 in Britain, taking over £500,000 at the box office, thus already making a profit for ABPC within a few months of its release.

When it was released internationally it was also a hit in the countries which had provided crews for the original 617 Squadron: Canada, Australia and New Zealand. The use of real Australian actors like Bill Kerr probably helped here. In Canada, the Deering family attended the premiere in Toronto, at which Richard Todd was present and posed for press pictures with Samuel Deering.

But the film did not do very well in the USA, much to Todd's annoyance – he thought that ABPC wasn't putting enough muscle behind it. He arranged a private showing for some of his Hollywood friends, including the producer Darryl F. Zanuck, who is reputed to have said, 'Gee. That's one hell of a picture. Is that a true story?' When Todd replied, 'Absolutely' (English understatement again!), Zanuck asked, 'Then why doesn't it say so?'[135]

The overwhelmingly positive reaction to the film ensured that *The Dam Busters* now has a permanent place in British cinema history. Anderson was always proud of this part of his work and its continuing influence. In a 2013 TV interview he described the first time that he heard composer Eric Coates play the 'Dam Busters March' and knew instantly that this was the music for the film. He also praised Sherriff's script, a 'masterpiece of understatement', something that he was keen to preserve in his direction. He died in 2018, at the age of 98, a few weeks before the seventy-fifth anniversary of the Dams Raid.

Time has not been kind to some 1950s British war films. However, this is not the case with *The Dam Busters*, which many critics have now taken to re-evaluating. It appears regularly in lists of best British

---

135 Ramsden, *Dam Busters*, p.115.

films (No. 68 in the one published by the British Film Institute) and is widely seen as an important influence. George Lucas based the sequence in *Star Wars* showing the attack on the Death Star on *The Dam Busters*. It will remain Michael Anderson's greatest legacy, and for that alone, he should be saluted.

★ ★ ★

There is a final coda to Paul Brickhill's work on *The Dam Busters*. He had become one of the best-known authors in the world with three huge bestsellers to his name. These had also been made into films, netting him even more income.

By the end of the 1960s, however, his personal circumstances had changed. He had been hit by large tax demands and had ended up leaving his native Australia for years at a time. His marriage had broken up, and his wife had cited physical assault as one of the reasons for their divorce. He had also suffered several episodes of poor mental health, not helped by periods of heavy drinking.

He eventually returned to Australia in December 1969, where he planned to get back to work. He told a reporter that he wanted to take on a number of projects but the only one he would ever finish was a revised edition of the Pan Books' paperback of *The Dam Busters*. During his travels, he had spent time in London going through some of the now declassified official records about the raid. The information he gleaned from this mainly concerned the fact that the Barnes Wallis-designed weapon used to attack the dams 'bounced' and then skipped when it hit the surface of the lake. This was hardly a secret anymore, since it had played a central role in the 1955 film, but until Brickhill sat down to write a revised edition, anyone reading the account in his book would have found vague references to the bomb 'working', without any clarification of exactly what this meant.

It was very hard work, particularly as he was still dependent on prescription drugs and alcohol, and it took him eighteen months. However, at the end he had inserted another 12,000 words into a new manuscript, which he sent to Pan, and in early 1971 he finished correcting the proofs. The book was published in 1972.[136] Unfortunately, the Pan Book archives don't have either a list of changes or a copy of the revised manuscript, so the only way of working out what revisions were made is by comparing the two published editions.

Although his biographer refers to Brickhill importing the new material from the declassified files, it is likely that a lot of the additions were in fact from Brickhill's own notes compiled for the original edition. He would have been given a lot of information for the book off the record, particularly by Barnes Wallis and Mick Martin. His recreation of the scene at Manston below, for instance, reads as though it is a story told to him by Martin – one he would have recorded on disc at the time and then had transcribed. He is likely to have kept all his transcripts from the early 1950s and worked through them at the same time as he was incorporating the classified material.

The original text reads:

A couple of days later, on May 8, Gibson, Martin and Hopgood flew three [Lancasters] down to Manston, and Martin and Hopgood watched goggle-eyed while a bomb was loaded into each. Two dummy towers had been put up on the water at Reculver, and the three aircraft had a run at them, dropping the bombs with the quaint plywood bombsights. It was beautiful to watch. Three enchanting direct hits. Micky Martin came in a little low on his run and the spouting water hit his elevator and tore one of them loose.[137]

The revised version shows the deftness of his changes:

A couple of days later, on May 8, Gibson, Martin and Hopgood flew three [Lancasters] down to Manston, and Martin and

---

136 Dando-Collins, *Hero-Maker*, pp.356–70.
137 Paul Brickhill, *The Dam Busters* (Pan first edition) (Pan Books, 1954), p.63.

Hopgood watched goggle-eyed while a bomb was loaded into each. Two dummy towers had been anchored in the water at Reculver. Wallis had already worked out a new drop-range and the quaint plywood bombsights had been adjusted for a risky range of 600 yards and lowered air speed of 230 m.p.h. (The fore and aft height lights on all the squadron aircraft incidentally had been adjusted to converge at 60 feet.) All three aircraft had a run at the towers and it was beautiful to watch. Three enchanting direct hits. Three times in a row the great black barrels skipped and skipped over the water until they ploughed between the dummy towers. Micky Martin came in a little low on his run and the spouting water hit his elevator and tore one of them loose.[138]

That there are such substantial differences between the two editions of *The Dam Busters* is not widely appreciated. Some historians have only looked at the earlier version before using it as a source. It is a wiser choice to use the 1972 edition.

If there is a criticism to be made of Brickhill's work, it is that it underplays the flaws which his principal characters displayed. Roger Bushell (the mastermind behind *The Great Escape*), Guy Gibson and Douglas Bader were only human; each of them could be said to be single minded and not to suffer fools gladly. By being uncritical of their personalities, Brickhill made them heroes. The truth is a little more complicated than that, and it has been the work of later scholars to reveal this. Brickhill was, however, a writer of gripping narrative history and it is this which is still remembered today.

The consequence of Brickhill's and Bob Sherriff's work is that the Dambusters 'myth' is now so strong that the general public's knowledge of the raid is almost completely derived from the film, and clips from it are regularly used in news items and documentaries about the raid, sometimes without even an explanatory caption. This has

138 Paul Brickhill, *The Dam Busters* (Pan second edition, 25th printing) (Pan Books, 1972), p.78.

been noted in some wry comments by those who took part. Bill Townsend, the pilot of AJ-O, who won the Conspicuous Gallantry Medal for his attack on the subsidiary target of the Ennepe Dam, told an interviewer in the 1980s that 'until that film was made, it was just another operation, wasn't it?'[139]

In fact, the myth and the film have become entwined and form part of the collective definition of 'Britishness'. There is no other event from the Second World War, whose memory is frequently used by politicians to evoke this 'quality', which is actually framed by a film dramatisation. When one thinks of Dunkirk, the Battle of Britain, El Alamein or D-Day, the moving-picture memories are of black-and-white newsreel, not of scenes shot in a studio ten years after the event.

---

139 William Townsend, interview, 24 October 1984, item 8,341, IWM
    Collections. I am indebted to Victoria Taylor for this reference.

Afterword

The last chapter of Guy Gibson's *Enemy Coast Ahead* ends with Gibson and his crew successfully crossing the Dutch coast on their way home, and their feeling of relief as they reached safety beyond the coast. 'Nice work,' says Trevor-Roper to his skipper from the rear turret. Gibson asks Taerum to give him the course for home, and the book's last line is simply, 'We would be coming back.'

The Dam Busters film takes the narrative forward to cover what happened in the next few hours. This is summarised in a sequence which must be one of director Michael Anderson's finest pieces of work. It's daylight as the crews begin arriving home, and a snatch of the 'Dam Busters March' is heard on the soundtrack. Then the music fades. The first aircraft we see arrive is that of Mick Martin, with visible flak damage. He and his men climb out and head for the briefing room, where they swig cocoa and prepare to be debriefed. From there, Martin and Leggo head for the room they share and crash out on their beds without saying a word. Then we see Gibson and his crew getting out of AJ-G, the last time the six actors playing the crew appear. They light cigarettes as BBC announcer Frank Phillips's voice is heard reading the official communiqué, just as he had done in 1943 on the radio. His voice continues over the next few scenes. Gibson walks briskly away, accompanied by senior officers. A man climbs a ladder to chalk the word 'MISSING' on the crew board. A waitress brings breakfast to four or five men in the dining hall, with many empty seats seen in the background. The camera pans back as the announcement concludes: 'Eight of the Lancasters are missing.' Then there is silence. A Committee of Adjustments officer stands in Dinghy Young's bedroom, looking at some papers. He leaves the room, and the camera zooms in on Young's name on his Boat Race oar, hanging on the wall. In Maudslay's room, the hands on his alarm clock show it's just after 6 p.m. Again, the camera closes in, and the sound of the tick gets louder and louder. The whole sequence takes nearly four minutes and not a word of dialogue is spoken. It's a beautiful, understated masterclass in sound and visual editing.

Then follows the final scene: Barnes Wallis seeks out Gibson on an outside pathway, loping into shot. He is distraught at the loss of fifty-six men. Gibson reassures him: even if all the men had known that they wouldn't be coming back, 'they'd have gone for it just the same. I knew them all and I know that's true.'

'Get some rest,' he advises, 'ask the doctor to give you a sleeping pill.'

Wallis swallows. He fiddles with his glasses again. 'Aren't you going to turn in, Gibby?'

'No,' says Gibson. 'I have to write some letters first.' They part, no further words spoken. Gibson marches away, resolutely. He salutes a passing airman. The music arrives and swells fast. He marches on. A crash of cymbals and – 'The End.'

But, of course, it's not the end of the story in real life. It would have been interesting to read Gibson's account of the aftermath. He didn't start writing *Enemy Coast Ahead* until his return from America, so what happened to him over the months that followed the raid could have been added to his narrative. Without it, for this book I have had to construct what happened to him – and to the other six members of 'My Crew' – from other sources. All seven men had much more exposure to the public eye in the few months left to them after the Dams Raid than they had individually received in the two decades before. They had each started their air force careers as one of thousands of new recruits. By a series of coincidences, they had found themselves in an exalted role, part of a team with a singular place in history. In this book, I've tried to be fair to all of them. I leave it to the readers to judge whether I have succeeded.

Acknowledgements

My thanks go to the relatives of all the men who are the principal characters in this book. I would particularly like to thank six individuals: Charles Trevor-Roper (Richard Trevor-Roper's son), Rob Taerum (Harlo Taerum's great-nephew), Colin Hutchison (Robert Hutchison's nephew), George Germain (George Deering's nephew), Nicola Tyson (John Pulford's great-niece) and Helen Lakly (Frederick Spafford's family). I was in touch with all of them at some point during the process of writing this book, and they were all very helpful in allowing me to use personal photographs.

There are others who have also helped me with information and comments on my drafts. In particular, I would like to thank: Malcolm Bellamy, with his help on John Pulford and his family; Mark Evans, with help on George Deering's service; and Wg Cdr Jack Harris OBE DFC, with help on the Taerum family.

I would also like to give special thanks to: Clive Smith, who read the whole manuscript and made many individual comments; Dave Birrell, who also read the manuscript and sent me many photographs from the Taerum family archive, which is held under his stewardship in the Bomber Command Museum of Canada, Nanton, Alberta; and Robert Owen, the academic doctor to whom people routinely turn for guidance and advice, and who dispenses this so frequently with wit and wisdom.

I would also like to thank the people who run Wikipedia and all those dedicated to keeping the internet free and accessible to all. The people who run Wikipedia are one large community, described here: en.wikipedia.org/wiki/Wikipedia:Contact_us.

Those who gather around the RAF Commands forum (www.rafcommands.com) are a smaller bunch but no less dedicated.

I have found both sites absolutely indispensable over the twenty years or so in which I have been conducting my own travel around the shark-infested world of Dambuster Studies.

Finally, I want to extend personal thanks to those who have helped me in the six or seven months between finishing the final text of this book in mid-December 2022 and it going to press in August 2023. In between these dates, on 12 January 2023, I had a haemorrhagic stroke – an unexpected and dramatic medical emergency – which the medical team at St James's Hospital in Dublin dealt with with great skill and patience. Amy Rigg and Alex Boulton from The History Press took this setback to the schedule in their stride, producing the result which you now have in your hands, and I thank them for everything they did.

And of course my family. My cousins, John Maltby and David Blackburn, for their continued interest and support. My brothers and sisters, George, Andrew, Jane and Sarah, who have kept on helping me personally and also supplying information. My children, Patrick and Aisling, now mature young adults who live away from home. However, they continue to support me with much more loyalty than I deserve, as does my wife, Jacqui Kelly. It has been her who has got me through these last trying months, and to whom I continue to owe everything.

Bibliography

Several attempts have been made to write a popular history of the Dams Raid. However, none have superseded the book first published forty years ago, and updated in the early 2000s: John Sweetman, *The Dambusters Raid* (First edition, Jane's 1982; Revised edition, Cassell, 2002 and 2012). This is an authoritative account of both the build-up to the raid and the raid itself, and his first edition has the advantage of being written while many of the men who took part were still alive.

Guy Gibson's book, *Enemy Coast Ahead*, was published by Michael Joseph in 1946. The story of how Gibson was asked to write about the Dams Raid and lead up to it being published is told in Chapter 17.

Enemy Coast Ahead went through many later reprints, the most recent being a new edition in 2019 published by Greenhill Books in association with the RAF Museum (where Gibson's final manuscript is lodged). This new reprint also contains a foreword by James Holland, which gives an overview of Gibson's brief life. But, most importantly, it also contains an extended section, nearly fifty pages long, which contains more than 200 notes on the text. These notes were compiled by Dr Robert Owen, the 617 Squadron Association official historian, and can only be described as a tour de force. His knowledge and scholarship are evident throughout as he corrects and explains Gibson's errors and omissions. With the addition of these extras in this edition, Gibson's text can at last be relied on as an important contemporary account.

Over the years, several biographies covering Gibson's short life have appeared. The most authoritative is the 1994 account *Guy Gibson*, written by Richard Morris, published by Viking that year and by Penguin Books in 1995. Also useful is Susan Ottaway's book, *Dambuster: The Life of Guy Gibson VC*, which has been through several editions. The most recent by Thistle Press in 2017 contains substantial updates and new information coming directly from the Gibson family. Gibson's time as Commanding Officer of 106 Squadron is comprehensively covered by Clive Smith in *The Great Men of 106 Squadron*, published by Admiral Prune in 2022.

These are the five books discussed above:

Guy Gibson (with James Holland and Robert Owen), *Enemy Coast Ahead* (Greenhill Books, 2019).
Richard Morris, *Guy Gibson* (Penguin, 1995).
Susan Ottaway, *Dambuster: The Life of Guy Gibson VC* (Thistle Press, 2017).
Clive Smith, *The Great Men of 106 Squadron* (Admiral Prune, 2022).
John Sweetman, *The Dambusters Raid* (Cassell, 2002).

These books were all extensively used as source material here, and this is generally noted in specific notes on many pages. However, in order not to clog up every page, it's generally stated at the beginning of each chapter where it is the usual source of information.

Many other books were consulted for the text of this book. These are listed below:

Max Arthur, *Dambusters: A Landmark Oral History* (Virgin, 2008).
Stephen Dando-Collins, *The Hero Maker* (Vintage Australia, 2016).
Ted Barris, *Dam Busters* (Patrick Crean/HarperCollins, 2018).

Kevin Bending, *Achieve Your Aim* (Woodhall, 2006).

Dave Birrell, *Big Joe McCarthy* (Wing Leader Publishing, 2012).

Patrick Bishop, *Bomber Boys* (Harper Press, 2007).

Colin Burgess, *Australia's Dambusters* (Australian Military History Publications, 2013).

Jan van den Driesschen with Eve Gibson, *We Will Remember Them* (Erskine Press, 2004).

Jenny Elmes, *M-Mother* (The History Press, 2015).

Jonathan Falconer, *The Dam Busters* (Sutton, 2003).

Jonathan Falconer, *Filming the Dam Busters* (Sutton, 2005).

Max Hastings, *Bomber Command* (Pan, 1999).

Max Hastings, *Chastise: The Dambusters Story 1943* (William Collins, 2019).

James Holland, *Dam Busters* (Corgi, 2013).

Harry Humphries, *Living with Heroes: The Story of the Dam Busters* (Erskine Press, 2003).

Richard Mead, *Dambuster-in-Chief* (Pen and Sword, 2021).

Martin Middlebrook, *The Nuremberg Raid* (Penguin, 1986).

Martin Middlebrook and Chris Everitt, *The Bomber Command War Diaries* (Midland Publishing, 1996).

Leo McKinstry, Lancaster: *The Second World War's Greatest Bomber* (John Murray, 2009).

Richard Morris and Robert Owen (eds), *Breaking the German Dams* (RAF Museum, 2008).

John Nichol, *After the Flood* (William Collins, 2015).

Robert Owen, *Henry Maudslay* (Fighting High, 2014).

Malcolm Oxley, *A New History of St Edward's School* (St Edward's School, Oxford, 2015).

John Ramsden, *The Dam Busters* (Tauris, 2003).

John Searby, *The Everlasting Arms* (William Hill, 1988).

Tom Simpson, *Lower than Low* (Libra Books, 1995).

Clive Smith, *Lancaster Bale Out* (Tucan, 2013).

John Sweetman, *Bomber Crew* (Abacus, 2005).

John Sweetman, David Coward and Gary Johnstone, *The Dambusters* (Time Warner, 2003).

Walter Thompson, *Lancaster to Berlin* (Goodhall, 1985).

R.A. Wellington, *Pathfinder Pilot* (Pen and Sword, 2020).

Hugh Trevor-Roper, *The Wartime Journals, edited by Richard Davenport-Hines* (Tauris, 2012).

Roland Wales, *From Journey's End to The Dam Busters* (Pen and Sword, 2016).

Chris Ward, Andy Lee and Andreas Wachtel, *Dambusters* (Red Kite, 2003).

Chris Ward and Clare Bennett, *Dambuster Deering* (Bomber Command Books, 2020).

Online resource recorded:

No. 50 Squadron Royal Air Force in World War Two, 'The Diary of a WWII Bomber Squadron – Part 1 to Part 4, 1937 to 1942', www.no-50-and-no-61-squadrons-association.co.uk/history-of-no-50-squadron/ [accessed 22 August 2022].

Gordon Cruickshank, 'Memoir Flight Lieutenant Gordon Cruickshank D.F.M. RAFRO', ibccdigitalarchive.lincoln.ac.uk/omeka/collections/document/17702 [accessed 9 September 2022].

www.bombercommandmuseum.ca/chronicles/ken-brown-cgm-dambuster/ [accessed 3 October 2022].

Eric Fry, 'Spafford, Frederick Michael (1918–1943)', Australian Dictionary of Biography, National Centre of Biography, Australian National University, adb.anu.edu.au/biography/spafford-frederick-michael-11737/text20985 [accessed 4 July 2022].

RAF Air Historical Branch, Manning Plans and Policy, app. 1948, www.raf.mod.uk/our-organisation/units/air-historical-branch/second-world-war-thematic-studies/manning-plans-and-policy/ [accessed 1 November 2022].

Other books, archive material, journal articles and websites consulted are recorded in the footnotes.

Index

(References to images are in **bold**)

The History Press
The destination for history
www.thehistorypress.co.uk